*Winding Paths—
My Spiritual Pilgrimage*

# *Winding Paths—*
# *My Spiritual Pilgrimage*

Life Stories of a Disciple in the Making

VERNON T. JONES

RESOURCE *Publications* • Eugene, Oregon

WINDING PATHS—MY SPIRITUAL PILGRIMAGE
Life Stories of a Disciple in the Making

Copyright © 2024 by Vernon T. Jones. All rights reserved. Expect for brief quotations in critical publications or reviews, no part of this book may be reproduced in any manner without prior written permission from the publisher. Write: Permissions, Wipf and Stock Publishers, 199 W. 8th Ave., Suite 3, Eugene, OR 97401.

Resource Publications
An Imprint of Wipf and Stock Publishers
199 W. 8th Ave., Suite 3
Eugene, OR 97401

www.wipfandstock.com

PAPERBACK ISBN: 978-1-6667-8847-1
HARDCOVER ISBN: 978-1-6667-8848-8
EBOOK ISBN: 978-1-6667-8849-5

The Scripture quotations contained herein are from the New Revised Standard Version Bible, copyright © 1989 by the Division of Christian Education of the National Council of the Churches of Christ in the U.S.A. Used by permission. All rights reserved.

This book is dedicated to all of those faithful people who have walked with me through my life. They have been with me in both large and small ways, some for a short time, others for an extended period, and a few for a lifetime. None of us can make it through this earthly walk alone without many people, events, and experiences forming us into who we are today. I am so grateful and feel very fortunate to have had so many that have helped, loved, encouraged, and supported me. My spiritual pilgrimage has been far from perfect. However, God's love shown to me through many people has helped me to make it through life's trying times. Some of these same individuals have shared my mountain-top experiences as well. A number of these wonderful folks and events are noted in this book, but it is certainly *not* an all-encompassing list because of a lack of space and time. All of them are nevertheless a part of my journey, and I am eternally thankful for all of them.

Trust in the Lord with all your heart, and do not rely on your own insight.
In all your ways acknowledge him, and he will make straight your paths.

   —Prov 3:5–6

## Contents

*Preface* ix
*Introduction* xi

| | |
|---|---|
| ONE | My Beginnings 1 |
| TWO | Personal Foundations Being Established—Not Always Perfectly Done 15 |
| THREE | Growing into Young Adulthood—With All of Its Opportunities and Challenges 41 |
| FOUR | Beginning the Challenging World of College 56 |
| FIVE | Rev. Ward's Words Come to Fruition 65 |
| SIX | Taking Another Leap of Faith 84 |
| SEVEN | Dealing with the Highs and Lows of this Life Pilgrimage 108 |

*Photos* 128

| | |
|---|---|
| EIGHT | The Human Mind Plans the Way, but the Lord Directs the Steps 144 |
| NINE | Judy's Second Operation 153 |
| TEN | A Dark Valley 162 |
| ELEVEN | A Hopeful but Unknown Future 185 |
| TWELVE | The Beginning of Our Mutual Ministries 208 |
| THIRTEEN | A Message 219 |
| FOURTEEN | One Final Move—Going West 233 |

*Acknowledgments* 241

# Preface

WHILE DIRECTOR OF SMALL group ministries for Christ Lutheran Church in Louisville, Kentucky, I was leading a small group and talked about my spiritual pilgrimage to that point in my life. I noted that when I was intentional about striving first for God's kingdom in my life things worked out differently for me than when seeking my own agenda. I was trying to get the point across that for me striving for the Lord's kingdom before anything else was critically important, and a lesson that had to be learned repeatedly.

However, what some people heard was that my life was nearly perfect, without any trouble or pain while trying to do God's will. Of course, that was not what I meant to say, but that is what some understood me to express. Thus, I must be very careful when referring to my own spiritual pilgrimage. My life has had many challenging times, as is the case with most of us. I do know, however, that things would have been much more difficult without having the faith to trust God with my daily life.

When one studies the life and times of the spiritual saints of former days or of today, we sometimes see them from a devout perspective. This may make us think that they were different from ordinary people like you or me. They could be seen as having lived a more righteous life and had more spiritual practices than we do. It may seem that they were able to write about and share more insights about walking with God, which we then come to admire and appreciate. Often these saints give us encouragement, support, and discernment by how they have lived their lives. Thus, we then have a habit of putting them on a pedestal and making them to be a god-like figure.

However, when we look more closely at their personal lives, they were just as fallible as any of us. Even as they tried to live a spiritual life, they had doubts, fears, and experienced pain, sorrow, and losses that trouble us as well. The point of this is that when someone reads my books or online blog, one might think that my spiritual journey is without the highs and lows of this earthly walk. Thus, I wanted to share with you that my life has not been without its share of heartaches, drama, and life's troubles faced by all humans.

Writing about my personal life allows the reader to see how people have helped me in my life, for I did not get to where I am today without lots of love and assistance. I offer my reflections in the hope that they will be an encouragement to those trying to live out their call to be a lifelong disciple of Jesus Christ. I also want to share some of the wisdom and insights gained in my journey.

Please note that what is written is not so much a reflection of what a wonderful life I have had but, rather, how grateful I am to be a beloved child of God who has been given so much. This is not because of what was done or not done in my life; but rather solely because of God's grace, love, and mercy. My prayer is that what you read here will enrich you and will offer something that aids you on your spiritual pilgrimage.

# Introduction

As one looks back over their life, there are a wide range of emotions and events that have been experienced. We are made up of the people and events, both the good and bad, that we have known and gone through. All of these have helped shape our very being, whether we want to admit it or not. Much as we might like to forget the awful people who have crossed our path, as well as the tragic or painful events of our past, they are still within us, just as the fun, successful, wonderful happenings and loving individuals are still a part of us. All aspects of our history have helped form us, even if we try to forget them or cannot even remember them. They have helped us get to where we are today. They also assisted us in developing the lens through which we look at life's occurrences, decide our actions, and function daily.

As I enter another phase in my life this is the case for me also. In my books and in my online writings, I often include people and events that have influenced me. These have also helped form me into the person that I am today. By sharing some of the individuals and happenings that have helped mold me, my hope and prayer is that it might encourage you on your journey to look for the people and events in your life through whom God works. Socrates wrote many years ago, "The unexamined life is not worth living." I believe that it is helpful to write about the people and events of our lives. In so doing it is often surprising what we remember and can then reflect upon. We also may be given insight into how God has placed others in our path to walk with and assist us.

This is not my entire life history with every mundane detail, but moments that reflect the times in which I have grown. Both of my marriages have been very essential to me. My late wife, Judy, and now Shirley are great examples of how God's love is shown through the people that we encounter on our earthly walk. Regardless of what I have done, or will do, having been married to these two wonderful, spirit-filled women has been central to my life and faith journey.

On the other hand, I have learned and grown through my errors, short-sighted decisions, etc. As fallible humans, we all have faults and shortcomings and wish we could change some aspects of our lives that have haunted us over the years. I am in this boat, *big time*! This book does not have enough space to list all my flaws and failings; however, some will be noted. Even as I have become able to trust God more and more about my journey, I still make mistakes, have pain and sorrow, and basically do *dumb* things. But there is also joy, contentment, and peace in my life, for which I am deeply grateful.

## BREAKING BARRIERS

The good Lord has used my life in many different areas, and one of them I want to record here. This is not done to necessarily pat myself on the back for doing something that no one else had been able to do before me; but, rather, to indicate how God can use ordinary people like me to do something meaningful for God's kingdom and our society.

I was the first African-American to fulfill certain jobs with several specific companies. One could say that I was there at the right time when a change was needed. It could also be noted that, apparently, I was gifted with the right personality and with enough talent and skills to do the job necessary to have some measure of success. Some could say that the good Lord knew how I would react in certain situations, so I was used to pave the way so that other minorities could follow me and could benefit from working at these positions that previously were unavailable to people of color.

For whatever reason, I was chosen to become that individual. Someone had to be the first one and I was blessed to be that person; after that it is easier for those who followed. Working in those various positions became part of my spiritual pilgrimage and helped in my quest to become a lifelong disciple of Jesus Christ. In doing these jobs I had to have faith in myself and in God, that no matter what I was called to do, the love and support of the good Lord would be with me. I also learned skills that would be used later in my life in other times and places, abilities such as being able to work with people from various backgrounds, races, and cultures, and the capacity to be able to listen to other's views to facilitate getting a task done.

The names of some of the companies have changed over the years due to mergers, and in certain cases some no longer exist. However, these are the names of the firms when I worked there. To my knowledge, I was the first person of African-American heritage to work in the positions noted below:

- Youngstown Sheet and Tube Company: First person to take a shift as a third helper in the Open Hearth Department: Second person to become a bona fide third helper, Youngstown, Ohio, Campbell Works.
- St. Paul Insurance Company: First marketing person, Denver, Colorado, and San Francisco, California.
- CNA Insurance Company: First marketing person, San Francisco, California.
- Crum and Forster Insurance Company: First marketing person and service office manager, Columbus and Cincinnati, Ohio.
- Merchants Insurance Company: First marketing person and first person in management, Buffalo, New York.
- Auto Club Insurance Company (later to become American Commerce Insurance Company): First marketing person and first person in management, Columbus, Ohio.

I was fortunate to have had people who helped me to succeed in these roles. My late wife, Judy, was extremely supportive and willing to move our family to take advantage of what was offered to me. I feel very privileged and honored to have been used to aid in opening doors for others in the business world. Additionally, my time with these organizations gave me skills that continue to be used on my journey and in my ministry.

Additionally, over the years, I have visited and worshiped in several churches where I was the only person of color. My son, Kevin, and I were the first persons of African-American heritage to become active members of Epiphany Lutheran Church in Pickerington, Ohio. After I married Shirley and she finished Trinity Lutheran Seminary, she was called to serve two churches as pastor. In both cases, I was the first and only person of color to become a member of St. Paul Lutheran Church in

Louisville, Kentucky, and St. Paul Lutheran Church in Alpena, Michigan. Both congregations were welcoming and supportive of us. I will always treasure my time with all the faith communities in my life and appreciate how they supported me.

## OVERCOMING LIFE'S DISAPPOINTMENTS

Throughout my life I have learned to trust God during life's disappointments. I grew up in the inner city of Youngstown, Ohio, which back then was primarily a steel town. My parents were divorced and both sets of my grandparents were divorced. During most of my growing up years my family did not have a lot of material things. Two months after high school graduation I got a job in the Open Hearth department of Youngstown Sheet and Tube Company and stayed there for eight years and eleven months. I started taking college courses a year after starting with YS&T, but was expelled several times for having too low of a grade point average. I persevered, went part time, and after eight very long years earned my undergrad degree.

After getting my college degree and beginning to work in the insurance industry, I started taking insurance courses, studying in the evenings and on weekends to learn more and hopefully be able to advance myself. After some years, I completed the course work to earn my CPCU (Chartered Property and Casualty Underwriter) designation, but only after I failed several of those exams. In order to pass those tests, I had to again learn skills that would help me later in my journey. Earning my CPCU designation was a huge deal for someone with my background and race at that time. The title is widely considered the most distinguished designation offered in the property and casualty insurance industry.

Over my lifetime, I have tried numerous times to lose weight, stay healthy, and tried several diets, as well as changing my eating habits many times. However, I have gained and lost countless pounds as I have a hard time keeping the weight off. This battle is one that will probably go to the grave with me.

Both of my marriages have been with someone of a different race and background than me. In both cases, there were some challenges that had to be dealt with, other than the usual ones for most married couples. I was reared in an African-American Baptist environment from the east side of Youngstown, Ohio. Judy, my late wife, and her parents, Stella and

Vito Buonavolonta, were Italian-Catholics and lived in Ashtabula, Ohio. Both of Stella and Vito's parents were born in Italy and came to the United States at a young age. She spent a couple of years in a religious order in hopes of becoming a Catholic sister but left before taking her final vows.

When I met Shirley Ross at Trinity Lutheran Seminary, she had plans to become a Lutheran pastor. Shirley has a varied background of Scottish/Welsh/Irish/ English/Eastern European heritage. Before she was a Ross, her maiden name was Villwock, and she was raised in South Bend, Indiana. Shirley had lost her late husband, Bob Ross, in an accident. She had lived most of her adult life in southwestern Michigan before going to Trinity. At both of my weddings, some of their family members did not attend. However, both Judy and Shirley were willing to confront any issues with a faith that God would walk with us in anything that we had to face.

Like many families in our postmodern society, I have had my share of financial stresses. While my late wife, Judy, was alive I was working in the insurance industry. On one hand I was gainfully employed earning a good income with benefits. This afforded my family a comfortable standard of living. We were able to live in several different locations and were always able to buy homes that we wanted. However, some poor fiscal decisions were made that caused us some major challenges, which severely strained our situation and then took a few years for us to recover from.

I worked for several insurance companies and, overall, most turned out well for me. However, I had to overcome two very negative job situations (one in Buffalo, New York, and another in San Francisco, California). On the outside, these companies appeared to be a good fit for me, but they ended up being just the opposite. However, through those experiences I ended up making some changes in my life. Thus, both of those positions, though starting out less than positive, did impact the person that I have become.

Something that has caused me the most distress in my life, besides Judy's final few years, was my daughter, Elizabeth. This situation also involves her children, my biological grandchildren. What Judy and I had to go through is something that I would not wish on anyone. Some of the decisions that we had to make before Judy died, and now what Shirley and I have had to handle, have been some of the most trying times in our lives. This is an area that has been very nerve-racking, and caused my family and me much pain, financial strain, and overall heartaches. There are parts of this story regarding my grandchildren that I do not want to go into much detail about now, for things are still unfolding and are subject to change. I believe that their lives can turn around and work out for the best for all concerned in the years ahead. However, I will share about what transpired with my daughter.

As noted, right up there as really difficult times to handle was when Judy was diagnosed with brain cancer. That period greatly impacted my life, and still does daily. The two surgeries to remove the tumors over a three-and-a-half-year period, her recovery, her treatments, the time in hospitals, nursing homes, doctor offices, and the time under hospice will be covered in more detail in this book. Things were the most stressful when she went under hospice care. However, with the assistance of the hospice staff as well as from our friends/family and people from our Christian communities, we were able to keep her at home for her remaining days. This was an extremely difficult time for all of us and changed us in a lot of ways. But through it all and over time all of us knew that God's love was with us and shown to us in so many ways.

## MAY THIS BOOK ENCOURAGE YOU

In all my life's journeys, I have been fortunate enough to have met some wonderful, Spirit-filled people, who have enriched, supported, and encouraged me. I have also been lucky to have lived in several different places, each with their own distinctive characteristics. Additionally, with my various marketing positions, I was able to visit many unique places and interact with a wide range of peoples and cultures. On the other hand, I have encountered my share of folks and situations that have either drained me or have become a barrier to my striving for God's kingdom daily. However, to be honest, more times than I care to admit, it was my own shortcomings, failures, or poor decisions that were the biggest obstacle to my becoming the person that God wanted me to be at any moment. However, as noted before, all these relocations, people, places, encounters, and even errors on my part are a part of who I am today, *all of them*! I am sure that all of you can say the same thing about your life experiences.

This book is about some of the major events of my life and how my spiritual pilgrimage and life journey were full of winding paths. My trek has included its share of detours, curves, bumps, and sometimes even flat tires along the way. Reflecting on things that I have done and barriers that had to be overcome are recalled to acknowledge that, even if I was able to successfully do a few things, I continually needed the Lord's help and guidance to make it every day. God's support came from family members, coworkers, friends, and sometimes from people or places I had not previously known.

My journey has had some events similar to that of others, but my specific experiences are totally unique to me and have helped shape me into the person I am today. My prayer is that sharing what I have been through might encourage you on your life walk. I would urge you to look back over your past and reflect on some of the situations and people that are part of your story. This pilgrimage/journey is never perfect, nor is it ever finished on this side of God's kingdom, nor lived without life's ups and downs, as we strive to become the person that God wants us to be. May you be able to feel God's love all around you, walking with you, sometimes carrying you when you cannot take the next step on your own. *Blessings on your spiritual pilgrimage!*

# ONE

# My Beginnings

> For everything there is a season, and a time for every matter under heaven: a time to be born, and a time to die; a time to plant, and a time to pluck up what is planted.
>
> —Eccl 3:1–2

## A TIME FOR EVERY SEASON

When my late wife, Judy, and I were married, one of the Scriptures read at our wedding was from Eccl 3:1–8. We felt that we needed to try as best as humanly possible to embrace all the seasons of life with its highs and lows, while at the same time putting our trust in the future on God's grace and mercy, versus our own wisdom and knowledge. We did not know how our life as a married couple would turn out. We had some major challenges when we first got married, in addition to the normal adjustments that all newly married couples face. However, we tried to believe that whatever confronted us, we could handle it together with the Lord's help.

Having a time to be born and having a time to die are mere words in a book until they are lived out in the real world. When we began our life together it was like a new birth, and it was a wonderful time. Little did we know that less than twenty-nine years later, it would be a time to die. When Judy passed away after several years of struggling with surgeries, cancer treatments, hospital stays, and a stint under hospice, it was time to deal with the second part of this verse. Of course, we had lots of moments in between these periods that were both high points in our life together and some challenging periods as well. However, nothing we had encountered before these final few years of her life can compare to what we had to deal with once she started having brain tumors.

For everything there is a season and a time for every matter under heaven. One of the main aspects of my spiritual pilgrimage and life journey that keeps occurring repeatedly is that life does not happen in a straight line, all perfectly traveled with no bumps along the way. There are times of new birth with all its joys, and there are times of death, pain, and sorrow; sometimes the joy and pain are intermingled.

All of us have births, deaths, and everything in between as we walk along our path. Trying to remain faithful to our calling to become lifelong disciples of Jesus Christ is always a daily, hourly responsibility. These events can be small births, like starting a new job, or small deaths, like losing a pet. They all impact our lives and become part of who we are. The seasons of life help shape and mold us to become the persons God created us to be. Thus, it is important to celebrate all the seasons of our life and enjoy each moment that we have.

I know that I enjoyed the birth of both of my children and felt honored that we were privileged to be given these gifts of new life. Being married, and then becoming a parent, is something that I shall never take for granted. There are many who have not been able to experience these treasures of life. I, of course, did not know what my parents felt when I was born, but hopefully they enjoyed that moment and knew that they were blessed as well.

Obviously, I have not faced my own death yet! Thus, I want to write about my beginnings and my life while I can still function. But as Judy's father, Vito, used to say, my bags are packed and as ready as I can be if it is my time to go. This chapter is about the beginning of my seasons of both births and deaths that will continue until my final pilgrimage to the next life.

When we announce a birth of someone, there are countless unknowns about this new individual. Will this person have good health, what will her/his character or personality be like, how will they look, or will they do something great for humankind? Of course, no one knows the answer to these or any other questions that could be wondered about anyone just born. We cannot judge how someone will turn out based on where they were born, who the parents happened to be, what race they are, or what their ethnic background may be. It is most surely a mystery to project out ten, twenty, fifty, or even seventy years concerning how anyone's life will develop. The most we can do is wait and watch the child's development.

Looking back over one's life allows a person to see how things have evolved. Of course, over time certain particulars may be forgotten or misremembered. We tend to see things from our perspective, while others witnessing the same event may have a totally different recollection of what happened. But for the person recalling the occurrences their opinion is the only one that counts. I do not think that I have a good memory for a lot of detail about past events. However, that has forced me to write things down to record facts that I want to remember. Others in my family can recall things from the past much better than I can. However, this work is based on my recollection and recorded history.

My life's journey is probably quite different from what others may have thought possible based on my beginnings. I was the son of parents who lived on the east side of Youngstown, Ohio, living in my grandmother's house. My parents were later divorced, and my brothers and I were raised by my single mother, and we all had many challenges to overcome. I know that I have been fortunate, lucky, blessed with God's grace, to be where I am today, versus how many others from my neighborhood and environment ended up. Many events and people have helped me along the way, and I know that I did not get here on my own.

## THOSE WHO CAME BEFORE ME

None of us are where we are today solely because of our own actions. A lot of people, events, and experiences came into play through the years. Having some knowledge about our family history, and some of the challenges that our ancestors faced, helps us to better help understand how we ended up where we are today. Concerning the roots on either side of my family, both my maternal and paternal families left the southern part of the United States and migrated north, in hopes of a better life. They were like numerous other people of all races and colors who have done the same thing over the centuries. That is how our country grew and continues to do so. In this case, my relatives were of mostly African-American descent, and thus they were also searching for a more equitable way of life. The great migration from the South to the North during the early part of the 1900s changed the landscape of America. At the same time, it also impacted the lives of many families, for they had to adjust to the industrial North, after generations in the agricultural South.

In today's world, a lot of attention is given to one's roots, heritage, or blood lines. I was able to obtain some of that information about my family. I want to share that data to show that as humans we are all connected in one form or the other. It should not matter so much what color we are, or who our parents happen to be, or where we come from. In the Lord's eyes, we are all beloved children and should be accepted as such. However, having said that, in my mind it is still important to know one's origins.

When my late wife, Judy, and I moved across country, away from our extended family in Ohio, we were not able to see them very often. Thus, we hung photos on a wall in our home of our parents, grandparents, and great-grandparents. This was done so that our children would know their roots and their ancestors. Therefore, as part of the listing of my family tree, where available, it will also include the composition of the individual family members. Their genetic makeup has helped mold my other family members and me into the persons we are today.

My mother's family was from the state of Virginia, and her mother, Madeline (Nanny) Murray, was born in Mechanicsville in 1900. I only knew her as Nanny; perhaps we called her Nanny because she was our grandmother. Her family moved to Richmond, where she got married. Her mother was Julia (maiden name Johnson) Murray, who died in 1912 at a very young age. Nanny's aunt, Nancy Johnson, helped raise her. Her father was Clyde and was said to have owned a saloon and several other businesses. Clyde and Julia had two boys and Nanny.

I have many wonderful memories of Nanny, for she was a very loving person who was always willing to help those in need. But at the same time, she could be tough and did not put up with any nonsense. While she was alive our extended family was very faithful about getting together on major holidays. After she passed away in 1960, those events did not happen as often. I remember her being short in statue and having a very light complexion. Her genetic makeup was half Caucasian and half African-American. One of the many ways that Nanny impacted my life was that she was a very faithful member of Jerusalem Baptist Church on the east side of Youngstown, Ohio, after her family moved up north. Nanny made sure my mother and her sisters and brothers always attended church, and my mother did the same thing for my brothers and me. Attending some congregation wherever I have lived is still something that I do today. That church-going habit is a great example of how what one generation does has an influence on the following generations.

My mother's father, John W. (Monk) Coleman, was born in 1882 and was from Clover, Virginia. I only knew him as Monk. The family story is that Nanny and Monk had nine children and my grandfather did not want people to know that all those children were his. So, he started having everyone call him Monk, versus Dad or Pa. He always seemed tall to me and was light skinned like Nanny. His genetic makeup was a quarter Native American, a quarter Caucasian, and half African-American. Monk served in World War I. His father was William Coleman and everyone called him Pa Billy. Pa Billy was a porter on the railroad and a tobacco farmer. He died in 1974 and was at least one hundred years old. Monk's mother was Betty Lax and together she and Pa Billy had twelve children.

Monk and Nanny were married in 1916; Nanny was only sixteen. Around 1923, Monk went to Youngstown, Ohio, to get a job in the steel mill and later sent for his family. The family moved from Richmond, Virginia, and settled on the east side of Youngstown. Monk got a job at Youngstown Sheet and Tube Company, the same steel mill that I would go to work for thirty-nine years later after finishing high school. Eventually, Nanny and Monk got a divorce, which was a challenging time for our family. However, like a lot of grandchildren, our view of Monk was different than that of his children. We saw him in a much more positive light then my aunts and uncles did, for he was always good to his grandchildren. On Sundays after worship, my brothers and I would catch a bus to his apartment. We would visit for a while and he would give us money to go the movies that afternoon. We would get back on the bus and go downtown to the show. That was a big deal for us and something that I will always remember.

Nanny and Monk had seven daughters and two sons, and for the most part the siblings seemed to all get along. I have fond memories of our extended family gatherings; I liked all my aunts, uncles, and cousins. My mother's brothers and sisters often helped us out over the years. They were supportive of us when my brothers and I were growing up, and their assistance continued even after I got married. My extended family helped to mold me and thus will always be a part of who I am.

My dad's family also came from the South. His dad ended up being called Henry Jones and was born in Arkansas in 1886. Family history has it that he had to change his last name to Jones from Jennings when he left Arkansas. He took the first name, Henry, from his brother. Supposedly, "as the story goes" he shot a Caucasian man because the man and he had a falling out over some cotton deal. As you know in something like this, the true facts can get mixed up over the years, but whatever happened, he ended up leaving his home state and changed his name. After he came to Youngstown, he became a self-employed painter, roofer, and fix-it man. Apparently, he always wanted to get paid in cash so he would not be found. I always enjoyed being around him for he was a fun person and loved to play the guitar. His genetic makeup was totally African-American.

My dad's mom was Nellie McKay, born in 1891 in Louisiana. Her father was James McKay, who was the son of an Irish slave owner, and James's mother was a slave. Apparently, the family's roots go back to Ireland. Her mother was Nellie Gasaway. My grandmother, Nellie, was the first of her race to become a woman barber in Ohio, and the first woman barber in Youngstown around 1927. She ran her own barber shop for many years on the north side of Youngstown. Her genetic makeup was a quarter Irish-American and three quarter's African-American. Nellie and Henry settled in Youngstown and had one son, my dad, Bennett, who was the oldest, and three daughters. At some point, Nellie and Henry were divorced. All of these family divorces caused all of us to have to overcome challenges along the way. However, these situations influenced me to be more determined to try and work hard at my marriages.

All of these people are a part me, my children, and grandchildren. They continue to be inside of me and continue to mold and shape me. They were an assorted mix of folk who were not afraid to make physical and emotional moves and changes. This was done in order to remove themselves from harmful situations and to seek a better life for themselves and their families. They were a mixed group of individuals of various economic levels, colors, and religions.

My heritage as told to me by my ancestors includes people from the Irish/Caucasian-American, Native American, and African-American backgrounds. Of course, this can be said of countless others in the United States and across the entire world. However, through AncestryDNA, I learned my true ethnicity, which is:

England and Northwestern Europe, 26 percent
Nigeria, 16 percent
Cameroon, Congo, and Western Bantu Peoples, 14 percent

Ivory Coast and Ghana, 13 percent
Scotland, 10 percent
Benin/Togo, 6 percent
Mali, 4 percent
Senegal, 4 percent
Wales, 3 percent
Nigeria (east central), northern Philippines, Sweden/Denmark, and Spain, each 1 percent

Often as humans on this planet called Earth, we fail to recognize that we all are connected in so many ways. God loves all of us, no matter what color/race we are, or where we are from, or who our ancestors were. My family is not perfect but are people with faults, who sometimes did dumb things, and whose journey has been a winding path. But they accomplished some wonderful, life-changing things and were very loving to their family and others in their lives. They were not much different than people in our society today. I have tried to continue what my ancestors started, and, hopefully, I have been able to honor their legacy.

## MY LIFE BEGINS

My life did not begin much differently than most people my age. Two of my three brothers and I were born at 441 South Forest Avenue on the east side of Youngstown, Ohio, rather than in a hospital. This was my grandmother Coleman's house, which was not too far from one of the many steel mills that were in town. Being born in a house can have its drawbacks, but it worked out fine for me. I have been blessed with good health for most of my life. Up until now I have not had any major issues health-wise, and it was not until I was in my sixties that I was hospitalized overnight. I do what I can to take care of my body by exercising and trying to eat right (most of the time)! But many other people have done the same things and still have health issues. For example, my late wife, Judy, died from cancerous brain tumors. Also, my oldest brother, Bennett, had to endure decades dealing with multiple sclerosis, which robbed him of a very healthy and active body before he passed away.

Dr. T. A. Lander delivered my brothers and me. Dr. Lander was an extremely close friend to our family, helping us out in several ways whenever he could. Looking back now, his support aided our family through a few challenging times. I am sure that his assistance allowed me to end up as healthy as I am. My life began as a post-war baby, after my father came home from World War II. It was the first year of the so-called Baby Boomers. My parents went to East High School together, the same school I would go to years later, on the east side of Youngstown, Ohio. My parents graduated East High in 1941 and were married in October of 1942.

My dad, Bennett Neil Jones Sr., was in the Army from 1942–45 and served in a few different African-American companies and was involved in a number of battle fronts. He was trained to work on supply trucks and was part of "The Red Ball Express" providing supplies to the front lines. He was able to rise to the rank of master sergeant. Learning to work on trucks in the Army gave him the skills that allowed him to spend the rest of his working life around cars as a mechanic. He was quite good at it, and in time would own his own gas/service station. Later, he was able to get a job at the General Motors' Lordstown plant as the first African-American mechanic to work for them. After he got out of the service in 1945, I was born a year later in 1946.

My mom, Emma Burnett (Coleman) Jones, was a stay-at-home mom for many years while raising her sons. She stayed with her mother while my dad was in the service. After he got out, my dad moved in with the family on Forest Avenue. I have three brothers, Bennett Jr., three years older than me, Randolph, two years younger, who was the baby in the family for many years. Brian changed that when he became the baby of the family eleven years later. Eventually, while I was still very young my parents separated and ultimately divorced. I do not remember much about my dad during those early years. However, we did see him, visit him, and have some contact with him. My dad in time got remarried, but more about that later.

My mom was the center of our lives throughout most of our younger years. My dad was involved with us, but the person who directed us and was with us every day was mom. She fed us, made sure we stayed out of trouble, taught us life lessons, and disciplined us the old-fashioned way. Raising four sons sometimes required her to get in our faces and show us who was the boss. She was not afraid to use strong punishment to get her point across, so that we understood her rules and how she wanted us to conduct ourselves. Of course, she was not perfect, but she fully lived her role as a mother.

We did not have much from a material standpoint, but mom was always there and did not give up on us and walk away. In my book, she did an outstanding job in raising her family, especially considering the environment she lived in and the limited financial resources she had to work with. Looking back, it was probably God's grace and mom's love and support that kept us pretty much out of trouble while growing up. This also gave us a good foundation in becoming productive adults. One of the most important things that my mother did for all of us was to be sure we went to church and Sunday school, no matter what. Again, she was old school in this regard; if we did not go to church, we could not do anything else that day. If we were too sick, tired, or grumpy to attend, then we could not go to the movies on Sunday afternoon or do any other fun thing. She was tough with most of her rules, but that one was the strictest of them all.

However, in the long run that worked out well for me. Being involved in the church community allowed me to develop a lot of skills that I have used throughout my life. It was the beginning of my spiritual pilgrimage that is still ongoing today. Additionally, my habit of always attending some worship service, no matter where my family or I have lived, also is maintained. Again, that rule of hers is still in me and part of my very being.

We lived with my grandmother on Forest Avenue until sometime in 1950. Then the four of us moved to a housing project on the north side of Youngstown. The place was a second-floor walkup with two bedrooms, one bathroom, a kitchen, and a living room area. Yes, very small but enough space for us at the time. I do not remember much about that time, except for the blizzard during the winter of 1950, when we had snow piles taller than me! While living in the projects we did not know how poor we were. My two brothers and I slept in the same bed for some time as young boys. I guess that worked out because we did not know any better. Trying to go to sleep with two others so close by could be a real challenge. For many years I would place my pillow on top of my head, in an effort to block out the noise and distractions.

You can image the struggles that occurred trying to get three young boys to quiet down at the same time every night. But my mom was firm that when it was time to go to bed, it was time—so just do it! Besides putting a pillow on my head, I have always liked my own personal space while in someone else's home or in a hotel. I am not comfortable trying to sleep in dorm-like settings. That time definitely influenced my sleeping habits for life. We slept this way until mom was able to get bunk beds for Bennett and Randolph while I was given a single bed. Even though we all were still in the same room, we thought we had died and gone to heaven!

As we grew taller, these beds were needed and were a true blessing to us. It was still a struggle to get all of us to quiet down so others could sleep, but at least we each had our own space.

I attended Covington Street School within walking distance of where we lived in the projects. I did somewhat okay at this school and seemed to get along with my teachers and other students. The one teacher who stands out to me the most during this time was my sixth-grade teacher, Mr. Tony Davanzo. I remember that he helped me with school work, encouraged and supported me. He was just a nice person to be around and one who I could trust. Of course, most of us can name teachers, coaches, and mentors who helped us, and without their support none of us would be where we are today.

In the sixth grade, I was a patrol person who helped students cross the streets going to and from school. It was a neat thing to be chosen to do that. Each year one patrol person from the school was selected to go Washington, DC, with a group from around the area. In the sixth grade I was the one chosen to go. That was a very neat thing to be chosen, and an even more wonderful experience to go. That event gave me a broader view of the world than I had before going and most certainly changed me.

## MY LIFETIME STRUGGLE

A lifelong struggle of mine, that has probably consumed more of my time and energy than anything else that I have had to face, is my love of eating, especially sweets and foods loaded with carbohydrates. However, my body makeup easily stores fat and has a low metabolism rate. The fact that I did not get much exercise caused me to become overweight at a very young age. Boy, I loved to eat and I was also very shy; so, food became a form of love for me. When people offered me food, especially sweets, I interpreted it that they liked me. Being overweight continued until I became an adult and actively started doing something to control my food cravings. I have never totally overcome this battle in my life; it is just something I must daily deal with.

Like most people of my age, my mom was a firm believer about eating everything on your plate at meal time. Thus, she made us stay at the table and finish all the food on our plates, even if we did not like it, like green peas, *ugh*! I am not blaming my mother for my eating issues; however, to this day I have an extremely difficult time not eating everything on my plate, even if I feel full. Funny how small things that you did while very young can impact you for a lifetime; this is certainly true in my case.

In order to deal with this struggle, I tell people that I have been on more diets than one could ever think of, and over the years I have lost and gained countless pounds. This issue is a constant temptation for me, and one where I can be overcome by forces in and around me to overindulge on certain foods. For example, when I was a marketing representative in California my job was to travel around and visit the agencies who sold my company's insurance. I was on my own during the work day and would stop by a store or bakery to buy goodies/sweets and eat them all in my car, and a little while later would stop somewhere else to load up again (not a pretty sight, yes, so *dumb*). After years of positive thinking, prayer, and reading many books about my issues, it dawned on me that my physical makeup would not allow me to eat just one of these foods. If I ate just one that was one too many and I would be on the path to eating more and more!

I learned over time that the best thing I can do is to not eat anything that will cause me to continue eating. However, I cannot do this alone, for my impulse is to eat up and enjoy the moment. Thus, I need the support that comes from my spiritual pilgrimage/practices and others to help out when my food cravings attack. Being overweight caused me more than a few struggles when I was growing up. Besides being made fun of at various times and acquiring some unwelcome nick names, this also contributed to my low self-esteem. My shyness and being overweight contributed to that. People can be so cruel sometimes and often do not think about the damage their actions can cause. Nor are they aware of the long-term effects it can have on people during their formative years. No matter what size or weight that I am today, I will always see myself as being overweight. Not until I was in my late teens and early twenties and began reading positive thinking books did my self-esteem begin to improve.

## YMCA

Even with me being overweight and not always in great shape physically, my brothers and I tried to remain active. Sports became an important part of our lives. We did not need a lot money or material things to be involved in playing games and doing other things. I feel fortunate for that time because it was something that we could do as a family. To this day, whatever setting I am in, I am always ready to take part in some form of game or sporting event.

The YMCA was very near to our apartment and we were able to go there all year round. It was a wonderful place for my family and those around us because it provided a location where we could learn things, play, and hang out with others of our age and with similar backgrounds. Probably its most important function, as far as my mother was concerned, was that it kept us from getting into trouble. We still did at times, but could have possibly been in more, considering that we were boys without a daily male presence at home. Our mom filled both parent roles most of the time, and did them remarkably well. But knowing that we were at the "Y" and not on the streets must have been comforting to her.

One of the neat things that I learned there was how to play Ping-Pong. I note this because after becoming an adult and raising a family, a Ping-Pong table was kept in our homes for many years. We have played countless Ping-Pong matches and had lots of fun times at that table. It is something that anyone can play, no matter one's age or ability. This sport has been carried over from my childhood and my time at the Y. My brothers and I also learned how to play basketball and other sports at that time. During the summer, we spent hours at the local public pool. My mother could not swim, but she made sure all her sons learned how to swim. That served us well as we grew up, for we were not afraid of being in water.

During our summers after we got older, my brothers and I were lucky enough to attend Camp Fitch, a YMCA camp. At first this was challenging for me because we had to be away from home. A bigger concern for me, a person who has always loved his personal space and was shy, was that we lived in group tents. The tents were on a solid foundation so we did not have to be on the ground. But there about six to ten boys in a tent, and, of course, we had to share the bathroom facilities. That was not easy for me and others but, after some time, I was able to adjust and hang in there.

Once I got past my initial fears and concerns it was a great experience for me, and it helped me grow as a person. Thank goodness there were things like Camp Fitch for young people like us. At Camp Fitch skills could be learned and wonderful experiences were enjoyed. Additionally, we learned how to live without our parents, work with others to do projects, and have fun at the same time. Looking back, that was a marvelous time in my life with lots of great memories.

My mother enjoyed sports and would take us to the high school football games on Friday evenings. She also got really involved in the games and would support the team very loudly. For many years I also did the same thing, watching games at home or in person. As I got older, I toned down a bit. But that pattern was born out of watching my mom's enthusiasm at high school games.

Sometimes we walked to Rayen High School on the north side to get to the games when we lived in the housing projects. Also, we would occasionally get a ride to South High School. At that time in Youngstown games were played at either of those two places. We did not own a car, and my mom did not learn to drive until all of us were adults. So, we walked a lot, took the bus, or got rides from family members or friends in order to get around. I grew up liking all sports and especially football. I did not play many organized sports, except in the streets, or with the Parks and Recreation program, or the YMCA. To this day, I prefer watching sports on television rather than other types of programs.

My memory about specific things that occurred when I was growing up is not as good as my brothers. I know people who can recall specific events from their youth. My brother Bennett and my wife Shirley are two people who always amaze me about how well they can recall detailed experiences from long ago. Beside recalling the 1950 blizzard, I do remember going with our Sunday school on a train ride to Cleveland to watch the Cleveland Indians play a baseball game. In the 1940s and 1950s they were a good team and we loved to follow them. Going to a big-league ball field was really fun for our family. Additionally, riding a train was a big deal for us back then. Even though I did not travel much then, I have definitely done my share of traveling and moving around as an adult.

At that time, our Sunday school and church was a very important part of our lives, with a lot of things going on for our family and community. As noted, if we did not go to church we could not go to the movies on Sundays, so, of course, we went to worship and Sunday school. My brothers and I were involved in a lot of things around church. We took part in Sunday school classes, and Christmas and Easter plays, which included learning countless speeches that had to be performed in front of the congregation. That was very intimidating as a youngster! We also sang in a youth choir and began ushering at a young age. All these activities helped in our development as people and in our faith journey. When

I got older, my roles were more of a leadership function until I moved away from Youngstown years later. Overseeing certain aspects of that community life also helped me mature and grow in my self-confidence.

## MUSICAL INSTRUMENTS

Another factor that helped in my development was practicing and learning how to play the piano. My mother believed that we should all learn to play some type of musical instrument. I guess she thought it would enlarge our horizons, teach us some discipline, and give us certain abilities that some others from our surroundings might not have. We, of course, did not know it at the time, but it did do all those things for us, and more. However, we just whined and complained whenever we had to practice or go for our lessons. Our grumbling did not work with Emma B. Jones, for she could be a tough person when it came to dealing her sons. She just made us keep up with it and practice even when we did not want to.

I learned to play the piano, while Bennett played the clarinet, and Randolph the drums. After Brian came along, he took piano lessons as well. All of us taking lessons was somewhat of a feat, because money was not readily available. The lessons were downtown, and my mother did not drive at the time. Thus, we had to catch a bus to get there or bum a ride.

After starting I continued to go downtown taking piano lessons for eight years. They were given at Strauss's Music Studios, and I had the same music teacher for the entire time. Each session was for a half an hour and we had to pay every week before taking the lesson. Besides paying for the weekly lessons, another miracle in my mind was that my mom somehow got a piano for me to practice on. Even though I often hated to practice and continue with the lessons, it was good for me. Besides building character and discipline, it allowed me to do other things later. I played for my Sunday school, one of the choirs at our church, the dance band at the high school, and the high school choir during my senior year. Being able to play the piano allowed me to experience certain aspects of life that I would not have been able to take part in otherwise. Thus, it ended up being a good skill to have.

TWO

# Personal Foundations Being Established— Not Always Perfectly Done

> Train children in the right way, and when old, they will not stray.
> —Prov 22:6

## BEING A SINGLE PARENT— NOT FOR THE FAINT OF HEART

Like most people my appreciation of the job that my mother did in rearing us grew as I got older. This developed even more so after becoming a parent myself. When Judy and I started having some major issues with our daughter, Elizabeth, I could see that it was nothing short of a miracle how my brothers and I turned out. We were not perfect by any means, but considering the barriers that all of us had to overcome, it was so amazing that things turned out as positively as they did.

This passage from Proverbs talks about training up a child in the right way, and when they are old, they will not depart from it. This does not always come true, or it may take a lifetime before it does. Nevertheless, we try to all do our best as a parent or guardian and set a good example for those we are parenting or mentoring. Like most of life, and especially regarding the spiritual pilgrimage, we must do our part and then leave the results and final outcomes to God.

As a parent, we do what we think is right for a particular moment or situation. We also try to look out for the best interest of everyone in the long term. But, sometimes, things do not work out as we had hoped. When we have done our best, unfortunately there still can be failure, poor choices can be made, and there may be some dreadful results. That does not mean that we should beat ourselves up or think of ourselves as failures.

At some point the child must mature and take responsibly for their own actions and life decisions. Living in today's world has challenges that at times can overwhelm us. Sometimes these events can have long and painful impacts on our lives. In my mind, next to being married, one of the more demanding things to do in life is be a parent/guardian/mentor. Now this is said realizing that many people do not ever get married or become parents, yet they have had countless barriers to overcome and deal with. But for me these roles are difficult to do. However, I will always be indebted to the foundation that my mom established for my brothers and me.

## A LIFE-CHANGING EVENT

My mom had a lot of hurdles to deal with in her role as a single parent. Having to discipline four boys, managing things financially, and making sure we mostly stayed out of trouble, plus helping with our school work, keeping us in church every Sunday, and basically raising us to be considerate and responsible adults—it was a huge undertaking. However, a very disturbing event happened while we still lived in the projects that caused her much pain at the time, and which still deeply troubles me today, all these years later.

As I noted before my memory regarding certain details about my younger years is not as good as I wish it were. However, there is one thing I am very clear about. Our youngest brother, Brian, was born on February 25, 1959; that is a known fact! Without that information, pinpointing this event would be more difficult. Approximately nine months before that date, my father came to our apartment in the projects and told my brothers and me to go outside. My dad did come by and visit occasionally, so that was not unusual. However, asking us to leave was odd, because when he came by, it always was to see us.

Thus, sometime in May of 1958, when the weather would have been good enough to be out doors, we were told to leave our small apartment. Even with my poor memory for details, I do remember this. Also, at that time we did not know what was going on. However, later we found out what had happened. My parents had officially divorced in 1956; my dad remarried but my mom never did. In 1958, my dad's wife was pregnant and my dad came by and had sex with my mom, who, nine months later, gave birth to Brian.

There is a lot that I can write about this, such as that Brian and Paula (my father's daughter) were born about the same time and looked a lot alike. However, I want to mainly focus on how this impacted my mom. There are so many things that she had to deal with because she was pregnant, unmarried, struggling financially, with three teenaged boys, and living in a very small apartment. Additionally, she had to go through the pregnancy without the support of a mate.

I have frequently mentioned how important my home congregation, Jerusalem Baptist Church, was to my family. However, during this time, some of the people there made my mom's life *extremely difficult*! That period was hard on us all, but she took the bulk of the negative comments. My father, on the other hand, did not attend our church and did not know what she was putting up with. But somehow, she did not give in and quit going to church, or singing in the choir, and she made sure that we continued going ourselves. In my mind, on many levels that was unfair for her to have to go through that basically alone. I am sure many other people would have left that church and gone elsewhere. My older brother, Bennett, has always said that is why he stopped going to Jerusalem, and began going to another Baptist church, because of how our mother was treated during that time.

The impact it had on me was that I felt *so* bad for her, because she went through that period, with only a few close friends and her extended family who stood by her. My brothers and I were too young and could not fully understand what she was going through. Because of this, and other things, I did not ever allow myself to get too close to my dad. However, when Judy and I had Elizabeth and Kevin, we wanted them know all their grandparents. I had hoped that their relationship with my dad would be different than mine. I never bought up what had happened in 1958–59 with him. I treated him with respect, as I would any other person. However, in my heart, I never saw him as someone who I looked up to and admired. I still have issues with this, even today.

This certainly influenced my life and impacted the person that I am today. My life has not been perfect, and I do not claim to never have made mistakes in my life. As you read further, you will hear about them. I know my father was not perfect as well, and I am not in any way trying to judge him or anyone else. I just know that in my mind, this did not have to happen the way it did. Brian is one of the nicest persons you will ever meet, and I am glad he is my brother. However, I struggle greatly with how my mom and Brian were treated and what they had to endure.

## JUNIOR HIGH DAYS—A LITTLE OF EVERYTHING

During my elementary school days, my grades were generally pretty good; I got mostly As and Bs without working that hard for them. I do not know if the work was easy or I could handle whatever came my way, but it did not seem that difficult. My days at Covington Street School were mostly fun for me, at least I do not have any negative memories about the time there. We of course walked to school every day, no matter the weather. At that point my mom did not drive or own a car, so walking was our only option.

When I started Hayes Junior High School, I had a rude awakening. Besides having to walk further to get there on time, the school was much larger and had a lot more students. One of the scariest hurdles that I had to deal with was that Hayes had lockers with locks on them! To this day, thinking about those days dealing with the combination lock still makes me nervous. For some reason, no matter how hard I tried, the stupid lock always seemed not to work right. It could take me multiple times to get it open. If I remember correctly, we only had three minutes between classes and that added pressure certainly did not help. I honestly think that issue affected me for a long time. Now I know looking back that was not such a big deal. But it was at the time, and I very clearly remember feeling stressed out about it.

That first year at Hayes was a challenging one for a few additional reasons. I was overweight as a young child and pretty much stayed that way until I was in my mid-late twenties. In elementary school being overweight was not such a big deal. Of course, things changed as I got older. Also, those I interacted with daily got older and were more willing to talk about people in a negative way. It did not help that I was shy, and my insecurity probably became more evident during that time. Consequently, I went further into myself because of those issues and the new surroundings.

I also had twin boys who were my best friends in grade school and we did a lot together. However, when we went to Hayes, we hardly interacted at all. I do not know if it was a race thing or not; they were white and I was not, so it could have been. Hayes was racially mixed, but we were never close again; this also impacted my transition to the new school.

I was in the seventh grade in 1958–59 when my mom was pregnant with Brian and then gave birth. As noted, that was an extremely trying year for all of us. Plus, I started a new school that I apparently was not prepared for. Additionally, I had the weight and self-esteem issues to overcome and the combination locks saga. That year was a very difficult year of transition for me. Consequently, I almost failed the seventh grade even though I was there every day. I usually enjoyed learning, but that year everything was a strain. I cannot totally blame it on the factors listed previously, for it was still up to me to get better grades. However, these issues contributed to my poor year.

At the end of the school year two of my grades were Fs. That should have caused me to repeat the seventh grade. However, one of my teachers gave me an "F in advance." That meant I still got credit for the course and could move on to eighth grade. However, it showed that I did not do enough good work to get a D. It was a good thing that did not happen in high school, for those grades would be on my permanent transcript. I am not sure if I was just lucky, if the teachers liked me and felt sorry for me, or if that was one of those miracles of life that are hard to see at the moment. But I was allowed to move to the eighth grade, and thankfully it was a better year.

At some point during my eighth-grade year at Hayes, my mom moved us back to the east side. We returned to my grandmother's (my mom's mother) house at 441 South Forest Avenue .I note the address because that is the place that I have a lot of memories. It was the house that my two brothers and I were born in. Before Nanny (my grandmother) died we had a lot of extended family get-togethers there. For a time, Nanny raised chickens in the back yard; I still remember seeing her catching and killing them. That was something a city kid like me was not used to seeing! That was the home where I became more involved at Jerusalem Baptist Church, the place where on Sundays after church we always had a big Sunday dinner. Later on, after we got older, we would invite friends over to eat with us.

I lived there until my early twenties and moved into my own apartment. I finished high school, got a job in the steel mill, and started college while living there. Our extended family always considered that house to be the homestead of the Coleman (Jones) family in Ohio. That was because Nanny was there and she was the solid rock whom we all loved and from whom we all sprang. After Nanny died, in my mind, it was never the same place; there was a large vacuum or hole that was never filled. However, it still held a warm spot in our hearts. I did not realize all this as an eighth grader, but later on when I reflected back upon those years.

That new year at Hayes was much improved for me; my grades were better and I played the piano for the school choir. I still had my fears about the dumb combination locks, but I learned how to deal with the time pressure between classes. I was still overweight and shy, but by that time I felt more comfortable in my school surroundings. Additionally, my family had gotten through some of the initial challenges and stresses of my mom's pregnancy and Brian's birth. I am not totally sure why my mom allowed me to do this, but after we moved back to the east side, I continued to attend Hayes Junior High School, which was on the north side of town. My mom allowed me to catch two city buses every day to continue at Hayes for that eighth-grade year. Neither of my school-age brothers did this, only me. Thus, every day I had to leave a little earlier to catch the two buses and would get home later, because of the bus ride. I am not sure if the school ever knew or cared, but I finished that year there.

The only thing I could think of is that the seventh grade was so hard on me that she did not want me to start another school so soon. By that time, I really enjoyed Hayes and was glad I was able to continue. On one hand, it was challenging to get to school, but, apparently, I never thought the strain of getting there outweighed the benefits of continuing there. It must have been an overall good experience for me.

All of the piano lessons and practicing the piano that I did, which I did not always care for, came in handy at that time. Besides starting to play for my church and Sunday school, I also played the piano for the eighth-grade choir. I seemed to enjoy doing that. It helped that I had a really good choir teacher/director who made it easy for me to play for the choir. However, I remember one time that catching the bus did not get me to school in time for a choir concert on a Saturday. I did not do enough research beforehand regarding the bus schedules and got to the concert late. The very wonderful director started playing the piano herself in order to get things started on time. I came in part way through the concert and finished playing for the rest of the performance. The director was really kind to me about it, but I was so embarrassed about being late. To this day, I always try to be on time for any appointment. I hate to make others wait, and I also dislike waiting for others when they are late.

## NANNY'S DEATH

Probably the most heartbreaking thing that happened during this time was when my grandmother, Nanny (Madeline Coleman), died on July 30, 1960. Her death impacted all of us, because she died too young at age sixty. Additionally, she was the rock and glue of the Coleman side of our family. Nanny had nine children, eight of whom were still alive when she passed away. Thus, I had plenty of aunts, uncles, and cousins from the Coleman side. We used to get together for a lot of events and were all close at that time. Looking back, Nanny was the center of it all. After she left us, we still tried to continue getting together, but as all of us got older and more geographically spread out, it did not occur as often.

I still remember the day of the funeral sitting in one of our cars waiting to go to the funeral. As I recall, it was a hot day, and all of us were having a hard time dealing with her death. But I can also still see my mother, sobbing and being very upset with Monk, her father, my grandfather. Monk left Nanny for another woman after she had given birth to nine children. They were married when Nanny was sixteen and Monk had brought their family from the south to the north for work. She gave her entire life to him and her family. I do not remember exactly what my mom said; however, it was something like this: that Nanny would be still alive if he had done more for her and had treated her better. My mom just let all her emotions out at the funeral, and she did not care who heard her. She was grieving and was very angry at her father all at the same time.

All of us would miss Nanny, but, additionally, because of the issues that my mother faced, Nanny had been a great support for her as well as others in our family. She pretty much raised two of my older male cousins. She could be loving and very strict all at the same time. One of the many gifts she gave to our family, and to me personally, was that she made sure her children, while young, attended church. That practice was carried on by my mom, and she made sure my brothers and I went as well. I continue today to attend some church community whereever I have lived. That routine goes back to what Nanny had modeled.

As a preteen and teen, being overweight and shy was not necessarily the best combination for anyone growing up on Youngstown's east side, which was basically a blue-collar town. Another issue was that my parents and grandparents were divorced, which had its own set of difficulties to handle. Dealing with peer groups as a teen is always challenging, but having these other aspects in my life did not help. Being a teen and having to function in this environment had a huge impact on me, but being a member of Jerusalem Baptist helped in my development and aided me in dealing with some of the other things that impacted my mind and spirit.

## MY TIME AT JERUSALEM BAPTIST CHURCH: A TIME OF GROWTH AND MATURITY

The first twenty-seven years of my life I belonged to and was a very active member of Jerusalem Baptist Church, which was on the far eastern side of Youngstown, Ohio. It was built near a steel mill and a number of the members worked in various mills around town. The vast majority of the families that were church members had moved to the area from the southern states to get jobs in the steel industry or some related business. My mother's family moved from Virginia to Ohio for the same reason and joined Jerusalem. The members were hard-working people who were looking for a better life for themselves and their families. The church was a very important part of their life and helped shape who they were. Jerusalem was also the cradle where my faith formation began.

Attending Jerusalem Baptist Church was generally a positive experience, which helped my brothers and I grow and mature. Except for the time when my mom was expecting Brian, that faith community was a place where we were welcomed and loved. Now do not get me wrong, there were still issues there like with any congregation. But it helped mold and develop me in so many ways. I was born into that church and over time became a very active member until I moved away to take a job in the insurance industry.

Even though I was born into this community, I did not officially join the church until I was baptized. This was an American Baptist Church, which believed in a believer's baptism. Thus, we did not baptize infants as liturgical churches do. Nor was this what Judy and I did with our children, because we had agreed to raise them in the Catholic church. But at

Jerusalem Baptist each person had to make the decision to join and be baptized on their own.

Near the end of all of our worship services we would have an altar call. The deacons would be in the front of the church inviting those who wanted to profess their faith in Jesus to come forward. It could be a stirring moment for certain people when they came up. Often adults would share their life stories of what they had been through to get to that point. Some of the accounts could be gut wrenching and filled with sorrow and pain. The feelings could be quite raw, especially after all of the praying, singing, and the hearing a long and passionate sermon. There could also be tears, people shouting, and occasionally someone getting "happy." The buildup was intentionally emotional to get people to respond to the invitation.

I can still see myself getting out of my pew on the day I decided to come forward. It was not something that I thought of doing beforehand, I just came up, for I knew it was time for me to do this. I was on the left side of the sanctuary facing the front of the church. On that day, I was not ushering or doing anything else. Normally the deacons or pastor would ask some questions of the person, to be sure that they knew what their decision meant. However, if I remember correctly, they only said that everyone knew me, and that I was already involved in lots of things around the church. Basically, they acknowledged that I was ready to take this step.

We had baptisms on the first Sunday of every month together with communion. Unlike some other denominations, communion was only once a month. We had a small pool in the basement of the church, and that was where one was baptized. The pool would be filled with water, and one was totally submerged. I was baptized at age fourteen, on February 6, 1960. After that I was able to take communion at Jerusalem and became an official member of the congregation. Rev. Anderson was our pastor at that time, and he was someone in my mind who was gifted to be a pastor. Being baptized was a huge deal for me personally and to those in our faith tradition. This was another important step in my spiritual walk.

Besides attending Sunday school and worship most every Sunday, I was involved in a number of different areas over the years at that small church. I starting ushering while quite young. At that time, we always had ushers helping out with the service. It was a very important role at Jerusalem. There was a proper way to stand, certain times you faced the front, certain times you faced the back when ushering people. Back then people could not walk in whenever they felt like it. There was a time and place for everything. The ushers had to respect the worship service or else they were told about it. Also, ushers had certain ways of dressing, so we all looked the part.

After I got older, I was put in charge of the Bud ushers, those who were not preteens yet. Yes, we started them out young back then. I must have enjoyed ushering for I still do it at times today. In many of the places I have lived as an adult I have filled in as an usher. I am probably one of the few people that can say that they have ushered in a Baptist, Catholic, Lutheran, and several other Protestant churches. Being comfortable with ushering started while I was at Jerusalem Baptist as a young boy. Sometimes I think of this Bible verse: "I would rather be a doorkeeper in the house of my God than live in the tents of wickedness" (Ps 84:10).

## SUNDAY SCHOOL

Our Sunday school at that time started at 9:15 a.m. with a song, devotions, and an introduction to the lesson for that day. From about 9:30 a.m. to roughly 10:15 a.m. we were in our separate classes studying our Bible lessons. From 10:15 a.m. to 10:30 a.m. someone did a review of the Bible lesson, we had announcements, and a closing song. I mention this time frame for at some point I did most every job in our Sunday school. My piano skills came in handy for the few years that I played for the Sunday school. As I got a little older, I became the teacher for the high school class.

About age eighteen or nineteen I became the youngest Sunday School superintendent that congregation had ever had. Being the superintendent meant being there on time to start everything, getting people every week to review the lesson, being sure we had materials for the classes, filling in when teachers did not show up, basically making sure things ran smoothly. I learned organizational skills that would be used the rest of my life. I also had a good grounding in the study of the Bible. In this position, I also came into contact with some spiritual-minded people who became wonderful mentors and role models for me.

Sometime after becoming Jerusalem's Sunday School superintendent, I became involved with a group of other churches and their Sunday schools from the surrounding area that worked together. We frequently had programs of interest that were offered to our communities. We often did things as an alliance that would have been challenging for the individual churches to do alone.

Eventually I became president of that association, and became more involved in planning those events. I remember a program that we put on one Sunday afternoon. We had two sisters from the Humility of Mary religious order come and take part in one of our panel discussions. Now it is important to be aware of the context of that event. The time frame would have been in the late 1960s in Youngstown, Ohio. The people in this federation would have been made up of 100 percent African-Americans. Most would have been from Baptist churches or from a similar denomination. The two sisters were Roman Catholic and both were of European descent. That was an interesting program from many different standpoints. The main thing was that the sisters were willing to do it, and our community was open to the idea and received it in a welcoming manner.

While I was taking classes at Youngstown State University, I was involved with the Campus Christian Fellowship group. Through them I met these sisters and others from their order. We became friends and they were willing to take part in this. This event was the one of the first times that I was connected to something that included people from different races, backgrounds, and religions. We are all God's children, despite the fact that some of us do not look the same or even have a lot in common. But we can come together, talk, and share when our hearts and minds are open in a loving manner. The panel discussion went well, and I will always be grateful for everyone who took part in it.

As president of that confederation, I enhanced my presentation, organizational, and communication skills, which still helps me today. Also, like some of the people at Jerusalem, I was fortunate to be helped and mentored by persons I met there. One such person was James Smith, whom I met through this alliance. He was the manager of the YMCA on the north side of Youngstown. He was full of wisdom about life, the church, and about walking the spiritual path. He influenced a lot of young lives in his role at the Y, and I will always appreciate the time he gave to me.

## VISITING OTHER FAITH COMMUNITIES

Another neat experience I had was my involvement with Jerusalem's youth and our trips to visit other worship centers. Because I was involved with people from different faith traditions when I was a part of the Campus Christian Fellowship group at YSU, and also teacher of the small Sunday school high school class at Jerusalem, I was able to connect the two parties together. Additionally, because I also was the Sunday School superintendent, I had the authority to take part in these happenings as long as everything was done in good order. These trips would have taken place in the late 1960s.

Again, our church was made up of African-Americans whose families moved to Youngstown for employment and a better way of life. Most would not have had much contact with people of different races or ethnic backgrounds, within their own faith communities. My thinking back then probably would have been that it was important for our youth to be exposed to people who were different than they were. It would have been the same for those with whom we came into contact. Having a little knowledge concerning people that are dissimilar to us goes a long way in understanding others and in time can change how we interact with them. Additionally, I wanted those teens to visit other faith traditions to learn about how others worshiped and something about their beliefs.

I am not sure I totally knew what I was doing when we started out on this particular adventure; certainly, I had no idea how it would turn out. This could have been a huge risk on my part if it had backfired. There may have been some really awful situations that we had to deal with, but, thankfully, for the most part it was a very wonderful encounter for everyone. As so often is the case in our spiritual pilgrimage, when we do things like this it means stepping out in faith, because so much is completely unknown. Inter-faith events had not been done before at Jerusalem, nor would I imagine that it had been done at very many other churches in the greater Youngstown area.

The youth from Jerusalem were really good students and were open to taking part in something like this. We generally took another adult along to drive and help out with things. Theodore Venable was one person who went with us on these trips. He was very willing to visit these other churches with us. Theodore also really knew his Bible. At one service, when the scripture for the day was read, he knew the passage from memory. He spoke the words from that passage along with the reader, without any notes. That impressed everyone there and me.

He was a wonderful example of God's love being shown to others no matter their race, religion, or ethnic background. When he met people for the first time, he was always friendly and welcoming. He told me the story of his walks around his neighborhood. He noted that this one person, who was of European descent, lived near him and, daily, when he walked, he would always say hello to this man, with no response back. But over time this man warmed up and spoke back to Theodore. He shared that story as an example of the importance of being open and welcoming to others who are different from us. By his model, he taught me the importance of being open to others and greeting them no matter who they are. He lived his faith, and that faith impacted how he treated others and how he went about his daily routine. He was the brother of Kenny Venable, who also had an impact on me. Kenny and I worked together in the steel mill.

With this small group of youth, we would worship with other churches and learn about their faith tradition. We even visited a Jewish temple, which, of course, was so very unlike the other Christian congregations we had visited. All of the communities we went to were of a European descent. One never knows how or when God will use activities such as these to break down barriers or cause people to be changed for God's kingdom. Pulling off these visits took a lot of work and faith-filled planning on my part and the community we were visiting. Probably the most awesome get-together we had involved a fellow student from the Campus Christian Fellowship group I belonged to at YSU. Steve Gifford was a member of this group and later on became a United Church of Christ pastor. He was someone who was open and friendly, and I got to know him well over time. In fact, when Judy and I got married, he did a reading for us during the service.

Steve's home congregation was in the outlying area around Youngstown. Nevertheless, he brought people from his church to worship with us after our small group visited his congregation. Now Jerusalem Baptist was a small congregation with a little building. Thus, when thirty to thirty-five Caucasian adults and youth appeared at our service to worship with us, that was a huge deal! It blew others in our church and me totally away. I can still see them all coming in and the looks of amazement on the faces of the Jerusalem worshipers.

It was awe-inspiring to see people of vastly different backgrounds, faith traditions, and races worshiping God together. There are many lessons learned from that day and from the other places we visited. I do not know for sure, but I think that God does not really care which faith tradition, or building, or format we use to worship and praise the Creator of all of us. The most importable thing is that it is done with a humble, loving, and grateful heart and soul, as opposed to us being hung up with all of the human-made structure we have built up and maintained over the centuries.

Hopefully, you have been fortunate enough to have taken part in something like this, and it was a positive and spiritual event that nourished your body and soul. When we take advantage of such opportunities, we become part of bringing God's kingdom into this time and place. In my mind and understanding about God's kingdom being brought forward in this present age, it happens whenever people of faith strive for this kingdom by their actions and deeds. At such precious moments the kingdom can be felt and experienced by those who are participating. When we planned to do this, no one knew how it would turn out. But thank the Lord, we were lucky enough to be a part of something magnificent for all involved and for the kingdom of God.

Being involved with the youth at Jerusalem was part of my growth as a person, and it also helped me on my spiritual pilgrimage. Besides taking them places, I also was their high school Sunday school teacher. Being good Baptists, we studied the Bible quite a bit, which required me to study and learn right along with them. The youth in my class were basically good students and I have fond memories of my time with them. I did not know it at the time, but teaching classes at Jerusalem started something that has continued most of my adult life. I am probably one of the few people who have taught Sunday school or youth religion classes in Baptist, Catholic, and Lutheran churches. It is something that I have come to enjoy and have felt that I have helped others in their spiritual journeys, as well as enriching my own knowledge of the Bible. In my mind, the study of the Bible is the cornerstone to growing in faith on our spiritual walk.

## WORSHIP AT JERUSALEM BAPTIST

Another important aspect of my time at Jerusalem was music. Besides playing for a while for the Sunday school, I also played piano for our senior choir during our morning worship services. Even though we were a small congregation, we had a number of choirs, from the youth on up.

I could read music pretty well at that time, and with practice could deal with most any music that they sang. This of course was due to my mom who made me go to lessons, *when I did not want to*, and also practice *when I did not want to*. I know practicing helped me with becoming more disciplined in my life, which has helped me on my life's journey. (That does not take away from the fact that I still disliked a lot of the lessons and practice!)

However, even though I could read music, I could not play by *ear*! Playing by ear meant that a person could hear someone singing, would listen for a bit, and then be able to pick up the key that was being sung. Then for those who were skilled enough could start accompanying those singing, and continue right along with them without sheet music. This was a very wonderful gift/skill to have, but I did not have it. However, for those who did, they could generally create some awesome music. In my mind being able to play by ear was a natural ability that you had when you were born. It was not something that could be taught or learned; you either had it or you did not. I always admired people who could do that. In churches like Jerusalem, people who had this gift and were also able to read music were always in demand. Talented gospel musicians added so much to the worship service.

The services that we had at Jerusalem were naturally long with a fairly lengthy sermon. The sermons were meant to get everyone emotionally involved in the service. It was used to get people who had not joined the church or made a commitment to Jesus to be their Lord to step forward and make that vow. Thus, that is why the altar call came right after the sermon. By that time in the service, with all of the praying, singing, and long sermon, those who sensed the desire to come forward were passionately ready to do so.

I was in worship most every Sunday, either serving in some role or sitting in a pew. However, over time I did not appreciate the long sermons as some others may have. I began to sense a layer of showiness that was used to get people to react based on the talents and skills of the preacher, versus a real life-changing event centered upon the need to have the love of Jesus become more of a factor in their lives. So much emphasis was placed on having this conversion moment. I grew to believe that getting people to come forward totally because of one emotional moment—maybe was not something that would last. If a person was not willing to change how they lived over the long run, hearing one fired-up sermon may not have really helped them in moving forward.

A concern with those who came down for an altar call is what would happen next. Without some faith practices or community backing, it would be very easy to not continue on this path. Staying on this walk involves getting support, having discipline, and making a commitment to make it be a lifelong decision. Thus, way back when I was at Jerusalem, I had concerns about the sermons and how they impacted those who heard them.

I do not fault the Baptist preachers that I heard; they were just following the methods of preaching that had been around for years. Of course, some were better than others, but I increasingly heard the flashiness and the watered-down Christian theology. Thus, I began to tune out the sermons and only half listened to them. I must add, however, that was not the case with me later on. Since Shirley and I have been married, before she retired, I timed her sermons and took notes during all of her sermons. That way I was more engaged with what was being preached.

Going through this experience has helped form the basis of my current ministry. That is, I feel called to help individuals and congregations in their spiritual pilgrimage. This journey means that daily we have to turn toward God, God's kingdom, and God's will in our lives. It is not a one-time happening. Every day we have to decide whom we will follow. Part of our role, in my mind and in the mind of many other spiritual writers, is to become lifelong disciples of Jesus Christ by what we do and speak. That role could include prayer, Bible study, and reflection, or whatever spiritual practices help move us toward this goal.

While at Jerusalem, I could listen to most of the music played there all day. The songs that the senior choir sang, which I played for, were not always the most upbeat. But when we had other church choirs singing, or had some guest choirs, or a dynamic, talented pianist, some of the songs they performed could light a fire in your soul and take you to a higher plane. Again, the music was meant to get everyone emotionally involved in the service. However, I did not look at our music in the same fashion that I saw our preaching. To me, the music could have more meaning and spiritual depth. Yes, it could just be an emotional reaction to what was heard, but in my mind, it was more authentic and soul changing. I grew up loving this type of music and have had a lifelong love affair with it. For my money, there is nothing better than some good spirit-filled, energetic gospel music. I like a wide range of music, but I have more gospel CDs, and I listen to more gospel than any other type.

I miss that part of the Baptist experience more than any other aspect of worshiping in that tradition. Since I left Youngstown, I have not had that many opportunities to take part in those types of services. Since then, I have had most of my worship experiences in the Catholic and Lutheran traditions. Their services can at times be uplifting and meaningful; however, for me it just is not the same.

Every faith tradition has things it does that are better than some others. I totally understand that, because I have had a lot of support in my spiritual pilgrimage from every congregation that I have been a part of. But, lively, soul-filled gospel music is in my bones and part of who I am today. It has continued to nourish and help sustain me on my journey. When I was caring for Judy after she went under hospice care, gospel music was a God-send, as it helped me make it another day. Music in whatever form that moves your soul is a gift from God. Music has enriched my life from earliest days until the present.

My time at Jerusalem Baptist laid the foundation for me in many ways. It helped me get through my earlier years when I was struggling with my self-esteem challenges (of course I still have deal with that part of my makeup even today). Because of my involvement with many different responsibilities there, I began to develop communication and organizational skills that have been with me ever since. At Jerusalem, I began my lifelong study of the Bible. That study and their worship services established the beginnings of my spiritual pilgrimage, even though I did not know what it was called back then.

I also learned firsthand that there is no perfect pastor, deacon, deaconess, church leader, or congregation. That everyone and every community will have failures, cause people to be hurt, and basically make unwise decisions. Of course, there are a lot of positive outcomes and spiritual aspects gained from being in a faith community. However, on this side of God's kingdom, all of us will come up short in some way at various times in our lives. But we have the promise of forgiveness for all that we do, and that assurance comes from the gift of God's infinite grace, love, and mercy.

The time at Jerusalem exposed me to men and woman who helped and supported me. By their lives, they gave me insight about how to act on a daily basis. I have already mentioned how Kenny and Theodore Venable were important role models for me. Another person who was an example of someone who daily lived out his Christian faith was Deacon J. R. Moore. I saw him as someone who was honest and forth-right and who tried to do the right thing, even when he was facing a lot of opposition in the congregation. Two of my mother's dearest friends were so supportive of my family. Mrs. Oliver and Mrs. Hickson were very loving and caring persons who gave of themselves to us and to those in our community.

I will always be grateful for the time at Jerusalem and for being a part of that congregation. By just being there I began a habit of always attending worship services no matter where I have lived. If my mom had given me the choice concerning if I wanted to go to church or not, my brothers and I would have probably slept in and stayed home. However, we were basically forced to go, but for me it stuck and that time helped mold me and get me to where I am today. Nanny and my mom, by their force of wills, instilled in me the awareness of the importance of being part of a loving, supportive community.

## HIGH SCHOOL DAYS—MORE MEANINGFUL INVOLVEMENT

In the fall of 1960, I entered the ninth grade at East High School. East, of course, was quite different from Hayes. It was much bigger, had more students, and there was more stress around being a student there. My oldest brother, Bennett, was already there and was well established. He was more outgoing than me, very confident of himself, and also was a lady's man. I continued to be basically quiet and shy and weighed more than I wanted to. Initially I had a tough time fitting in. Until I began to get more involved in activities around the school, I did not have many close friends. However, even though I was not as popular as my brother, by the time I left there, I had a few close buddies who I could count on, trust, and hang out with. Additionally, I had a wide range of people that I got to know and feel comfortable with from the groups and classes we were in together.

East High School was the same one that both my dad's and mom's family attended, when they were our age. Remarkably, we had a few of the same teachers that my parents had. I took college prep courses, even though I probably should not have because of my junior high grades. These classes were a real challenge for me, but at least I did not fail any like I did in the seventh grade. As with most of life, I had both positive and less than positive experiences at East. There were a number of teachers and staff that took a personal interest in their students and wanted them to flourish, both in the class room and in life.

I walked to and from East High School every day, like my brothers and most people that we knew. It was a long walk and, yes, sometimes we were able to get rides, but most days we walked, in rain, snow, or any type of climate. My mom did not drive nor own a car and to get around we walked, took the bus, or got a ride with people. To my knowledge, we were not late for classes and generally made it on time. The importance of being on time was ingrained in me at an early age when my mom made sure we made it to school on time every day.

I was fortunate to have been there for my entire four years of high school, and in time got to feel comfortable there. Looking back that was a big deal, for my own two children had to switch schools whenever I moved to change jobs. That can be a tough enough time in a young person's life without changing in mid-stream. But I did not have to move while at East, and for that I am very grateful. Those years molded me and helped me mature as a young man.

Being able to play the piano came in handy for me at East like it did at Jerusalem. I played piano for a while for the school dance band, the orchestra, and in the twelfth grade played for the a cappella choir. Again, being able to play allowed me to take part in events that others may not have been able to participate in. Being in these groups allowed me to get somewhat comfortable performing in front of people. As a basically shy person that was a really big deal for me to be able to take part in those concerts. Even though one never gets totally used to playing in front of an audience, it little by little takes some of the fear away.

I took part in a number of different clubs and activities during my high school years. As a senior, I was on the Senior Sales Committee that sold ads for the 1964 *Janus* (our yearbook). Even though I continued to be basically a shy person, I became good at getting people to buy ads. If I remember correctly, I was one of the best sales persons that committee had. However, as you know some details can get a little fuzzy over the years, but that is how I remember it. This may have been a foreshadowing of my career in the insurance industry where I spent the bulk of my nearly twenty-eight years in the marketing area, working with the agents who sold my companies' insurance. I basically became a company sales person to the agencies who sold our insurance.

Sports have always been an important part of my life. From an early age on, my mother took us to high school football games on the weekends. We also watched a lot of sports on the TV when we had one. I had a couple of older cousins who were really good athletes. They made their high school football teams and as a family we were there to watch them. My brothers and I played a lot of street football, and then recreational baseball, and swam at the local pool during the summer. I still loved sports by the time I got to high school, but was not that great of a participant for organized sports. I tried out for football and track, but did not have the drive, ability, or whatever it took to be very good. People said about me concerning football that I was not aggressive enough, which was probably true. I was known mostly for being a nice guy. It took a long time to just make the traveling team. I only got to play in one game, the one between East High School and North High School when it was already won, which was the last game of my senior year.

Track was not any better; I tried to throw the discus, but also was not good at that. I went to practice and hung in there but I just did not have what it took to be good at either. Back then, trying to be good at sports was a really big deal for me, but it just did not work out for me. As an adult, I know that we all have different gifts and cannot be good at everything. But I really wanted to do well in sports, and it caused me some pain and struggle when I could not be. However, as I got older, I got involved in recreational sports, which I took part in and enjoyed, like softball and soccer. I coached some of my children's teams, and eventually got into refereeing soccer. I went so far as to take the tests and in time became a licensed high school soccer referee, which I did for a number of years and really enjoyed it.

The biggest thing that came out of my lack of athletic abilities in high school was developing a lifelong habit of jogging. Because I have always looked at myself as being overweight, I began jogging regularly in my mid-twenties and continue until today. I started this to lose weight, to stay in shape, and to maintain a healthy body. Jogging has also become part of my prayer routine. During that time, I have various prayer practices that have evolved over the years. They mostly help keep my mind and soul focused on God's kingdom and doing God's will in my life. Thus, even though I was not good at organized sports in high school, which caused me some anguish, I have been blessed with a body that has been able to be physically active for all of my life. The lesson here is to not let what did or did not happen in our younger days prevent us from moving to where we are being led to go today.

During high school, I was also involved with a few clubs and the Prom Committee. However, nothing stands out to me about any of these today. I was also in the College Club, which is odd. I knew I probably wanted to go college; however, not until later on did I know how unprepared I was to attend. Thus, being part of the College Club did very little if anything to help prepare me for actually going to college. Later on, when I relate my early college days and the courses taken, you will understand. I did, however, take college prep courses. For some reason, they allowed me to do that, even when my junior high grades were not all that great. I always liked the social studies type courses, while courses like physics, geometry, etc., were a real struggle for me. During my senior year I got As and Bs in most of my courses except for physics, which I averaged a D in.

All of us have those moments in time when we can remember where we were in a certain situation no matter how much time passes. On November 22, 1963, I was in physics class when we got the word that President John F. Kennedy had been shot. I can still see our teacher, Mr. Amato, hearing the news and leaving us alone in class. He did not say a word; he just walked out. He was so upset about it that he had to leave. He never came back to our class until the next day. That was an extremely daunting and emotional moment for all of us, no matter what political party one belonged to.

One of my favorite high school teachers was Mr. Arthur Schwartz, my Problems of Democracy teacher. He was a bit older than some of the other teachers at East and he could be tough and demanding. I liked his course, and he taught me two important things about life that I still remember. I am sure he and other teachers helped me learn countless other things about life and knowledge about the world, but these two aspects bear noting.

One thing I remember was him helping me to learn facts and data that would be needed to pass certain exams. Because my memory is not as good as some others, he encouraged me to write down over and over the things that had to be learned. Especially those things that my mind had a hard time holding on to. I have used that practice for most of my life when involved in any type of study.

He was also a very wise person about life, and at some point, he said, "If you solve one problem, you create another one." Now I cannot tell you in what context he said this, only at some point he spoke those words or something like them. I realize that this short sentence is not all that profound. However, at that moment in time, it was something that made a huge impression on me and has stayed with me all of my life. At various times, I have recalled that saying and applied it to a current situation. I do not look at it as being a negative statement in regards to never trying to solve problems. However, my view is that life is forever revolving, being created anew, and that, unless you are in a grave, life is not stagnant. Amazing that I still remember Mr. Schwartz and his wisdom after all of these years; he is most certainly a part of my life's story and journey.

As any of us look back over our school years, we realize that it was a mixed bag of emotions. Those days could be seen as the best of times right along with the worst of times, often in the same day. It basically was like our adult daily lives, where the ups and downs merge together on our life journey. I know that was the case for me. I faced difficult times there because of my weight issues, being rather shy, and from being a teenager. Some of the challenging moments also came about because of my home situation, being raised by a single mom, with all of the financial shortcomings that we faced.

However, I was also able to have some close friends who helped me get through my tough times. Additionally, I had some really wonderful happenings which were a positive for me. People who knew me saw me as a nice guy who tried to get along with everyone. I wanted to try and please those around me and be a helpful person. Looking back on the notes written in my yearbook that seems to be the common theme, being a nice guy is what was noted the most. I probably still try to be a nice person; thus, my basic personality is the much the same as when I was younger. That is undoubtedly who I am at my core.

## THE HIGHS AND LOWS OF HIGH SCHOOL

Talking about having a negative and positive occurrence in the same day, that happened to me one day in the boy's gym locker room. As background for this let me bring up again that I had attended church and Sunday school since I can remember. I had learned all of the Bible stories about how God loved us and would be with us no matter what was going on in our lives. All of that learning came into focus for me one day after gym class.

This defining moment for me came probably when I was in the tenth grade. Guys would often make fun of me when I changed clothes because of my excess fat from being overweight. This did not happen all the time but enough times for me to dislike being in those settings. To this day, I still have a hard time being in situations like that. Of course, I am not made fun of anymore, but I do have an emotional scar from those experiences that still impacts me today. When I played football, I would always want to get dressed quickly after practice to keep the comments from happening too often. Those gym times were not fun moments for me.

However, this one day I prayed that God would stop them from talking about me and you know what—*they did*! This was the first time I knew that God could directly answer my prayers. One minute they were making fun of me and the next they were not. I was still overweight and they could pick at me again, but at that moment I knew God was there and cared about me. All of those days in church hearing about God's love came into focus for me at that moment. Now please know that my life did not suddenly become perfect and I was able to walk off in the sunset free of life's struggles. But my faith grew on that day, and, hopefully, it has continued to grow every day since.

Another memorable high school moment revolved around my playing the piano for the a cappella choir during my senior year. I mostly enjoyed being a part of the choir, and with practice I was able to do an okay job accompanying the choir. I also liked the director, Mr. Campbell; he was demanding, but we sounded really good. Occasionally, we would do a concert away from our school. Of course, we always practiced the pieces that we would be doing in our performance. However, at one outside event, we were going along and doing rather well when Mr. Campbell suddenly decided the choir should sing another song that we had not scheduled. Because we had not intended to sing "The Lord Bless You and Keep You," I had not taken the sheet music with me. As you may recall I did not play by ear, without music, and always played from printed music.

However, he felt the urge and told us to go right into this song. In my mind, a miracle happened because I started playing the introduction to the song from memory. The choir came in when they were supposed to and, from my recollection, we sounded fantastic. I continued to play without music and we all finished together. To my knowledge that was the first time I had ever done that, and that never happened again. I can remember it being a huge rush for me when it was all over.

That event and performing in general were a real boost to my ego and self-esteem. To this day, even with my shyness, I still enjoy being in front of people speaking or teaching. I do not perform any longer but those days playing the piano in church or at high school helped mold me and gave me confidence about not being afraid to be in front of people. While in the work force and now in my current ministry I have done presentations frequently. Those earlier days helped prepare me for my current roles.

Looking back, overall, my high school days were just okay in my mind. There were of course highs and lows, but I do not think of those days as being that wonderful, magical period. I was not one of the more popular people, certainly was not a sports jock, nor a class leader, nor one of the better students from a grade standpoint. I was just Vernon T., all-around nice guy. I had some friends and people that I could do things with, but was not someone who people just had to be with.

For any number of reasons, I did not have any real girlfriends, even though I would have loved that. I had females who were friends, but not "girlfriends." I fell in love often, almost daily whenever a pretty girl walked by, but nothing ever came from that. One female classmate, with whom I tried to get a relationship going, ended up hurting me very badly. I thought we had a connection, and she sort of led me to believe that, but she only strung me along. After a while another good friend of mine finally told me what was happening, and that this other person did not really care about having a relationship with me. That was really a crushing blow for me, and one that took a while to get over.

I did not learn to drive until I was out of high school and that of course really limited any dating I could do. Additionally, my mom did not drive or own a car at that point. However, if my memory serves me right my mom found a young lady, not from my high school, to go the senior prom with. My mom wanted me to enjoy my senior year and to take part in any activity that I wanted to be a part of. My friend Carl Murray did have a car and drove me to the prom with him and his girlfriend. From what I can remember, I had an enjoyable time. I was glad I was able to go, for I was on Prom Committee and had invested time in the event.

## MY PARENTS DURING MY HIGH SCHOOL DAYS

From what you can tell, my mom was a very important part of my life and the glue that held our family together. However, until I got out of high school and started working full time, we would be considered fairly poor from a financial standpoint, throughout most of my growing-up years. But when I was in high school there were more monetary demands on us, versus having all of us being in grade school or junior high.

My mom did not work out of the home until most of us were gone and on our own. Those years were often extremely difficult for all of us, especially as teenagers. It seemed that we were always short of money and when we did have some cash flow, we spent it on food and the basic elements of living, and then it was gone. The bottom line was that we were really poor money managers, with no long-term vision. I remember periods when we were not able to pay our gas bill and were without heat for a time during the winter months. I also recollect having to heat water on the stove to wash up with, plus other unpleasant things that we had to do. I know that everyone has had to deal with things in life that are not always fair and I also understand it could have been a lot worse if my mom had not been there making sure that we did what we were expected to do and staying out of trouble.

I recall that my mom and dad had many discussions about the child support he was supposed to pay. Apparently, he was often late or not giving the required amount. I am not totally blaming my dad for the situation that we often found ourselves in, for I did not know all of the factors that went into our financial condition. But my mom was with us all the time, and I do not remember him being with us that much, especially when we were younger. He had remarried and had a daughter. But I will always side with my mom in cases like this one.

We are all gifted in different areas and being a good personal money manager has never been one of my strong suits. While in the insurance industry I generally managed well the company's funds and the budgets for which I was responsible. However, my own individual financial matters could be a challenge for me.

While I was in high school, my dad ran a service station on the east side of Youngstown. He owned this station until he left to go to work for General Motors at their Lordstown plant. The summer between my junior and senior years in high school I worked at the station pumping gas and helping out around the station. My dad was well known for fixing cars and he specialized in repairing automatic transmissions, which is where the station made the most money. Selling gas was just a side line for him. I also worked for him after my senior year, because I did not have any firm idea about what I wanted to do once I was finished school. I left that job once I went to work in the steel mill, which offered a steadier and better paycheck

My dad was really good around cars and knew how to fix most anything on them. However, my brothers and I did not follow in his footsteps in that regard. I like new cars and what they can do, but I never had the urge to fix them for a living, nor work on my own cars, except for very basic stuff. My dad had a really strong work ethic, and I think that is one quality that I received from him.

When I graduated from East High, my dad bought me a new suit for the graduation. I mention this because, in my view, it was a big deal for him to do that at that time. In my opinion, my dad was not an important factor in my young life; that is how I saw it then and still see it many years later. He treated us fine when he was around us. But in my mind, he did not try hard enough to become more involved in our lives when we were younger, unless it suited his schedule. After we were older, growing into young men, he seemed to be more visible. Thus, when he got me that new suit, I was amazed.

THREE

# Growing into Young Adulthood—With All of Its Opportunities and Challenges

> But strive first for the kingdom of God and his righteousness, and all these things will be given to you as well. So do not worry about tomorrow, for tomorrow will bring worries of its own. Today's trouble is enough for today.
>
> —Matt 6:33–34

## STRIVING FOR GOD'S KINGDOM—TOUGH AT ANY AGE

This is one of my very favorite Bible verses while at the same time being one of the more challenging ones. It has been a key part of my faith journey for the majority of my life. For me it holds so much truth about what our focus should be during our pilgrimage. Striving for God's kingdom before anything else in our lives is so easy to say, but so incredibly hard to do daily. The truth is right there in front of us in plain sight. Jesus talked about this kingdom more than any other topic. He gave us many parables about it and referred to it often in his teaching.

I know this lesson well in my head, soul, and heart. However, getting the spiritual and physical facets of my life in alignment to live out this message on an hourly and daily basis is one that I will probably take to the grave with me. I cannot begin to tell you how many times I have tried to do things in life where my focus has been on myself versus God's kingdom. Then, at some point, I eventually wake up and turn toward God's kingdom and will in my life. When I do this, my attitude and emphasis changes, and what and how things are done changes, because my motivation is more on God's kingdom and not on myself. When this is done the results belong to God and not me, and I am freed from my self-centeredness. What then comes from my actions is in God's hands and not in mine. I am less concerned about how things turn out as long as I am doing what I think God is directing me to do.

Now do not misunderstand, my life does not suddenly become perfect, and I walk off into some paradise sunset. I still have failings and faults and make countless mistakes. However, over the long run when I strive for God's kingdom versus Vernon T.'s agenda, I have more inner peace, even when going through some very demanding situations. I bring this topic up now because, during the next period of my life that I will be recalling, God's kingdom and where my attention was placed began to play an increasingly important role in my life. After I started taking college classes and for the rest of my life, Matt 6:33–34 kept coming back to me over and over again. It is very humbling for me to admit that this remains a constant unceasing lesson for me to learn.

## WHAT NEXT AFTER HIGH SCHOOL

After finishing East High School, I did not have a lot of direction about what to do next. Even though I had taken college prep courses at East and did pretty well in most of them, no one at the school, in my mind, helped me think about my future. Maybe they did try to guide me, but I do not remember anyone sitting down with me and saying "Vernon T., what do you want to do when you finish your high school years?" So, I never looked at or applied to any colleges, nor even looked into what other career options there were for me. I did not even know much about junior colleges or trade schools, and did not necessarily want to go to the armed forces, even though my older brother, Bennett, went that route. Maybe I should have been more aggressive about this myself, but I was not.

However, I went back to work at my dad's service station for a time. Thank goodness that was available, for it gave me something to do. Sitting around doing nothing without some goal or purpose would have not been good for me. Later that summer, my mom tried to come to my rescue again. As you know I was a member of Jerusalem Baptist Church, and she approached Mr. Melvin Dotson, a caring deacon at our church, for help in getting me a full-time job. He helped me get an interview at Republic Steel where he worked.

Youngstown, Ohio, at that time had a number of steel plants and many other businesses that worked with the steel industry. A number of the people at Jerusalem had jobs that were connected to this industry. You could not go very far in Youngstown without seeing, hearing, or smelling one of the plants. On certain days, the smoke from the plants could be seen for a long distance. Over time the EPA helped clean things up; however, much later on, most of the bigger plants closed down all together. This did not help Youngstown or the surrounding area. Countless people permanently lost their jobs and many had to leave town to find work. Youngstown is greatly reduced in size from the town it was when I lived there. But I am getting ahead of my story. Let us go back to my looking for a steady-paying job.

Because of my shyness, going out and trying to find a full-time job or discerning what I was meant to get involved in was a very frightening task. The steel industry was one that I knew very little about, and I had never been in a plant before. So, it took a lot of strength and faith on my part to enter this world. The mill environment could be very daunting as well as dangerous. Thus, interviewing for a steel job and then working there took me way out of my comfort zone. I eventually became somewhat comfortable in those surroundings; however, it was not very easy at first and took a long time before I became more at ease in going to work there every day.

My interview with Republic Steel did not result in a job offer. Later I interviewed at Youngstown Sheet and Tube Company (YS&T), at their Campbell Works location. They had two steel plants in the area, this one in Campbell, Ohio, and a plant in the Briar Hill area. The Campbell plant was near the east side of Youngstown where I lived, and Briar Hill was on the north side of town. From what I can remember YS&T offered me a job right after my interview. Republic called and offered me a position a few days after meeting with them. Apparently, that industry was doing well, as both of them were hiring at that time. This was a positive for me and for others who were looking for a job in the area. I decided to take the job offered by YS&T.

I knew very little about either mill, but was certainly guided to go with YS&T. Because they offered me a job right away inside of waiting, I felt that was the company to work for. I could say that I was guided by the good Lord to go that route. However, at that time, I am not sure that I was totally aware of how much God can lead us on a daily basis. But I do know that was the right choice for me at the time. At YS&T, I had steady employment, and was laid off less there than other places around town. Additionally, over time they also worked with me regarding my college class schedule, when I started school. Generally, the people there were very supportive of me, and I had a number of people who were wonderful mentors for me.

I need to be very careful with this following statement, because I do not want to give you the impression that my life has been perfect and that all of my major decisions have always turned out right. But, over my life, when it came to changing jobs, and I was ready to move on, I generally had only one clear choice to choose from. As in this case, going to work at YS&T was the obvious pick and ended up being the right one for me. After I left YS&T and over my working career, prior to going to the seminary, I worked for a total of five different insurance companies in four separate states. From what I can remember of each move, there was only one clear-cut option to select from. One could say that this was how things worked out, or one could say that God cares about where we work and live. Additionally, that God knows what is best for us as individuals and for our families. I tend to believe the latter reason because of how things have evolved for me. As I noted, at age eighteen, I did not fully understand this aspect about my life, as it became more evident to me as I got older.

I had finished high school in June and started to work for YS&T in August of 1964 as a laborer. When YS&T gave me their physical, I heard them talking that because of my size, the Open Hearth Department would be a good choice for me. Most of the jobs were around hot furnaces and they must have thought my extra weight would come in handy. For once, my being overweight helped me out. The Open Hearth Department ended up being a good place for me to work over the long haul. In order to begin work I had to buy a pair of steel-toed work shoes. They were expensive and a lot of money for me at that time. My dad loaned me the money to buy them and asked that I pay him back after my first full paycheck, which I did. I do not know how I remembered such a minor detail in my life, but maybe it was because that was how my dad was with all of us. If that was the only thing that he did like that, I probably would not recall it.

I rode the city bus back and forth for the first six months that I worked there. In time, I took driving lessons in order to get my driver's license. I saved money to buy my first car from my dad. At his service station, he had a 1958 red Ford Ranch Wagon, which I purchased from him for 225.00 dollars. That was not necessarily the kind of car that an eighteen-year-old male would think was very sporty. But, for me it was wheels and I did not have to ride the bus anymore to get to work. When I think back to that time, nothing was given to me; I worked and paid for it all, including all of my college courses. However, I know that I was blessed with the opportunity and ability to work and the initiative to continue working.

## LIFE AT YOUNGSTOWN SHEET AND TUBE COMPANY

There were seventeen to eighteen men hired on the same day that I started in the Open Hearth Department. As I noted things must have been going well for our economy in general and the steel mills in particular. There was one other African-American man in this group as well. In the mill at that time most promotions were based on seniority. Our seniority should have been based upon when we punched in at the time clock on that first day. However, from that time forward, whenever it came time to decide who got new jobs, the other African-American person and myself always came after the Caucasian men who started with us. Thus, our seniority on the job was at the bottom of the list of all those who began on the same day as us. This is a form of discrimination that probably would not occur today.

All of us started out with the title of laborer. That meant we did any and everything that we were asked to do. That first week, all of us worked the day shift. I do not remember much about that first week there except it was loud and dirty. That aspect of the mill never changed during the nearly nine years that I worked there; I just got used to the smell, noise, dirt, dust, moving equipment, and hot furnaces.

The mill attracted a very wide cross-section of people whom we all had to learn how to work with. At times, this could be extremely demanding depending on the person. Some were highly intelligent, maybe with a few years of college. One person had a college degree but could make more money in the mill than doing some other job. A few of us worked in the mill while we took classes or courses outside of the mill on our own time. Then, there were those who did not or could not finish high school and had a hard time with basic things like math and reading. However, in some mill jobs you could get paid well no matter what you knew.

There were also people who were not pleased that persons of color or other ethnic groups were working around them. However, on the other hand, there were others who were welcoming and open to all, no matter one's race or background. The trick was to find out who was good to work with and who you had to always watch your back with because they could not be trusted. Learning who was reliable could take some time and often you might discover the hard way the ones who were not dependable.

I learned how to work with most everyone there because I tried really hard to get along with everyone, even the pains in the rear end. I believe one of the benefits for me working there was learning how to work and deal with a really wide range of people. I know that skill was helpful in my insurance industry marketing jobs that I had after I left the mill. Working in that environment has also helped me in many other ways that I continue to use today. Looking back, I am surprised that I made it through that first week, for it was a shock to my mental and physical makeup. I am sure that my life would have been different if I left and found other work. But over time staying there worked out for me, because it allowed me to get my college degree and move on from there. Of course, I did not know that at the time.

Even though I do not remember much about the first week, the second week had more happening. I was told to report to the midnight shift the following week. At that time, this shift went from 11:00 p.m. to 7:00 a.m., the following morning. Needless to say, that took some getting used to, staying up all night when most of those around me were sleeping. Later on, I found out why I was put on that shift. That night I became the first African-American person to take a shift as a temporary third helper, on the Open Hearth floor of the Youngstown Sheet and Tube Company, at their Campbell Works. I did not know it at the time, *but that was a really, really big deal!*

I guess they were checking me out during my first week there while I was working with the rest of the laborers. I also assume that they had me take this first turn during the midnight shift so fewer people would know what had happened until it was all over. At night, there were generally fewer people around the plant as compared to the day shift. I was told later on that when something like this had been done before the other workers walked off the Open Hearth floor in protest.

## THIRD HELPER POSITION

The Open Hearth Department was one of the highest paying departments in the steel mill. Just being hired into this department was a positive situation for anyone lucky enough to get in. Compared to other blue-collar jobs in the area they had an above average pay scale. Additionally, working directly on the furnaces, as a helper, was among the best paid positions in our department.

The first helpers were the kingpins of the department and possibly in the entire mill. When you became one, you were highly paid, had power because you were in charge of a furnace, and basically had it made as long as you did not mess up. There were a lot of things that came into play in being a first helper. The steel produced there was worth a lot of money, and the furnaces were also expensive to build, operate, and repair, and had to be taken care of and run correctly. If you did not know what you were doing or if you were a screw up, you would not last long in that job. These positions were highly paid, but you earned your money, especially in the summer time. The furnaces would have to get really hot to melt the raw materials in order to make the steel. It is not a job for everyone and took a lot of experience and discipline.

The way things worked back then, once you became a third helper you could work your way up to the second helper position, and then up to first helper. Even though there were hundreds of people working on the floor, it could take many years for someone to move up the ladder. There had never been any African-Americans as any rank of helper. Therefore, by having me take that first shift as a third helper, the door was then opened to others that followed after me. Also, the path for becoming a first helper was now possible, for previously that avenue was never open to people of my race. Yes, this was an enormous event when it happened. I was just there at the right moment and did not give the powers to be any reason to not allow me to be the first.

If you have read things about me before, you may know that this is the first of several positions/situations that God put me in wherein I was the first person of my race to fill such a role. I know that I have been gifted with certain skills and have a personality by which I have been able to function in these environments, once I have become a part of them. However, I am very aware that what I was asked to do is nothing compared to what others have done in breaking down racial barriers. Many others have risked their life, the lives of their family and friends, their community standing, and their jobs and financial well-being in order to make a positive change in their surroundings.

Looking back, I am humbled and feel honored to have had a small part in making a path that others could follow and benefit from. I also consider this to be part of my spiritual pilgrimage, by going where I was led to go, even when I could not see where it would end up. When I went to work in the mill, I had no idea of what my becoming a third helper would eventually mean for other persons of color. I just know that was where I was supposed to be at that moment.

YS&T did have African-Americans working in other positions in the Open Hearth Department. They held jobs like running charging machines that loaded raw materials into the furnaces, operating overhead cranes carrying supplies and molten steel in various part of the plant, and brakemen who worked on the railroad that ran throughout the area. These positions were important and paid pretty well. Some of them required an immense amount of skill and dexterity in order to get and keep those jobs. The charging machine and overhead crane operators generally worked around the furnaces. Just like the first helpers they needed to do their jobs well, because of the potential large financial loss involved if they made mistakes. Also, like most positions around any mill or factory, the work could be very dangerous, and these workers had to be extra careful in carrying out their duties.

There was also a separate department that worked on and around the furnaces that rebuilt and repaired the furnaces when they were shut down. This was the Masonry Department, and they employed a number of people of color in various jobs. That point is so ironic, that they could work on these furnaces repairing them, but could not get a job as a helper on the furnaces to make the steel. Because of these jobs there were always African-Americans around this area, but not necessarily in the higher paying positions. I am sure those who were there when I started wondered how I was the one selected to take the first shift in this position. I just tried to do my job and not get caught up with anyone's issues about why me and not them. Later on, I talked to a number of people who were there before me, and got a sense about what an important step it was when I first worked as a third helper.

It was an important step for YS&T to allow this position to be done by someone of my race. However, this happened in August of 1964, and probably only came about at that time because of what was going on in our country and with our government. As you may know the Civil Rights

Act of 1964 was enacted on July 2, 1964. President Lyndon B. Johnson worked to have this passed. It was a landmark civil rights and United States labor law that impacted our nation. The act forbid discrimination based on race, color, religion, sex, or national origin. Would YS&T and other businesses have willingly moved to take down barriers without this act? Your guess is as good as mine. Because there were African-Americans already in the plant, it may have occurred at some point, but when, no one knows for sure.

Even though I was the first African-American to take a shift as a temporary third helper, I was not the first one to become a bona fide third helper. When openings came up for a certain position, people could put in for a specific job title. The titles were generally awarded based on seniority. Another African-American transferred into the Open Hearth Department who had more overall company seniority than me. He applied for and became the first certified third helper. I continued with the title of laborer until April of 1970 when I became a bona fide third helper, the second person of color with this title.

It could take a long time for people to move up the job chain. During that time those people who were hired on the same day as me, but given more time from a seniority standpoint, were awarded the third helper position title before me. I could work as a third helper whenever the plant was operating at full or close to full capacity. However, when things slowed down, I got bumped to other lower-paying jobs or could get laid off. As a bona fide third helper, you had more rights.

Working in a plant or factory could at times be dangerous besides also being taxing from a physical and mental standpoint. When I found out that I would be working in the mill, my mom's dad gave me his old leather working gloves, so I would not have to initially buy a pair of gloves. John Coleman Sr., Monk to his family members, had also worked at YS&T until he retired. He had moved his family up from Richard, Virginia, in 1923 to take a job there. He, however, never worked around the places I would be working. His leather gloves were okay for what he did, but not for me. Neither he nor I knew that 100 percent cotton gloves were required to work on the Open Hearth floor, because of the intense heat coming from the furnaces. Cotton gloves protected your hands better than any other type. Unfortunately, no one told me that when I started. Therefore, I ended up burning the back of my hand and had to go to the plant hospital. For many years that scar on my right hand was still visible.

I had some other things happen to me over the years while I worked there, but that was the most painful, physically.

Over time I learned how to protect myself from the environment. Because of the heat coming from the furnaces, most everyone wore long john underwear year-round, as an added layer of protection. These were used even during the summer, when it could get really *hot*! One of the jobs that had to be done after a heat of steel was ready was to *tap* the furnace. That meant going to the back of the furnace and pulling materials out of the tap hole, so that the molten steel could be emptied into a large ladle. From there the steel was poured into molds and then shaped into whatever product it was going to become. In order to *tap* the furnace, we had to wear a heavy wool jacket and face mask to shield ourselves from the intense heat and bright glow of the molten steel. Tapping a furnace was always something we had to be very careful in doing, because sometimes it could blow before we were ready, and someone could be severely burned and that was not good.

Like any mill or factory position, even if you were careful and wore all of the right equipment, accidents could still happen and people would get hurt. I was fortunate to leave that place without any serious injuries. Also, I was especially lucky and blessed (as of this date), to have no long-term issues from lung diseases, like so many others have had to deal with. That is remarkable considering that this was before everyone used breathing devices to help combat all of the dusk, dirt, and graphite that was everywhere and that we breathed daily. Also, it is surprising that my hearing is not any worse than it is, as we did not often wear ear plugs, and believe me it was one noisy place.

During my time in the mill, I did a number of different jobs, besides the ones done on the Open Hearth floor; a few other places worked on were called the Mixer, the Stock House, and the Pit. Being asked to do a number of dissimilar positions gave me the opportunity to be flexible and to learn how to function in new and diverse environments. These are some more of the traits that I picked up while there that still come in handy today. These are also wonderful characteristics to have on my spiritual pilgrimage.

Additionally, when the orders for steel slowed down, I was temporarily transferred to other departments in YS&T. I was also laid off at times, which meant being on unemployment benefits. Thank goodness, this did not happen too often or for really long periods of time. I knew that I was fortunate to be there, because other mill workers were often out of work more than me. In my opinion, I was known as a hard worker and was able to do all of the tasks assigned to me in an acceptable manner. I tried to help other people with their chores when time allowed, but also to learn how to do their positions. For example, when working as a third helper and I had free time, I would help some of the second helpers with their duties.

Especially during the warm months, the second helpers' duties could be a real killer. I would help them clean up the tap hole area after a heat was tapped. That task could be extremely hot and could drain one's energy very quickly. Normally they had to use a wheelbarrow to haul up to five hundred pounds of materials from the front of the furnace area to the back. When it was hot and they were tired from just tapping a heat, pushing that wheelbarrow could get really taxing on their mind and body. Some of the people who did this for a number of years ended up having bad backs or knees or feet. Here again I lucked out and did not have any such issues when I left. But, by giving help when I could, others would help me back when I needed it. Isn't that how life should be, each of us offering help to those around us?

Trying to aid second helpers sometimes ended up being a very undesirable situation for me. After a while I learned that some people did not want me being there because of my race and also did not want me around them or helping them. When I offered help to one second helper, he was very cold to me when I first started helping him out. Come to find out, he was one of those who would have rather not had me there. Probably in a time before I got there, he would have been one of the leaders that would have walked out to keep those like me off of those jobs. However, over time, he warmed up to me, and we got along on the job. Another lesson about life: sometimes when we do not know much about certain people who may have negative feelings about us, just a little firsthand interaction can go a long way to breaking down some of the barriers that have been set up. There were some unique characters whom I was lucky enough to work with. Some became strong role models and mentors for me while I was working in that environment. I will always be indebted to those individuals for what they did for me, probably without even knowing it.

## COLLEGE AND THE MILL

After I had worked in the mill for about nine to ten months, I was talking to my mom and told her that I wanted to do more with my life besides just working in the mill. She encouraged me to think about enrolling in college. She had never gone to college but knew that could help me in so many ways. That was one of the best pieces of advice that anyone had ever given me. I never thought about that before that moment. I did start taking college classes and continued to work full time in the mill, until I earned my degree.

As noted earlier, working for YS&T ended up being a really good situation for me for many different reasons. When I started taking college courses, I would occasionally miss one or two classes depending upon which shift I was working. Initially, I took evening courses but later on signed up for day classes. Over time, I moved up the seniority chain at work; thus, when the mill was operating at a good capacity, I was able to work most of the time in the third helper position. Then the mill management allowed me to do the third helper floater job every week, instead of working the three different revolving shifts (day, afternoon, and midnight). They basically froze me in that position, as long as my seniority allowed me stay in it. However, I could not move up the job chain, but that was okay for me because at that time I was more interested in obtaining my degree than making additional money.

Because it was expensive and labor intensive to shut down a furnace, the mill normally operated twenty-four hours a day. Thus, there were crews working around the clock, for an eight-hour shift. The vast majority of employees in Open Hearth Department worked three shifts, generally with the same group of people. They would rotate working the shifts for five days, then move on. They would work afternoons (3 p.m. to 11 p.m.) for five days, then move to nights for five days (11 p.m. to 7 a.m.), then work five days (7 a.m. to 3 p.m.), all after about two full days off. When I was the mill's third helper floater, I worked with a specific shift of people for one week. That is because at certain times these shifts had to work a six-day week. Back then, anyone who worked over forty hours was paid overtime, and that was something they tried not to do unless they had to. Thus, these floater positions usually kept them from having to pay someone overtime during this six-day work week.

The periods that I worked as a floater were generally the afternoon and midnight stints. This meant that I usually had to work Saturdays from 3 p.m. to 11 p.m. and turn around and start a new work week on Sunday night starting at 11 p.m. for the midnight shift. Bear in mind that I continued to be involved in things at Jerusalem Baptist. That could be a real grind for my body and mind. Because my body could not get into any steady, routine being constantly sleepy became a way of life for me. Becoming more and more well-organized was key for me during this period so I could balance my mill life and the class work at the same time. Needless to say, being a decent time manager is probably one of my stronger skills today.

Working this floater position allowed me to sign up for day courses and thus I was able to miss fewer classes. If I worked the midnight shift, I often went to class after working all night. If I worked the afternoon schedule, I went to classes before going to work. Normally my days off were in the middle of the week, allowing me to get more sleep and do my school work. Once every four or five weeks, the way the floater schedule worked out, my shift would be from Tuesday through Saturday afternoons, from 3 p.m. to 11 p.m. That seemed like heaven to me when it happened. I could get a full night's sleep every night and still not miss any classes. I would not suggest that anyone ever do what I did. It was a grueling way to get a college education.

I did not have any role models for what I was trying to do. No one in my family or at my church was working and going to college. I was breaking new ground for myself and had to figure things out mostly on my own. Needless to say, it was a really tough learning curve for me trying to work full time and attend classes as well and, yes, I screwed up a bunch. But the Lord gave me the will and faith to continue taking small steps along this path.

In trying to be a good steward of my time, I got in the habit of bringing my books to work. When I had free time, I would read and try to keep up with my class work. However, what I found out over time was that if I tried to take an important exam after I worked all night, I did not do well, especially if my studying was done during my working hours. After bombing out on a number of tests I got smarter and took measures to be sure I could pass them. I realized that it was better if I just reported off for a shift before a test and studied elsewhere, which allowed me to be fresher for the test and do better on it. There was something about being in a work mind-set and then trying to turn the brain toward my studies that just did not work. Others were able to do it, but not me.

I basically followed this routine after getting married and having a child, until finally getting my degree. Looking back, it was a faith walk to start taking the classes when I did not know how it would turn out. Also, there were many barriers that had to be overcome during the process. Some of the obstacles were in me, especially when I tried to focus on what I wanted, instead of on where God was leading me. Basically, was I striving for God's kingdom while trying to become the person that the good Lord wanted me to be, or was I intent on doing things my way? For me, these lessons are still being rediscovered on a daily basis today.

## IMPROVING MY SELF-ESTEEM

During the early days while working in the mill, I started reading a lot of positive thinking, goal oriented, or inspirational-type books during quiet times at work. I was looking for ways to have a better self-esteem and make more of my life. Because in my mind I did not have a lot of overall direction in my life, these books helped give me a more positive outlook about myself. They also helped me to begin setting goals about things that I thought I should be working toward. As mentioned, I also received support and guidance from my mom and people whom I was in contact with, mainly at work and at Jerusalem Baptist Church.

This was an age where many were going off to college or to the military with some goals in mind. Even if they would have changed their objectives during their twenties, at least they were heading somewhere. I did not know where I was going and at the same time did not feel really self-assured. Thus, these books aided me in a number of different areas over the long haul. I cannot tell you exactly tell how or why I started reading these; I just think it evolved over a period of time.

Of all of the books read then, *The Power of Positive Thinking* by Norman Vincent Peale was the one that helped me the most. That book and that author both helped my low self-esteem and aided in me becoming more goal oriented. It also helped me in my spiritual growth and I became more aware of how Bible scriptures could impact our daily lives. I read many of his other books and was on his ministry mailing list for a number of years. Many of the prayer routines and positive reinforcing habits that are still used were picked up from his writings. It is fair to say that Dr. Peale's influence on my life is enormous. I would not be the person that I am today without encountering him at my young age. I understand that currently many people may find some of his theology and methods questionable. But he was incredibly helpful for me when it was needed. However, I do not read him any longer and have a number of new favorite authors that continue to encourage and inspire me these days. However, he and other similar authors that were read at that time are part of my essence and spirit, even though they are not read now.

During some free moments at work, I starting reading a Bible. I kept a small pocket-sized copy in my wool furnace jacket. This came about for several different reasons. I was still involved with my church and Sunday school and taught our high school class. Throughout this period, I was also superintendent of the Sunday school and had to know things about the lessons that were being taught. Additionally, books like those written by Dr. Peale, while illustrating his philosophies, referenced Bible verses. Also, I keep going back to my low self-esteem; reading the Bible could at times give comfort, support, and guidance for me.

Thus, the Bible was always close to me and people also saw me reading it. Studying it became part of who I was and helped me on my way. As we daily walk on our spiritual pilgrimage, we are all fallible human beings with as many faults and warts as the next person. However, maybe, just maybe people around us can see our love for others and how we carry ourselves in the good times and the bad; and that might encourage others in their own personal journey. Looking back, that was a witness in and of itself. I did not have to preach to others about my faith. Hopefully, my reading of the Bible and positive thinking books and the way I carried myself on a daily basis were an example to others at work and during my time at church and at college.

FOUR

# Beginning the Challenging World of College

> Beloved, we are God's children now; what we will be has not been revealed. What we do know is this: when he is revealed, we will be like him, for we will see him as he is.
>
> —1 JOHN 3:2

## WHAT WE ARE TO BE HAS NOT BEEN REVEALED AND IS STILL UNKNOWN

WHEN STARTING TO WORK in the mill, I did not know how things would turn out. Likewise, when beginning to take college courses, I had no clue how everything would develop. As this verse indicates, what we will be has not been revealed. So much of life and this spiritual pilgrimage is all about *taking it one step/day at a time*. Of course, I also did not know that it would take me eight long years to get my degree. Nor did I have any idea about all of the obstacles that would have to be overcome. I might add that some of these difficulties were of my own making.

As has been written before, when we determine that we want to become a lifelong disciple of Jesus Christ we are in reality saying that the future is in God's hands and not ours. We begin to live each day making decisions and taking steps trusting that the Holy Spirit is directing our path. I am not sure that I understood that fully when I took the job in the mill or began taking college courses. But in reality, they were both faith walks, for the outcome was not yet determined. We never know where God may be leading us. Our task is to pray about it, contemplate on what is being given us, and then at some point take some action. Believe me, taking that first college course took me way out of my comfort zone. As time went by, I continued to be stretched and given new situations to overcome.

The bit of advice given to me by my mom, and me deciding to follow it, was a huge milestone in my life. Until she mentioned it, I had not thought of doing that, and quite frankly did not know how to go about getting started. However, by walking through that door, my life's direction was forever changed. By beginning to take college courses, things turned out so differently for me. Without taking those classes, I probably would have remained in the mill, and over time would have been out of a job when the mill closed down. My involvement with churches of other faiths would not have taken happened. I would not have met Judith Ann Buonavolonta and gotten married to her. Additionally, the over twenty-seven-year career in the insurance industry would not have happened. Plus, so many things would have turned out differently, without that discussion with my mom and me following her suggestion.

## YOUNGSTOWN STATE UNIVERSITY

When I first started the college was called Youngstown University. It had humble beginnings in 1908 when the local YMCA started offering law courses. In 1967, it became a state institution and was then known as Youngstown State University. While taking my first class there in the fall of 1965, it was predominantly a commuter school, with many of its students living at home. During my time there I never lived on campus. However, later on I did become involved in groups there, when I was able.

In the beginning, I took just one class in the evening; it was Communications 105, a basic English course. I remember it being held in a small room and taught by a young man. I cannot recall much about the instructor other than him mentioning that 50 percent of the people starting college would never finish. That was probably a true statement, but what a dose of reality to give someone when they are starting out! It hit home for me however, because I failed this first course. My writing skills were so poor, and I was not ready to do college work and was unable to do enough to get a passing grade. (*Not a great beginning!*)

YSU was on semesters back then, which ran for eighteen weeks. That was a lot of time to invest in a class without passing it. I remember a young man who was also taking classes at YSU at the same time, who was working in another department in the mill. He also failed a course about the same time that I did. He said that he was finished with that school and was not going to give them anymore of his money! He was majorly ticked off and used derogatory language as he blamed the school, and said that he was *done, done, done*! However, I signed up for another course and kept moving on. Again, that was an important step for me. I had a job and could have easily quit also. However, I was guided to continue on, even if I failed that course and had a lot of educational hurdles to overcome.

During the winter semester of 1966 I took a social studies course, 101, another basic class, and received a D in that one. It still was not a great grade, but at least I got credit for it. Back then, they had summer classes of five weeks each. I took a class during each five-week session. I retook the Communications 105 class that I had failed and got a C in it. I took another basic social studies course, 102, and also got a C in it. Still not wonderful grades but at least they were passed, and then I felt comfortable to continue with the classes.

## TWO STEPS FORWARD—ONE STEP BACK

One of the common themes running through my life stories is how I have to constantly learn the same lessons over and over again regarding certain aspects of my life. As a fallible human being, I know that I am not perfect, will screw up, and make mistakes. However, some of my shortcomings occur in the same areas—repeatedly. This was the case with me in taking these college courses.

After taking a few classes, I got into a routine and was able to get the course work done and get a passing grade. But, *oh no*, that was not good enough, and I continued to try to chew off more then I could handle, which resulted in problems with my grade point average, being on probation, and ultimately being academically suspended. Basically, it was about me thinking that I was smarter than I was, trying to seek my own agenda, in my own way, versus striving first for God's kingdom before anything else. Thus, I would do okay for a while, then try to do too much and have issues with academic probation and suspensions. The "two steps forward and one step back" refers to taking some courses and then not being able to take anything while suspended.

During the fall of 1967, after YSU became a state school it changed to a quarterly calendar. That fall I was put on probation for having too low of a GPA, and I took two courses and got Cs in both. During the winter quarter of 1968 I did something that was not too bright and took three classes, and got a B, a C, and a D, which obviously did not help my GPA rise enough. Because of the number of hours earned and with a 1.8 GPA I was suspended for the spring quarter of 1968. I could not take any classes that quarter, which was a very humbling experience, and one that should have taught me a lesson, but it did not. The first time that I was suspended I had to have a professor write a reference letter to get me back into YSU.

During the summer of 1968, after being reinstated, I took three classes and earned two Bs and a D and was able to continue on probation. However, during the fall of 1968, I did something really stupid again and took four classes. Cannot explain what I must have been thinking when I decided to do that! I was able to attend most of the classes because I was working the afternoon and midnight shifts at the mill. But that did not mean that I would have the time to do the class work and be able to have some good study time for the tests that were given.

My initial report card for that quarter showed all Cs for the four classes and indicated that I was suspended—yet again. By that time, I had earned 81.5 academic hours; however, my overall GPA was only 1.88. WOW! What a blow to my self-esteem. Looking back, I know that I did it to myself, but that still really caused me a lot of pain. However, in this case I was saved for the moment by one of God's angels. One of the professors that I had gotten to know and who was in the department of my major was Mrs. Edna McDonald. Over time she would become a personal friend of mine and she helped me a lot during my journey at that time. She was one of those loving people that God puts in our life to help, support, and offer guidance on our life's travels.

She was one of my professors during that quarter. I went to her with my problem and explained what had happened. She looked at my work that had been done in her class, and gave me a B- instead of a C+, which allowed me to stay in at that time. However, I remained on probation and had no room for error. I will always appreciate Mrs. McDonald and her willingness to help me out when it was needed.

Did I learn my lesson at this point? *No*! I was still intent on following my own agenda, versus using what I knew to be an important part of my spiritual pilgrimage. That was striving for God's kingdom first in my life, and all these other things would be added (Matt 6:33–34). During the winter of 1969 I took three classes, and one of them was Spanish. This is the guy who had a hard time with the basic communication courses. I fooled around and got a D in Spanish and could only muster up two Cs in the others, suspended again. This time it was a killer; I had to stay out the entire spring and summer quarters. Two steps forward—one step back.

That hurt, really bad! Besides not being able to take courses, I had lots of time to think about the position that I had put myself in. Thankfully that period humbled me a little and allowed me to learn more about where my focus was and what was needed to continue with my classes. I am sure some others would have quit at this point. I was working full time, making good money for someone with only a high school diploma, and also had good health insurance and other benefits from working a union job. However, something kept me going, even when I came up short.

After being out for two quarters, I had to write a letter to the dean of the College of Arts and Sciences asking to be let back in. Additionally, two professors had to write letters for me as well, asking that I be readmitted. Thankfully they allowed me back in. However, I was limited to how many credit hours that could be taken, and had to remain on probation. At that time, my overall GPA was still 1.88, and an overall 2.00 GPA was needed to get off of probation.

At that point, I had no other option but to take it slow with my class load. Starting with the fall of 1969 I took only one course a quarter for an entire year, on Friday evenings. I had to be really careful, for I needed at least a B in each class to maintain an improving GPA to not be suspended again. Because if that happened, I am not sure if I would have been able to get back in again. That was a really long year for me, taking one Friday night course a quarter. However, it needed to be done in order to stay in school. By the spring of 1970 I had an overall GPA of 1.98, getting close!

After I got married in June of 1970 things got better for me schoolwise. My wife, Judy, was a much better student then I was and was able to help me. She also became a student at YSU and continued to work on her college degree along with me. After taking two summer courses, I got my overall GPA up to 2.01, and my academic status became "Good Standing." I was no longer on probation—*that was a wonderful feeling*!! Thankfully, I never got another grade below a C for the remaining three years I was at YSU. I maintained a good standing status until I finished.

Of course, I still had many challenges to deal with and overcome. I was now married and Judy and I took courses together, continued to work full time, and did a number of things at my church. Our first child came along, and she went to school with us. We juggled many balls at the same time in order to get everything done. Getting through all of this would have been more challenging without Judy's assistance and the support and help from many others. It took a village of people to help me earn my degree!

Judy and I both earned our bachelor's degrees after the spring quarter of 1973. Thankfully I finished with an overall 2.33 GPA; considering that I was suspended twice and almost suspended one other time, it is okay. I do not take lightly that I was guided to start taking classes and even though I failed often, somehow, I continued and made it through. The lessons learned were many, but the most important one that has become a lifelong learning for me is *striving first for the kingdom of God before anything else.*

## YSU LIFE AWAY FROM THE CLASSROOM

Even with all of the challenges of my grades and classes, I began to get involved with social activities and groups on campus. Looking back, I am not sure how free time was found to get involved with them, but it was. Even with my full-time employment, attending classes, doing class work, and taking exams, and my continued work with my church, somehow I found time, amazing! I believe the first group I was connected to was the Social Studies Club. I was a sociology major and that seemed to be a good fit for me. From interactions with people in that club, I was led to attend the International Students Organization. Even though YSU was basically a small commuter university it attracted a number of international students. That was a real learning experience for me, being connected with people from different parts of the world.

Later on, I also met people who also attended YSU's Campus Christian Fellowship group and became a part of this group and that is who I spent the most time with from then on. I became very close friends with a number of people from there. Rev. Bert Cantrell was their chaplain and someone who I felt comfortable with and who had an influence on my life. Through this group I became friends with Steve Gifford who later became a pastor, and Steve was the one who brought a large number of his congregational members from his suburban church to my small inner-city Baptist church.

I also began a fairly serious relationship with a young woman from that group. This group had their office in Jones Hall, which was the most centrally located building on campus, where a lot of activity happened. Through this group and with our connection to Jones Hall, I also met my wife, Judy, there. At that time, she was a Humility of Mary novice (a Catholic religious order). She and a number of her sisters were taking classes at YSU, and Jones Hall is where they would hang out between classes. More about that later. Thus, the Campus Christian Fellowship and Jones Hall both had an enormous impact on my social, spiritual, and romantic life.

Besides Steve and Pastor Cantrell, I made a number of friends in that organization. We did things together socially and seemed to enjoy each other's company. Because of them I was able to make contacts that allowed me to take my small high school Sunday school class to different worshiping communities. In turn, some of those churches visited our congregation also. We were taking young people from an all African-American Baptist congregation to visit several all-Caucasian churches of various faith traditions. Needless to say, that was a learning experience for all concerned, and allowed those involved, who had an open mind, to have their worldview enlarged. We also gave my class exposure to the Jewish faith. My being a part of the Campus Christian Fellowship opened doors for me and those in my home congregation. It was mostly a very good experience and helped mold many others and me in many ways.

As I began to take part in the activities of this group, and hang out socially with them in my free time, I became really good friends with one young lady. Sometimes we would go out together as a group, but she and I grew closer as time went on. I guess you could say we became an "item" while we were in this organization. We started seeing each other occasionally apart from the group. We seemed to like each other's company and appeared to feel comfortable with each other. Her parents were of a German background and she lived in a suburb of Youngstown and drove in for classes.

We seemed to get along really well for quite a while. I became genuinely enamored with her, and I thought she felt the same way about me. However, she saw things differently. I did not realize that we had done very little as a couple around her family. We were mostly together with friends from the college. Back then my rose-colored glasses kept me from seeing how it truly was. We were moving right along (at least in my mind) until she had a death in her family. I think she lost a grandparent and I went to the funeral. I thought that since we were seeing each other I should attend the funeral and support her during her time of grief. However, my being there backfired for both of us.

Shortly after that she told me that she had to choose between her family and me. She apparently did not realize this before the funeral, but that event brought things to a head. She wanted to keep her ties with her family. She was not strong enough in her feelings for me to fight the battles with her family. Interracial dating was not generally accepted in the late 1960s. Needless to say, that really hurt me. I was emotionally devastated and it was a long time until I recovered. Even though this situation took its toll on me, thankfully I was able to continue doing what was required of me. Somehow, I was able to push on, taking classes, working, and doing the other things that I had going on.

Apart from my school life and other things going on in my life, something that was going around me was how much I helped my mom after I went to work in the mill. I still lived at home for a number of years after high school. She did not drive until she was much older, thus I ended up driving her to her job and other places when I was able. I also supported her financially. One of my mom's sisters, Aunt Ruby, was married to a Baptist pastor, Rev. Ward. He was a person who seemed to be an honest person who told things as he saw them. My mom's family knew how much I did for her and appreciated my efforts. Somewhere along the way Aunt Ruby told us that Rev. Ward said that because of how much I did for my mom, God would allow me to find a wonderful wife. At the time I heard that, I was not looking for a wife, but later on in my mind his words did come true.

My mother and I did a number of things together, and of course that could be both a blessing and challenge depending on how things went. I always loved my mom and was very grateful for what she did for my brothers and me. However, after a while I was ready to move on and be out on my own for a number of different reasons. That was a major decision for me, and really caused my mom a lot of heartache when I actually moved out. Thus, at age twenty-three, in 1969, I was able to find a second-floor apartment on Princeton Avenue on the south side of Youngstown. Besides being hard on my mom, it also a very difficult step for me, but one I felt that I had to make at that time. I continued to try to help her out, be involved with things at college, church, and work forty hours a week—I just fulfilled these roles from a different location.

FIVE

# Rev. Ward's Words Come to Fruition

*A capable wife who can find? She is far more precious than jewels. . . .
A woman who fears the Lord is to be praised.*

—Prov 31:10, 30b

## ANOTHER NEW CHAPTER IN MY LIFE

I HAVE OFTEN STATED that being married, staying in a long-term relationship, or remaining close to someone who is not a family member is one of the more difficult things to do in life. At least that is the case for me. In my mind, being a parent, guardian, mentor comes in as the second-most challenging task to accomplish in our personal lives. Again, that is how I see it. Along with being one of the most complex things to do, it can also be one of the most rewarding, loving, and joy-filled situations in life. But, isn't that the way most of life is? If you want to have a mountain-top experience, sometimes wilderness occurrences must be dealt with as well. The issue is, are we willing to go through the long rough stretches in order to have the joy that comes out of those tough periods?

I have been fortunate, lucky, or blessed to have been married to two different but both very spirit-filled women. They have loved me, supported me, and helped make my life better than it would have been without them. Hopefully, their lives were also enriched by being married to me. However, in both cases, there were some growing pains and difficult times. But, for many reasons, we were able to come through to the other side of the issues, remain together, and grow in our love and trust for each other. Being married or being in a long-term relationship takes a lot of emotional energy, love, patience, prayers, etc., to make it work. Remember, my parents and both sets of my grandparents were divorced.

Rev. Ward said that because of how I took care of my mom God would allow me to find a wonderful wife. Well, no matter if you believe these words or not, or if you think that God put Judy and Shirley in my life or not, I sincerely believe that both women are a gift from God to me. I found an answer (twice) to the question posed in Prov 31!

## JUDE CAME INTO MY LIFE

Sister Judith Ann Buonavolonta (aka Jude or Judy) came into my life when she was a novice with the Humility of Mary. The Humility of Mary, also known as the "Blue Nuns" because of their blue habits, was a Catholic religious order out of Villa Marie, Pennsylvania, which was not too far from Youngstown. The order sent their novices to YSU at the same time that I was there. The sisters would hang out between classes in Jones Hall on campus. Jones Hall was where the Campus Christian Fellowship had their office, and where I also could be found between classes when not working. Thus, members of this Fellowship group and I got to know some of the sisters and became good friends with many of them.

As mentioned, I was able to get my Sunday school high school class to visit other churches and also have these other churches visit ours. Additionally, because of my connection to the "Blue Nuns" I was able to get two of the sisters to appear on a panel discussion (Judy was not one of them). The panel discussion was held while I was president of the area Sunday school association. This association was made up of churches similar to Jerusalem Baptist, in that they had mostly Baptist churches with predominantly African-American members. Thus, having these two Caucasian Catholic sisters take part in this discussion gave us all a viewpoint that we may have not have thought of before. Again, the good Lord allowed me to be a part of something that was way ahead of its time. To my knowledge, something like that had never been done with that association before.

I might add that the "Blue Nuns" were fairly open and liberal at that time. The sisters seemed to be willing to try new things and were adventurous. The two sisters who came to the panel discussion had to get the approval of their superiors and had to get to the event themselves. Additionally, once while Jude was still in the order, she visited my Sunday school class at Jerusalem and talked to them about her decision to become a nun. Again, to my knowledge something like that had never been done at Jerusalem before. Later they invited me to visit their place at Villa Marie. They showed me around and gave me a tour. The highlight was when I was ready to leave, they broke out in song. An entire group of them sang "Let There Be Peace on Earth." "Let there be peace on earth and let it begin with me." I can still see them singing as I was leaving. To me that was a very meaningful event.

I had bonded with a number of the sisters; they knew that I tried to live my life as one filled with peace and love. It was one of those wonderful Spirit-filled times in life that only comes around every so often, if one is lucky or blessed to be a part of. This memory is still with me today because it showed that God's love and peace overcome any racial, cultural, ethnic, or economic barriers that individuals can institute or create. Also, that no matter how far apart we may seem to be as humans, God's love can bring us together if we are open to it. The sisters were willing to allow this love to be the most important factor that motivated them, rather than our racial or religious differences. It was so awe-inspiring and amazing!

Jude went into the Humility of Mary right after high school sometime in the summer of 1966. She had attended Catholic schools for her twelve years of schooling up to that point, and this order taught her for a lot of that time. Thus, when she thought about going into a religious order, the "Blue Nuns" was the obvious choice. For most Catholic families at that time, having a child who wanted to become a priest or nun was a really big deal; that certainly was the case for hers. Judy's parents, Stella and Vito Buonavolonta, were both first generation American-Italians. All of Jude's grandparents were born in Italy and then came to the United States, eventually settling in Ohio. Stella and Vito were very active in their home parish, Mount Carmel Catholic Church, in Ashtabula, Ohio. Thus, Judy's upbringing was about as Italian-Catholic as you could get.

When Jude first entered the "Blue Nuns" hers was a fairly large class; I believe well over twenty young women came in together. However, after a few years, for any number of reasons, people from her group started leaving. They were departing before they made their final vows to the order. That was hard on everyone; however, that life is not for everyone. A person has to give up a lot in order to continue. I know that it can be very rewarding, but it could also be very challenging. Eventually, Judy left also, which was a shock to me when I found out about it. Now hear this very clearly: *she did not leave because of me!* At that point, I never crossed any boundaries and only had the utmost respect for the sisters and their vocations and what God had called them to do in their lives.

After Jude left the Humility of Mary, she began going to Saint Louis University in Saint Louis, Missouri. She had been taking classes to become a physical therapist and wanted to continue on that track. She had a few friends at that school, and, apparently, they had a good program for physical therapy. At some point, we started "seeing each other." We liked being together, seemed to like a lot of the same things, and basically were comfortable with each other. More importantly, we had the spiritual aspect of our lives that connected us as well. I remember one time she even took me to see her parents. At that point, we were just friends and I was warmly welcomed by them. I even made a couple of trips to Saint Louis to visit her while she was at school.

Judy was a very loving-caring person, and I do not think she would ever knowingly hurt anyone. She was also strong enough in her own right, and was able to decide that being with me was more important than what others thought—that meant even her parents or her family. Thus, I did not know it at the time, but God gave me someone who would not choose her family over me. Remember my story about the teenage girl in high school that I cared about very deeply, but she did not feel the same way about me and that caused me pain. Also, the young woman at YSU who could not deal with losing her family by choosing to be in a relationship with me. As I noted, that situation impacted me in a negative way and, consequently, it took me a long time to get through that hurt. Judith Ann was someone who helped me to love by loving me, without some of the issues that I had experienced with these other two young women.

I think it is fair to say that our relationship was somewhat unique for any period of time, but most certainly for the late 1960s in our country. As I noted Judy was a second-generation Italian Catholic from Ashtabula, Ohio, which was a small blue-collar town on Lake Erie. Her father worked on the docks, as did a number of people. I was from an African-American Baptist family, with divorced parents who grew up in Youngstown, which is about one hour from Ashtabula. Youngstown was principally a steel town back then, and I was working full time in the mill, while going to college part time. By becoming a couple and eventually getting married we had the normal challenges that any young persons might have, plus we had the religious and racial barriers to overcome as well.

We did, of course, have a lot of positive aspects working for us. We both were on our own spiritual pilgrimage, attempting to become the persons God wanted us to be. We were very active in our faith traditions, fulfilling roles that we were guided to take part in. We were also open to taking bold steps in faith as guided by the Holy Spirit. Even though we did not know it at the time, we would begin a new adventure that would take us to places that we had never dreamed of. With all that being said, however, our early months of marriage were far from stress-free.

Some of the tougher obstacles of our relationship, of course, came from the external forces around us; however, one major difficulty we created by our own actions. As noted, Jude was taking classes in Saint Louis, but that still did not prevent us from getting together at various times, either there or in Youngstown. Even though we were faithful, loving people, we were still human, and Judy became pregnant before we were married; and that, of course, put a lot of stress in our lives and caused us to rethink all of our plans at that time. Discovering that she was pregnant was a nerve-racking time with lots of unknowns. Judy was in Saint Louis when she got the results that she was expecting. For a time, we had to deal with this new situation over the phone. It was, of course, hard on her because she was away and still having her class load to deal with. I was living on my own and was working and taking classes.

Sometimes, God puts angels into our lives to help us at moments such as these. I was fortunate, lucky, or blessed, however you want to see it, to have Mrs. Beth Brewer in mine. Mrs. Brewer worked at YSU in the office of my favorite professor, Mrs. Edna McDonald. I had gotten to know Mrs. Brewer through my dealings with Mrs. McDonald and through the campus groups that we were all involved with. Mrs. Brewer was one of those up-beat loving people, full of energy and gentleness, with a very caring ear. I remember telling her about Judy being pregnant, and how disturbed I was about what the future held. I do not remember exactly what she said, but only know that sharing that situation with her helped me get through that period. I will always be grateful for her love and kindness to me at that time. She continued to be a wonderful support for Jude and me after we got married. In my book she was an angel sent by God to help me through that very stressful time.

We started to plan what we were going to do next, via long distance, which was a challenge. Thankfully, we tried to be patient with each other and were willing to make sacrifices in order to make things work. We decided to get married after her school term was over and she came back to Ohio. Talk about starting out a new life together with a lot of hurdles, an understatement for sure. Some of the issues we created ourselves;

however, we had some that were imposed on us by those around us. Up until that time I had been welcome in her parents' home. When we decided to get married, her parents had a hard time accepting what we were going to do. Of course, who could not blame them, because prior to that they were supporting Jude in college in Saint Louis, and now she was marrying me in Youngstown. That was a shocker, and a lot for them to take in. Initially they were hurt that Jude was marrying me, but in time they would come around (more about this later).

## OUR WEDDING

We were married on June 16, 1970, at Immaculate Conception Catholic Church on the east side of Youngstown, Ohio. Judy wanted to be married in a Catholic church as opposed to Jerusalem Baptist where I belonged. I was willing to go along with that for the Mass was always very important to Judy. Additionally, we were very fortunate to have Father Bernard (Bob) Bonnot as the priest at Immaculate Conception at that time. He was a very caring, loving, and open person and he helped me feel comfortable with getting married there.

In order to get married in a Catholic church, the non-Catholic (that is me) had to sign a paper that I would not interfere with Judy bringing up our children in the Catholic faith. When we had premarital counseling, Father Bob talked about the importance of having one faith practice that our children could be raised in. At that time Jude and I felt that we would just allow our children to decide for themselves which faith tradition that they would follow. However, Father Bob talked to us about a coat hanger being like one's faith and how it was something that you could hang things on. He said that a young child would not be able to decide which faith tradition to hang on to or become a part of—the Baptist or Catholic faith. He said that if we decided which faith to bring them up in that would be their coat hanger. If at some point when they were older, they decided something different, they would have been given a solid foundation upon which to build.

That sounded fine to me at that time and I agreed in writing to bring our children up in the Catholic faith, which we did. Thus, we were able to have the wedding in a Catholic church. I might add that many times in my life I have used Father Bob's example of the coat hanger and one's faith in explaining things about one's spiritual journey. I know that his being in our lives at that time was a real blessing for us as a couple and for me individually as well. His wisdom, concern, and loving manner continues to be a part of who I am today.

Our actual wedding day had some highs and lows. Because of the circumstances around us getting married no one from Judy's side of her family came to the wedding. Needless to say, that was extremely difficult for her to deal with. She was strong enough to go ahead with the wedding even without the support of her family at that time. She did have many of her friends there to support her, including a number that she knew from the Humility of Mary Order.

Even though we were not able to get formal invitations out we had a lot of loving souls show up at the wedding. My mother got up at Jerusalem Baptist during the Sunday worship service the week before the wedding and invited the entire church to the wedding! Thus, a large number of members from Jerusalem attended the wedding. I had been involved with that church my entire life, and even with all of its faults, like any community, there were a lot of loving individuals there who were connected to me and wanted to share that event with us. We also had a number of mutual friends who came, some of my family members, and folks from the YSU community. A real cross-section of people attended.

Thus, we had people at the wedding from different racial, religious, and cultural backgrounds—many of whom had never met before that day. However, they all came to share in that moment in time with us. But is not that how God's kingdom on earth is supposed to be? It should not matter how we look, or where we worship; God's love transcends any human barriers that can be constructed. When God's love is able to flow freely, it is amazing what can be accomplished. While I know that our wedding brought people together who would not normally be with each other for an event, I also know that it is God's love that made it happen in the way that it did, and it was not so much that Judy and Vernon T. were these special people. We were just the vessels for this loving event to happen.

Those who took part in the ceremony itself were also a diverse group. Father Bob Bonnot was the Catholic priest who actually performed the marriage. However, my minister from Jerusalem Baptist, Rev. Clyde Murray, was able to be involved in the service. Additionally, Steve Gifford, a friend from YSU who later became a minister, took part. Again, we were blessed, lucky, whatever, to have Father Bob be there for us at that time. Some other clergy would not have been willing to allow people of different faiths to be involved in the service. Judy's very good friend, Martha

(Marty) Logan, who she met in the Humility of Mary Order, stood up with her. My older brother, Bennett N. Jones Jr., stood up with me.

In my mind this illustrates how God's kingdom can become present in a specific moment in time when God's love brings different peoples together in a loving, Spirit-filled manner. We still knew that we had many challenges to deal with moving forward, but we felt God's love with us through all of the love that we felt from those who attended this service and the reception afterwards. We were very grateful for those who came and supported us.

Besides all of our friends, classmates, church members, and my family members who were there, we also think that we had one of God's angels at the wedding. In the back of the church sat a middle-aged Caucasian male dressed for a wedding; he was there for the entire service. The church was located on the east side of Youngstown, where you would not normally see this type of gentleman. We do not know exactly how he looked, and no knew who he was. We are not sure if anyone saw him come in or leave, only that he was there. Looking back on that day Judy and I felt that this individual was an angel. We knew about how angels could be used by God for various purposes. We felt that this angel had been sent to be with us at the beginning of our marriage. We thought it was a way of showing us that the good Lord was with us then and would continue to be during our marriage. Now, you might ask, are we sure that this person was an angel? Well, we did not ask him who he was, nor did anyone do an in-depth interview with him; however, we believed that he was an angel and we continued to hold on to that thought.

## STARTING A NEW LIFE TOGETHER

As you would imagine, prior to our wedding we had a lot of stress, worry, and concern about our future. But the wedding was mostly a very positive, loving, and affirming experience for both of us and, we believed, for those who came. We were glad that we decided to have a wedding where my family and our friends could attend, instead of just eloping; we would have missed so much! However, afterwards we did have to again face reality. Even with an angel being at the wedding, and with all of the spiritual aspects of the event and the affirming love and support we received, we still had challenges to overcome and deal with; we were feeling anxious about what the future held. When couples start out together there are always growing pains. Being in a long-term relationship with someone who is from a totally different background from you carries with it a unique set of difficulties from those who come from similar cultures. A key aspect in any marriage is the ability to compromise in order to make everything work. Judy and I had these issues to deal with plus a few others.

I was still working full time in the mill and taking college courses with many more credit hours to take. She had not finished her degree yet; she was expecting, which carried with it a unique set of circumstances that had to be addressed. She did not have her mother nor her family for support during her pregnancy. We also worshiped in different faith traditions. I had been raised with three brothers, and her brothers were much older than she was. Therefore, getting used to having an individual of the opposite sex in your personal space took some getting used to, probably more for me than her. Additionally, she was always open about sharing her feelings and I was someone who found that extremely hard to do, so that became another enormous learning curve for our relationship. Thus, even though we loved one another, and knew that God loved us and would be with us no matter what we went through, we had our struggles to overcome. Everything was not a bed of roses!

One of the initial things that we had discussions about was college. At first Jude said that she did not want to continue taking classes. Because of everything that we were having to deal with, her pregnancy, me working, and us starting out, she was okay not taking any more courses. However, I felt that we should try and honor her father's strong desire for her to graduate and the financial help he gave her, after she left the Humility of Mary. He had assisted in paying for classes while she was in Saint Louis and even got her a car to help her get around. (We returned that car to him after we decided to get married.) After much discussion, we agreed that she would continue, even if she could not finish the physical therapy degree she was working on. Getting some type of degree was better than dropping out altogether. It was very tough to do, but within three years she had her degree in psychology.

We lived in the apartment that I had moved into when I left my mom's house. The address was 444½ West Princeton Avenue. I always get a kick out of the address being ½; that is the only time I have had a ½ as an address. The apartment was on the second floor of a two-story house on the west side of Youngstown. We were not there very long, but had some good memories. That apartment was where we had the reception for our wedding, the home our daughter, Elizabeth, first lived in, and where we had her baptism.

Elizabeth was born on December 19 and came home right before Christmas. We had not done much in the way of getting the place fixed up for Christmas, but Jude wanted a tree, so I went out looking for one. However, most of the tree lots had closed down by the time I got there; it was Christmas Eve. I eventually found a really sick-looking tree left on a vacant tree lot. I took it and left a couple of bucks, in case the owner ever came back. The tree was not much to look at, but I know that it helped get us into the holiday spirit.

An additional important memory, and in my book a miracle, also happened while we lived in that apartment. It was the first time I lit a candle and said a prayer and asked God for something. Now, lighting candles while saying prayers is a long-held tradition in the Catholic church. However, it was not something that was done in the Baptist church that I was raised in. However, one day I was guided to light one and pray for Jude's parents, Vito and Stella. At that time, we had not seen them since we told them that we were getting married. I went to a Catholic church and lit a seven-day candle and prayed for them, and, yes, *seven days later*, they appeared at our apartment. They showed up with food for us and stayed for a short visit. It was a bit uncomfortable being together, especially after not seeing each other for a while. However, after that visit things slowly improved, and we continued to have contact with them from that period on. Luckily, Vito was a really strong Spirit-filled person who showed us both a lot of love. He was very open to being a part of our lives, and Stella followed his lead.

That was the first time I used candles as a form of prayer. I do believe that the good Lord always hears our prayers, loves us, and only wants the best for us. I also believe that the answers from our prayers may not always be in a manner that we expect or want. Sometimes the response may be no, or wait a while, or the reply might come in a way that causes us to change. However, to this day, I frequently will light a candle and pray for my family and close friends, and ask that God be with us. To my knowledge no prayers have been fulfilled quite like this first one was, but I continue to use that method in my prayer life. Yes, you could argue that Vito and Stella would have shown up anyhow at some point, because of their love for Judy. However, I believe that lighting the candle and my prayers helped get them there when they did come.

## ELIZABETH'S BAPTISM

I am glad that Vito and Stella came around when they did, for they were able to take part in Elizabeth's baptism. In the Baptist church we practiced believer's baptism, which meant a person decided on their own when they were ready to be baptized. This could be at any age, like myself, who was baptized as a teenager. For the Catholic church, infant baptism was the norm. Therefore, since we had agreed to raise our children in the Catholic faith, Elizabeth was baptized as an infant. She was born on December 19 and was baptized on January 17, 1971, in our apartment. Father Bonnot, the priest who married us, did the baptism, along with doing a Mass as well. This ended up being a mixed blessing for me, and for some of those who attended. Many years later, while I was a student at Trinity Lutheran Seminary, I took a class in which we studied about baptism. I wrote a letter to Elizabeth about her baptism and how it was a mostly wonderful event. Below is that letter so that you can see as well about how special that day was.

>Nov. 20, 2000
>
>Dear Elizabeth:
>
>At our Teaching Class at Trinity, the subject of baptism was covered as we did our teaching models. The student teacher asked that we bring in something to remind ourselves of a baptism memory of ours. I brought in pictures of your baptism. The more I thought about it the more I realize what a neat experience it was for our family.
>
>First of all, the way I was raised we did not have infant baptism, but we promised to raise our children in the Catholic faith, thus it was something we would be doing. To me it was neat because we had many different people at the event—all people that were special to us. I want to tell you about the people who came (using pictures from that day).
>
>You know about Stella, Vito, my mom, and Aunt Julia. Rev. Clyde Murray (from Jerusalem Baptist Church) was there, you know for a Baptist Minister he was a fairly opened-minded person. He read at our wedding and was willing to take part in your baptism. Fluorine, his wife, and Kerry their daughter was there as well. Kenny and Voncile Venable from my church were a couple that had accepted you, Judy and me before many others did. Mrs. Hickson and her daughter Teresa were there; Mrs. Hickson was like a second mother to me. She helped your mom and me is so many ways, especially by just loving us.

Karen and Carl Ansevin, the young-looking couple in the picture, were fellow students at YSU and were close to us. Mrs. McDonald the shorter woman was a professor from YSU, who was very supportive of your mom and me, in countless ways. Mrs. Brewer, worked at YSU, and helped us a *lot* at various times. Her daughter Linda, is seating next to her. Linda was our age.

The priest who did not get in a picture was Fr. Bob Bonnot, who married us. He was a great human being who was able to treat us as individuals along with doing the Catholic thing.

All of these people helped to welcome you into the Lord's family, but they were also a wonderful loving support community, for your mom and me. At this baptism we had black and white; Catholics, Baptist, and Methodist, but we were all Christians and came together to share in a special moment for us; your baptism.

Love, Dad

Yes, this baptism was another one of those moments that we humans get to experience that reveals a bit of how God's kingdom is manifested around us today. Having people of different races, backgrounds, and faith traditions come together to share in this event was really awe-inspiring. However, I have to be honest and note that there were a couple of uncomfortable moments as well.

Mrs. McDonald, my YSU professor who was a strong Methodist, did not say some of the responses during the Mass. The baptism was just part of the full Mass that was going on. Afterwards, she told me that there were certain parts of the Catholic liturgy that she did not agree with. Even though she was okay attending the service because we asked her, there were certain parts that she could not say. That was an eye-opening point for me, and I took a hard look at the responses, and from then on, I also did not repeat parts that I did not agree with.

The most embarrassing moment for all of us was when it came time to taking communion. I did not tell the non-Catholics that they could not take communion beforehand, and my pastor, Rev. Murray, went up to take it when it was time. However, Father Bonnot, being a good Catholic priest and knowing that Rev. Murray was not Catholic, refused him communion. Even though Father Bonnot was right in doing what he did, that still impacts me today. That hurt Rev. Murray, me, and I am sure everyone else in that small group who saw it. This also changed how I acted at the Masses I attended. I always tried to attend worship with Judy and my family where ever we lived. However, I did not take communion.

This action stayed with me so much that, at Judy's funeral Mass, I printed in the funeral bulletin that communion would only be for those of the Catholic faith, but that everyone could take part in the singing, prayers, and funeral dinner afterwards. I did not want any of our non-Catholic friends being hurt again.

Thus, for me this baptism had both high and low points. I was glad we did it the way we did it in our apartment with a small group, and was also very grateful for all of the loving Spirit-filled people who came and took part. However, even though we could come together in certain areas, there were also aspects of the event where barriers were established that could not be removed. I felt sorry for how certain people were hurt, but I know that their love for us and for their Lord helped them get through their discomforts. Thank God for that!

## THE FIRST OF MANY MOVES

The second-floor apartment served us well for a short time, but we decided more space was needed. In the spring of 1971, we moved to a single family dwelling we rented at 375 Cool Street. Yes, what a *cool* name, it was still on the west side of town. We rented from a lady that we met through a friend of ours from my church. The house was down the street from the Oliver's. Mrs. Oliver was one of my mother's best friends. We stayed there until we finished college and moved out of town. We did a lot of work to the place and it looked really good. We painted it up and cleaned up the yard. Jude was very creative, plus she was a hard worker and knew how to decorate on a budget. This was the first of many places we would fix up and, at some point, leave, as we relocated around the country.

We were blessed to have received help from various kind people as we were starting out and becoming established as a family. We were very thankful for all of the people who helped us out in small and large ways during that time. We got furniture and items from family members, friends, and my mom. We were especially aided by Mrs. Hickson, two of my aunts on my mother's side, Aunt Ruby, and Aunt Mary, who were all so helpful. Yes, it takes a village to help us make it in life!

Aunt Mary and her family lived in Cleveland about sixty miles away and she gave us a refrigerator to use. Thus, I had to rent a small trailer and pull it with our VW to get it back to our home. I remember that being a really big deal to haul at that time. Jude painted the refrigerator yellow so it looked better. She made my life more colorful in so many ways.

Those few years seemed to pass by rather quickly. In my mind it is nothing short of a miracle that we remained together with all of our challenges: our fairly new marriage, our baby (who quickly became a toddler), my working full time, both of us taking college classes (with me having issues with my GPA and a number of really difficult courses to take and try to pass), and with my continued involvement at Jerusalem Baptist. Plus, our families wanted to see us, especially because they wanted to be a part of Elizabeth's growing-up years. On top of that, for a while we tried to attend two church services on Sundays, so we could both worship in our own traditions. That made for a really lengthy day because of how long the Baptist service would run.

Somehow, we slowly began to get to know each other as a young married couple. We had our good times and some difficult moments as well with our families, our financial matters, and the overall daily pressures of life. However, Jude and I tried to work things out. For sure God was with us, because there was no way that we would have survived without the Lord's love, grace, and mercy to support and guide us.

One of the fun things that occurred during this time was an overnight retreat that we did together. Jude became involved in a youth religious education program at her church, and I was still connected to mine. Now this would have been in the 1971–72 time frame. We took a class of African-American Baptist students and a group of Caucasian Catholic students overnight and had a great time together. Again, this was another example of how God's kingdom can break into our lives. Everyone seemed to get along, and I am sure it was a great event for those who took part in it.

I was on a real high after the retreat, but still had to show up at Jerusalem Baptist that Sunday to fulfill my role as Sunday school superintendent. I was singing songs from the retreat, including my favorite, "Day by Day," and ran into another car because I was not totally paying attention to my driving. I was still in the retreat mood, and was basking in the glow of what we just went through. Oh well, it was still a wonderful retreat.

Another unique thing that we did together was to put on a very small performance of *Jesus Christ Superstar* at Jerusalem Baptist. Judy and I worked with the high school group at Jerusalem and got them interested in this. In late 1971 *Jesus Christ Superstar* was becoming very popular and Judy and I really went out on a very shaky limb to pull this off. You might image that this was a real stretch for our congregation to be a part of something like this. I am still amazed today that we were able to do that.

## FINAL FEW YEARS OF COLLEGE

Even with these activities at Jerusalem, during my last few years of college, I began to back off somewhat on helping out with things at Jerusalem. I found it increasingly more difficult to have a good marriage, be a loving parent, work full time, do the course assignments, and at the same time give quality time to the extra things at Jerusalem. I still remember telling Pastor Murray what I was going to do, and he of course did not like it because of all of the things I had done there.

That is when I began to learn about how hard it can be to say "no," especially to someone or something that has been so much a part of your entire life. However, I realized that if I wanted to earn my degree and do what I thought God was asking me to do, something had to give. Isn't this how it is for anything we want to do in life, letting go of something behind us in order to reach for what is ahead of us? This is especially true for those of us on a spiritual pilgrimage and attempting to become the person that God wants us to be. Being able to say no and letting go of past situations allows us to better strive for God's kingdom in the present.

Philippians 3:13b–14 states it very clearly: "But this one thing I do; forgetting what lies behind and straining forward to what lies ahead, I press on toward the goal for the prize of the heavenly call of God in Christ Jesus." I did not totally forget about Jerusalem Baptist until we moved out of town; we attended worship services there and at Judy's church. But I was not as active in other areas there which freed up time for me to focus on the other things that I needed to concentrate on. I let go of some things in order to work on others.

Additionally, after I got more serious about my college studies, I did not have as much time for family events on either Jude's or my side. Because on free days or on days off, we had to study. Plus, I was not necessarily off on holidays because of the shift work that I did. We did try to help my mom out by driving her places, because at that time she still did not drive. Balancing all of the balls that we had to juggle was an effort, but, somehow, we pulled it off and learned as we went along how to make that all work out.

As I was getting closer to finishing the work for my degree, I tried to get an office job at Youngstown Sheet and Tube. However, none were available for me, at least that was what I was told. I also applied for a supervisor's position in the department that I had worked in for over eight years, but that was not about to happen either. At some point a friend of mine told me that because I was in an interracial marriage they were not going to allow me to be considered for any of those positions, even if I was better qualified than others there. It did not matter that the color line had been broken in a number of areas; it was still a very race-oriented place.

Most African-Americans were still stuck in certain positions with little room to move up. I was fortunate, lucky, or blessed to have been in the right spot at the right time to do what I did do and break the color line for third helpers. I was also fortunate to be able to move up as far as I could. Hindsight is always twenty-twenty and it ended up being a very good thing that I did not get another higher-level position in the mill, for the good Lord was looking out for my family and me.

In 1977 (we left Youngstown in 1973), YS&T pretty shut down. A lot of people were permanently laid off and out of a job. Many of the people that I had known and worked with for years were on the streets. That really hurt all of Youngstown and Mahoning County. YS&T employed a lot of people and now nearly all were unemployed. A lot of workers only knew mill work and did not have the skills to do anything else, and some had very little education. If I would have tried to stay and not left, I would have been out of a job as well. However, I was willing to leave and go elsewhere, when I had the chance. One could ask, Didn't God care about all of those people who were out of a job, and why did the good Lord provide me a way out? I cannot answer that, but I believe that God opened a door for me, and I was willing and able to step through that door to a very different life that I had not known before.

There were a lot of different dynamics operating in our lives as we neared the end of our college journey. Many people at the mill and others believed that after I received my degree I would stay there in some form or fashion. Even though the job had its drawbacks, we had great union health benefits, which paid for almost all medical expenses; I knew the work and the pay was fine for what I did. Others in the past had stayed in the mill even with a college degree. Jude's dad, Vito, said that I should stay there because I had over eight years invested in the mill. He had been employed on the docks in Ashtabula, Ohio, most of his working life. He thought I should not give up my seniority but continue working there.

However, over time the way things worked out, I was able to leave because of how God directed me, and opened doors for me, and then placed a desire in me to try something else. Additionally, Judy was willing to leave to find a different life elsewhere, definitely a faith journey thing—going into the unknown, only knowing that God is leading the way. Looking back, we had a lot of great people to help us and God was with us for sure as we discerned our next step.

## LIFE AFTER THE MILL AND COLLEGE

As I approached graduation and could not get any managerial offers from YS&T, I started dealing with YSU's Campus Placement Department. They attempted to sign me up for some interviews. I also mailed a lot of resumes out to anyone who might be interested in me. However, my GPA was so low, most did not say, "This is a person we have to get." But St. Paul Insurance liked to interview people from YSU because a number of their graduates worked while in college and showed discipline in doing so. This was something they liked. I interviewed initially with their local claims representative on campus. Then I was asked to go to their Cleveland branch office to have another interview and meet several of their staff. There they told me about their operations and a little about the insurance industry, which I knew nothing about. That was a very wonderful experience for me; they also took me to lunch—my first business lunch. After this second interview, I thought things went well.

Remarkably, they then asked me to fly to Saint Paul, Minnesota, to meet with staff in St. Paul's home office. That was another amazing adventure for me, as it was my first time flying and having to stay overnight on business. I met with a number of different people there. The one thing I remember was part of my conversation with the vice president of marketing. I asked him why he would take the time to deal with a potentially low-level trainee. He said that if they were able to hire the right people in each area, he had a better chance of being successful in the home office.

They were interested in me for their marketing department. They were not as concerned about my GPA, but that I had worked full time while going to college and had shown self-discipline. Because marketing people generally operated on their own, they had to be trusted and able to function without day-to-day supervision. Additionally, the VP of marketing said that, if they hired me, they could send me pretty much anywhere to work, except for the southern part of the US because of my race. They felt that it would be too difficult for me to be successful in that part of the country. They were probably right about that. At that time the insurance industry had very few minorities in staff positions in their branch offices. Also, St. Paul and other similar insurance companies did not have any African-Americans calling on agencies, working hand in hand with them fulfilling the marketing or field representative function. I do not think that, at that time, St. Paul nor any other major insurance carriers had any women in marketing as well; this would come much later.

During this process, and after I was hired, overall, St. Paul was very fair with me. However, I filled a need for them at that time. They wanted minorities because at that time everyone was searching for good candidates. Times were changing and the property-casualty insurance industry was slow in adapting. Back then the overall industry was mostly Caucasian, male, and overly conservative. After I was hired, I became the first person of any color to become a marketing representative for St. Paul, and possibly the first in any main-line insurance company.

Leaving the mill to take a job elsewhere seems to be an easy decision looking back at it today. However, it was not all that straightforward. The mill had great benefits, and in 1973 their health insurance was extremely good. St. Paul and the rest of the insurance industry's benefits were not nearly as good as we had through the mill. When I left, I was making about twelve thousand dollars a year in the mill and started with St. Paul at a salary of nine thousand dollars. Of course, the mill had its downsides; it was dangerous, hot, and dirty work. I was guided, however, to leave the mill and in time take the offer from St. Paul, which opened a new door for my family and me.

What I am about to say may seem odd to you, but I truly believe that for my entire life God has only shown me one way to go in my career. Whenever I have changed positions, and I have done so quite often, it always seems that one choice stands heads and shoulders above any other. So, why would the good Lord care more about my new jobs than someone else's, who may have many opportunities/offers to choose from? I cannot answer that. I only know what has happened to me. St. Paul was the only offer I had after I finished my degree, and going to YS&T was a clear choice for me after high school. There you have it, believe it or not. Do not think for one minute that my life has been perfect without all of the challenges that others have to face. But, in this one particular area, I firmly believe that God has directed my steps.

Looking back, it is hard to believe all that went on during my early adult years. I ended up being employed at Youngstown Sheet and Tube for eight years and eleven months, from July of 1964 until June of 1973. It took a total of eight years going part time to obtain my undergraduate degree from Youngstown State University, from September of 1965 until June of 1973. Jude took a total of five years to finish. We both received our BAs on June 16 (our wedding anniversary date), in 1973.

Needless to say, that was a really awesome moment for both of us and our families and friends. It took a lot of hard work, persistence, and faith to get us to that point. But we know that we would not have made it without the support and prayers of those around us and a belief that God's grace and guidance would be with us through the ups and downs of our journey. It was a time that had a bit of everything. But little did we know that is how the rest of our life's pilgrimage would be. We can only actually live the present moment that is given to us. The difficult part for all of us is to trust the future to the Lord and just take each next step, each day as it comes.

Even though we were very thrilled to have earned our degrees, there was also some pain to go along with it. Jude's father, Vito, who had so badly wanted her to finish college, could not make it to the college graduation. He became ill and was not able to come, which was so sad, because that was something that he really wanted to be a part of. Vito and his wife, Stella, had become a big part of our lives, and it was a real disappointment that he could not physically be there to celebrate our accomplishment. A neighbor brought Stella to the graduation. Vito got us a TV as a present for our graduation; he was very generous and supportive of us. In my mind, he was quietly a very spiritual person and, overall, a wonderful human being. He was one I came to respect, and I learned a lot from him about how to be a family and how to treat others in a loving and caring manner.

# SIX

# Taking Another Leap of Faith

*I hereby command you: Be strong and courageous; do not be frightened or dismayed, for the Lord your God is with you wherever you go.*

—Josh 1:9

## LEAVING OUR FORMER LIVES

IN MY MIND, GOING to work in the mill, beginning to take courses at YSU, getting married, and having a child, among other things, were all very meaningful new life stages that presented some hurdles for Jude and me and those around us. However, just thinking about leaving Youngstown was going to be a major change for all of us. Physically moving elsewhere would end up being a challenge, not only for myself, Jude, and Elizabeth but also for our families, especially my mom and Jude's parents, our other family members and friends, and our church families.

However, I was very thankful that Jude was willing to leave Youngstown, northeast Ohio, and the mill in order to enter the next stage in our lives and to do what we thought God was leading us to do. I am sure that if I had been married to someone else, they would have not been so open to leaving their family and friends. However, she had already done that twice, once when she went into the Humility of Mary Order after high school, and then later on when she went away to college in Saint Louis. We had our share of doubts, for we were entering into a world that neither of us knew anything about. This verse from Joshua talks about being strong and courageous. I am not sure if, in fact, we were really strong and courageous. The only thing I know is that when the time came, we went, trusting that we would be okay and that the good Lord was indeed with us wherever we were.

After waiting for what seemed to be forever when I had done all of their interviews, St. Paul Insurance Company offered me a job. *It was great to finally get that call.* As noted, they were the only company that offered me a position out of all of the places I had contacted and mailed resumes to. Originally St. Paul said that they wanted me to go to their Detroit branch office to be trained. I did not know anything about the insurance field, and they were going to have to educate me from the bottom up. At that time, we were willing to go most anywhere to begin our new lives. However, something came up with the personnel in their Detroit office, whereby they did not have a spot for me there, so they offered me Denver, Colorado. *Wow!* What a fortunate, lucky, or blessed turn of events for us. Detroit would have been closer to our folks, but Denver turned out to be a wonderful experience for us.

## ST. PAUL FIRE AND MARINE INSURANCE COMPANY

St. Paul paid to relocate us from Youngstown to Denver, which at first was a big deal for me. However, I came to realize that this was something that most companies did when moving people from one part of the country to another. When we moved to Denver, we thought we had died and gone to heaven for many reasons. We lived in a motel for about a month on company expense until we found a place to live and moved into an apartment. We had our issues with learning our way around a new and large city and finding a place to stay; however, overall, it was a very good experience.

Another reason that this period was such an amazing time for us in Denver was that I only worked a day job and wore business clothes to work. I did not get dirty and have to deal with the smell and dirt in my clothes, as was the case in the mill, and was a given a desk, and basically for the first few months had to read and learn about the insurance business. This was such a contrast from the life that had been known while in Youngstown, and I did not have to work those afternoon and evening shifts and also deal with my class assignments. Things were so different for us and we had so much to be thankful for. Jude did not work outside of our home or go to school; she took care of Elizabeth and helped support me in this new undertaking. I will always be grateful for her willingness to do this; *I could not have done this without her*! We of course missed being near our families, and we had to get used to this new city and our new life, but overall, we felt really blessed and we enjoyed ourselves.

The Rocky Mountains were and still are a beautiful sight to behold, especially for people like us who had lived most of our lives in northeastern Ohio. We, of course, had never seen anything like that before and fell in love with them! That period during my St. Paul training will always be remembered as one of the best times of our lives. While we lived in Denver, we also did a fair amount of sightseeing in the mountains and various areas around the state. There were so many wonderful things to see in that colorful state. We found a place to live on South Parker Road in an apartment complex, southeast of Denver, which was a distance from the city. We were in Denver from late summer 1973 until November of 1974.

The staff of St. Paul's Denver branch office were extremely helpful, friendly, and supportive. They did not let the fact that I was the only person of color in their office overly affect how they treated me. They always seemed to be honest and respectful in their interactions with me. I was hired as a marketing trainee, and trainees were moved to St. Paul's branch offices to educate them in an office environment.

Additionally, trainees would visit St. Paul's home office to take some required classes. After one to two years the individuals would be placed in a permanent position, usually in another branch office. It was a time-consuming and expensive process for St. Paul. However, because they were so conservative in their operations and underwriting practices, they chose to teach their new employees the company's ways of doing business. In their mind, they believed that it was more effective than hiring an experienced insurance person who would have to be retrained in their practices. Because this training covered all of the departments and product lines that St. Paul was involved with, anyone who finished this program was well grounded in not only what they did, but they had a good handle on the overall insurance business. I was very fortunate to have been trained by them; it helped me greatly for the rest of my insurance career.

At that time St. Paul's Denver branch office handled all of Colorado, Wyoming, Utah, and New Mexico. Thus, they had a large staff, with lots of business being written and transactions being handled on a daily basis. As I noted, they had some neat people working there who were very friendly and supportive of me. The branch manager was Fred Sheldon, and the marketing manager that I reported to was Ken Brocklesby. These men had been with St. Paul for years, and were sort of "old school" in some of their thinking and methods. However, they both were very gracious to me and my family, and tried to make my stay in their office as comfortable as possible. I will always be grateful that I was sent to train under their watch, for I know it could have been much more challenging in other places.

St. Paul, like other main-line insurance companies, was trying to bring more minorities into their organizations. For instance, in the Denver branch office they had a female package underwriting manager and two female package underwriters in that department. That was very rare back then. From what I could tell I was the first African-American to be hired to be a marketing representative to call on their agencies. St. Paul had a few African-Americans (in other locations) and women in staff-line positions, but none in marketing. Thus, God used me to break color lines in two different industries before I was thirty. I know that I was given the personality, skills, and just enough talent to be chosen to do this. I also broke additional color lines in other areas throughout my life.

When I first got to St. Paul and began my training, I spent time reading and learning about insurance; thus, I would just show up for work and spend the day reading. In September and October of the first year I was sent to St. Paul's home office to take part in a four-and-a-half-week trainee class. This class was made up of trainees from all over the country. It was like we were back in college classes again, but the total focus was on insurance and St. Paul's products. About halfway through this training session in St. Paul, Jude came up to visit me. She drove by herself from Denver to St. Paul; friends of ours from the apartment complex watched Elizabeth for those few days. It was neat that she could do that for it was great to see her. After the classes were over, she drove up again, but this time with Elizabeth. Looking back that was a really big deal for her to do that drive alone, from Denver to St. Paul with a three-year-old. Our plan was to drive back to Denver together and then do a little sightseeing on the way back; we also wanted to go to Mount Rushmore.

## MORE ANGELS

Now this was the middle of October in 1973 and we did not expect any bad weather. However, we ran into a really awful snow storm one evening after dark. I was driving and as always thought I could drive through it.

But it just continued to snow and got increasingly worse the farther we drove—it was dreadful and scary. I thought we had enough gas in the car and remember the gas tank showing about a quarter full. However, the car died right there on the interstate in this horrific snow storm.

Jude, always the person to do things quickly, got my flashlight out of the glove box, put it in my face, and told me to do something! I normally would not be so bold that quickly, but without thinking things through, I got out and waved the flashlight at the oncoming traffic. Guess what? The next vehicle that came by stopped. I do not remember how the car looked, except that it may have been a truck or some type of Jeep-like automobile. Two men got out, again, do not remember how either of them looked. But they had a large can of gas that they gave us and they would not take anything for it.

Now what are the chances that someone would stop at night to help out, in a really terrible snowstorm, and would have extra gas? The only thing that we could figure was that God did not want us going any farther that night. Additionally, the good Lord did not want us stuck on the freeway either. What we determined was that they must have been angels sent to help us out. Maybe our second encounter with angels sent by God? After they helped us out, my car started right up and we drove off. We got off at the next exit, and looked around for a few minutes in an area that we knew nothing about. Eventually, we found a motel, which surprisingly had rooms available; it seemed like heaven to us. It was an inexpensive place, normally used by truckers, but it was clean and warm and we were very thankful to have found it. The next morning the storm had passed and the roads were much better to travel on.

Looking back, no telling what may have happened to us if we would have continued on. It was much better for us to stop when we did. I will always be thankful for Judy's action, and God's angels helping us out. You might be wondering, did not God care about all of the other people on the freeway that night, or in other similar situations? I believe that God is love and cannot help but love all humans, and all of creation, and probably did help others.

## LIFESTYLE AND EDUCATIONAL CHANGES

After returning from the training class in St. Paul, I decided to go on a diet in order to lose weight. I counted calories and tried to stay under twelve hundred calories a day and also did not eat any sweets. I lost a bunch of weight for the first time. Because I was only working with no studying, and did not have as much stress as before, thus, I was able to really focus on the diet. I did well on the diet at that time. However, I tell people that I have probably gained and lost hundreds of pounds over the years, because I can do well for a while, then fall off. My eating challenges and weight issues will more than likely go to the grave with me, for that is something that always will have to be dealt with.

Also I got really serious about jogging, to help with my weight issues and overall health. I have continued to exercise through the years, and my jogging routine has been done pretty faithfully since then. Thank goodness, I am still able to do that, for if not, no telling what shape my body might be in, since I am not always disciplined as I should be when it comes to eating. But, with all that being said, I have been lucky, fortunate, or blessed to have had a really healthy life, and know that many around me have had life-threatening health problems to deal with.

In the fall of 1973, I began taking insurance courses in addition to the class work I was involved with during the day-time hours at St. Paul. Because I was not working and going to school at the same time, I found that taking a self-study curriculum on my own time was manageable. Additionally, St. Paul and most any such other companies love it when their employees take continuing education classes. After some discussion with the people around me, I signed up for the Insurance Institute of America (IIA) courses. These insurance courses were basic insurance classes and could eventually lead one into taking the more challenging CPCU courses, which I eventually did.

I studied the materials on my own for ten weeks and took their nationwide exam for the fall period of 1973 and passed IIA 21! Thinking that I was smarter than I really was, and being in a hurry again and not taking it one step at a time as I should have, I then took two courses. During the winter period of 1974, I passed IIA 23, but failed IIA 22. I know one would think that I would have learned my lesson from the trouble I got myself into while always on probation at YSU. But *no*, still had not learned how to pace myself and leave the future to God. However, one thing you can say about me is that I keep trying! In the fall period of 1974, I retook IIA 22, and passed it. At that point I was awarded the Insurance Institute of America Certificate, and was glad to have finished this course. St. Paul was happy as well because it showed that I was willing to invest my own personal time into becoming an insurance professional.

## TRAINING CHANGES

The first nine months or so of their training program went along fine for St. Paul and me. I did what was expected of me and the people in the office continued to support and encourage me. However, at some point St. Paul decided to change the agenda of what they had given me, when I first started. They felt the marketing people who were coming out of their program did not have a strong enough underwriting background. Thus, the curriculum was changed mid-stream and all of the marketing people had to spend more time working an underwriting desk. I had already spent time in the underwriting department and felt I understood that area of the business. But management wanted me and others to actually work a desk as an underwriter.

This upset me at the time, and I was not happy that now it would take longer to finish. As an imperfect human being, one of my learning edges is discerning how to be patient and to let things develop in God's timing. I was very eager to get out and start working on my own as a field representative. Additionally, in my mind it was not fair that they altered what they had promised me, but I did not have any choice but to just deal with it and move on. Over time I was able to let go of my negative feelings and put my focus on the tasks in front of me.

However, I did get through that part of the process, and during the fall of 1974 I was given the title of field representative and received my first ever business cards. I was the first African-American in that role for St. Paul, and probably, at that time, the first for most of the other mainline insurance companies. During my last few months in Denver, I was given a small territory to handle with a few agencies to work with. That part was fun for me and I really enjoyed it. My personality, knowledge, skills, and discipline allowed me to do well in that position. I had some successes with the agencies that were given to me to call on. I was able to help them out, solve problems for them, and was also was able to increase the amount of business that they gave to St. Paul.

The additional fun part was that during some of my overnight trips I was able to have Judy and Elizabeth travel with me and we could see some of the beautiful sights of Colorado. One time the three of us went to Leadville, Colorado, to make an agency visit. Leadville is the highest incorporated city in the US at over ten thousand feet. That was a very unique place to travel to and visit. We also visited other parts of the state. One of the nicest places we saw as a family was the Four Corners area in southwestern Colorado, and we got to see the Native American cliff dwellings. Because Jude was a stay-at-home mom with Elizabeth, she could be flexible when we wanted to travel like we did. That time in Denver allowed us to grow as a couple and as a family. We did miss being close to our extended family but there were so many positives for us living in Denver. I will always be grateful to Jude, for being who she was. I would not have been able to do what I did without her. She was definitely a God-send to me.

While in Denver, we all attended the Newman (Catholic) Church services, on the campus of Denver University. That was the beginning of us attending a wide assortment of churches and faith communities over the years. We always made the effort to find somewhere to worship wherever we lived. After we left Youngstown, I never attended another Baptist church on a regular basis. From time to time, I visited several, but never found one that was comfortable enough to join.

## ALCOHOL AND ME

St. Paul liked that I was a hard worker, tried to be a good team player, and was focused on what was required of me. However, one never knows what aspects of a situation may cause people concern and think, "That's odd." I do not drink alcohol of any kind and that was something that several in the office had a hard time understanding or getting their head around. I do not drink to this day and sometimes that makes me stand out from others who I may be working or socializing with.

My decision to not drink goes back to my early teen years. I was raised in a Baptist church, but that is not the main reason why I do not drink. My mother did not drink and I never liked the taste of alcohol the few times I have tried it. In my mind, the principle reason for this lifelong decision goes back to when our family lived on Forest Avenue on the east side of Youngstown. Forest Avenue was a dead end and at the corner of Wilson and Forest there were a couple of bars. Often, I would see men about my father's age just hanging around or out in front of these bars. I wondered, Why were they not home with their families and children? Those images really impacted me. My own father was not as active in my life as I would have liked, and I became upset seeing these men just hanging around. I thought drinking and alcohol had too much of a hold on those men, keeping them from doing more constructive things. From those impressions, at some point in my life I decided that alcohol was not a good thing, if you lost control of how it affected your life. Thus, I have only tasted alcohol when someone tries to make me try a drink that they think I will like, but never do. Because of this practice, I sometimes have to do a lot of explaining of my actions to certain groups of people.

That was the case when I started work as a marketing trainee for St. Paul. At that time, marketing people were expected to take agents out to lunch and sometimes order a couple of drinks. Every so often, the lunch and drinking could end up lasting all afternoon! That was more or less a standard business practice. The management and marketing staff in the Denver branch also would go out for lunch and sometimes would have too much to drink. They had a really hard time getting used to the fact that I was going into marketing and *I did not drink*! Some of them really thought that I was weird. At first it was sometimes uncomfortable for me when they would drink too much, and I did not drink at all, but over time I got used to it and could deal with it. But believe me it was a shocker initially for some of the people there. However, we all lived through it.

I still do not drink, and I have added another reason to why me drinking would not be a good idea. Sometimes, when I fall off of my good eating habits and I start eating sweets, my body cannot stop, and I crave more and more. I know that happens when the sugar goes to my brain and wants more. Now I realize that alcohol would do the same thing. Because of how my body is wired, once I started drinking, there is no telling if I would ever be able to stop. From a career standpoint my not drinking ended up being just a minor topic of discussion. The main concern for the company was whether I could fulfill my role and do what was required of me, and, in most cases, I think the answer was a definite yes.

Things were going along fine for me as a field representative in training when Judy became pregnant with Kevin. There were not any jobs for me in Denver, so sooner or later we were going to have to move. Management did not know if they had any permanent positions available for me to transfer into elsewhere. Jude was expecting in February of 1975 and we felt that if we did not relocate prior to the new year, we would travel too close to her due date. Thus, I asked that they try and find something for me before it got too late. Plus, as always, I was in a hurry to get on with the next stage of my business career, and begin handling my own territory. But Judy's pregnancy changed the timeline for me looking for a permanent spot.

We were lucky, fortunate, or blessed to have a position in St. Paul's San Francisco office open up. That is right folks, San Fran! I made a trip there to go through the interview process. The branch manager was Tony Ria, and the marketing manager was Bob Regan; both liked me and asked me to work for them. This was another very large branch, doing lots of insurance business in a very charming part of the country. One of the fun things from this was that they gave Jude and me a trip there for a week to look for a place to live. We were able to leave Elizabeth with a good friend and neighbor while we were gone. That was a great and awesome trip. The company flew us there and took really good care of us. We were in a wonderful area, at a nice hotel, and on an expense account. This was the beginning of an entire new adventure for us.

## CALIFORNIA, HERE WE COME

Leaving Denver was quite difficult for both of us, and it held a special place for us because of all the pleasant memories we had while there. I think that is so because it was the start of a totally new life for us: after having to deal with college classes, working, beginning our marriage, and starting a family. We enjoyed the mountains, the state, the people, and overall St. Paul was very fair to us. However, we needed to be settled into wherever we would end up before Jude delivered. Additionally, I was eager to begin working with my own set of agencies. So, we had to go but it was not without some pain and sorrow for leaving what we had while there.

We moved in December of 1974, which maybe was not the best time to be going through the mountains. I remember driving from Denver to California and we ran into another snowstorm, and I still recall going through the mountains leading into Salt Lake City. We were fortunate this time to be able to pass trucks on the interstate that could not make it up those hills. We had a little Mazda wagon at that time and it drove well in the snowy conditions. We were lucky to make it, and we were also able to stop over in Salt Lake City for one night.

When we arrived, we settled into the apartment that we had picked out when we made our earlier visit to the Bay Area. Kevin was due in late February, so Jude had to begin taking it easy while getting us set up in our new home. Our place was in Concord in a second-floor apartment, a complex around many other apartment developments on Adelaide

Avenue. This was the fourth residence we had lived in together since we were married, a lot of changes for us in a few short years! Thank goodness, we were learning how to work together and could feel God's love with us, no matter what was happening in our lives.

Kevin was born in February of 1975, shortly after we moved into our apartment. Thank goodness that we had been able to move and I had started my new position before he was born. The move would have been much more taxing if we had waited until after his birth. We were also blessed to have a wonderful couple in our apartment complex. They offered to watch Elizabeth when Judy went to the hospital to deliver Kevin. We did not have any family around, which was hard, but God provided us with someone to help us out.

Jude had Kevin by the Lamaze method, at John Muir Hospital in Walnut Creek, which was the next town over from Concord. I got to go into the delivery room, and guess what—I did not faint! This is the guy who generally dislikes hospital rooms, or medical stuff, or needles, etc., and has been known to get light headed when being around those type of things. It was a neat experience and we still have pictures of me holding Kevin immediately after his birth. We were also blessed that Kevin was born heathy even with the stress of the move on Jude and him. I have to give Jude a lot of credit, praise, and thanks for how she handled all of this. She had to move close to her due date and switch doctors, and she dealt with everything really well. Again, I was very blessed to have been married to Judy; a lot of women may not have been able to deal with what she did.

## A NEW MARKETING TERRITORY

Work wise, I continued with the field representative title that they gave me in Denver. I started operating out of St. Paul's San Francisco office in January of 1975. After demonstrating that I could continue doing what was needed to fulfill the role, I was promoted on August 11, 1975, to the field supervisor position. It was still the same type of job, but with a higher-level title and salary. Again, to my knowledge I was the first African-American to hold that position for St. Paul.

The San Francisco branch was one of the largest offices in the country for St. Paul. It handled all of Northern California, and wrote a large amount of commercial line and personal line business. Because of the shipping industry nearby, they also had a good-sized ocean marine department that serviced that industry. This location had more people than Denver had and gave me a great opportunity to learn more about the insurance business and business in general. The skills picked up in the mill regarding how to work with a wide cross-section of people came in handy there. Because St. Paul was a very conservative company, sometimes it took a lot of effort to get them to try anything new. It took a while, but people in positions of authority began to trust me and I was able to get some things done that others may not have been able to do.

My initial marketing territory to call on was the Oakland/East Bay Area plus some places south and north of there. I also went further north to Redding, California, several hours away and additionally had one agency in Mount Shasta, near the Oregon border. At first, I spent time familiarizing myself with the new area and the branch operation. I also tried to learn the background of that territory. There were of course some common aspects concerning most agencies. However, the agencies in Northern California had some different characteristics than those in the Denver area. The California ones were on average greater in size, and handled more and larger commercial accounts. They were also more progressive in their thinking and aggressive in their management styles. Thus, I tried to get a handle on their methods and history before calling on them.

Around this time, in January/February of 1975, St. Paul and the entire property and casualty insurance industry began going through some difficult times. The term that is used to describe this type of period was a *hard market*, which happens when insurance companies begin to restrict their insurance writings and tighten up their underwriting guidelines to be more selective about the type of accounts they will write due to higher risk factors. This was the environment that I started working with in my new territory.

Hard markets produced cut-backs in the percentage of compensation paid to agencies/agents, which was not a popular decision or an easy sale. Also, St. Paul was a fairly conservative company, but one of their advantages for many years was that they offered professional liability coverages to their agents, which many other companies did not. However, when St. Paul began to pull out of that market, they lost some of their edge over their competition. I had to explain these changes in person to the agents. It was a tough job to do but during times like that being a marketing representative meant you took a lot of heat and negative comments. Thus, for me, in my very first call to these forty-five to fifty agencies, I had to reduce their income and take some previously available insurance products from them—not the way to make friends and influence people on the first visit!

The disappointing part for me was that my marketing manager did not go with me to these first calls. I had never worked with these agencies before, nor had I even been to their offices. I had to figure out how to get to them—all in cities that I had never been to previously. This was before GPS; I got lots of maps of the area in order to find my way around. During those first few months just getting around added a lot of stress to my job. Then on top of that I had to deal with the issue of decreases in commission and with the product changes. Looking back, I think more could have been done to support my initial calls since I was a novice marketing representative in a brand-new territory, and had to deal with those less than popular modifications. This was a definite baptism by fire. I continued to learn more about good presentation skills and how to remain cool in tense situations, for I did have a number of upset people to deal with.

However, with all that being said, I only had one agency president refuse to sign the new commission schedules. I remember the call to this day, for he made me extremely nervous, when he would not accept the changes. The agency was a very large and successful one in Berkeley that was not going to accept this adjustment from a rookie like me. In this case my marketing manager had to get involved because there was no other choice. On the following visit the amendments were signed. All of the other agencies signed the revised contacts. After that, I felt that I could handle most anything that would come up during an agency visit.

I acknowledge the fact that God had blessed me with the skills, knowledge, persistence, and a personality to be able to do what was done then and what has been done since. But, think of this for a moment: You have an African-American individual from Youngstown, Ohio, brand new in the position and territory, making calls on middle-upper income Caucasian males (at that time there were no women in management positions in the agencies that I called on), who were principals in these successful Northern California agencies, who had never had any persons of color make calls on them before. My very first call was to get them to take an income reduction. At the same time, I was also reducing the number of professional liability coverages that they could market with St. Paul. I know that none of that would have happened unless the Lord was guiding me on those calls.

## ANCIENT PRAYER AND BIBLE QUOTES

One of the things that helped me on a regular basis to make agency visits was a couple of ideas that I picked up from reading materials by Norman Vincent Peale. He wrote many books, but the main one for me was the *Power of Positive Thinking*. Some of the practices that I learned from his books are still very much used in my life. Two of those routines were used on my daily agency calls. He quoted a very ancient prayer when asking God for guidance in one's life. The prayer is "I believe I am always divinely guided. I believe I will always take the right turn of the road. I believe God will always make a way where there is no way." He wrote about how this prayer could be used. Over time, I began repeating this prayer prior to going into an agency visit and sometimes repeated it during the call, depending upon how things were going. *Now*, just because I said this prayer did not mean that I always had wonderful, successful calls. Believe me, I had my share of unhappy, grumpy people and negative situations to deal with over the years.

Because I was *the* company when walking into our agency's offices, anything that was done either incorrectly or well, I would hear about it. Occasionally, I would walk into a situation that I did not see coming and had to react quickly to address the concerns. In some cases, I could not do anything about the issues, only listen and lend a caring ear. Sometimes I could correct the problem, which I got good at doing. However, if I went into a call knowing that no matter what happened God would guide and be with me, my attitude was one of being hopeful and helpful, rather than one of being doubtful. I still use this prayer today at various times.

Something else picked up from Dr. Peale's materials was writing positive thinking quotes and/or Bible verses on the back of old business cards and placing them on my car's dashboard. He wrote about a sales person who did this so that person would be reinforced and encouraged during their work day. I started doing something similar and obtained quotes from various people and Bible verses that I liked and wrote them on business cards. Once a week I would attach one to my dash, so I could see it while driving. For years I have memorized a Bible verse every week, and those would be the verses that would be placed in my car.

This routine did a couple of things for me. As much as humanly possible it kept my mind focused on positive thoughts and how I was not alone in my car, God was with me. Additionally, it helped my attitude in going from one agency visit to the other. If I had a really bad call, I did not want what had happened earlier to impact my next visit. But, being a fallible human person, sometimes I could not help but let this occur. However, having these Bible verses and positive quotes allowed me to deal with more negative situations than I would have been able to handle without them. The card stayed there, regardless of who rode with me in my company car. Thus, the cards became a form of witness to my faith. Occasionally, people would ask about them or make a comment about them. Those cards helped in my role as a field representative and in my spiritual pilgrimage.

Having these business cards in my car continued as long as I was calling on agencies, no matter where I worked, or what company I was employed with. One of my many career stops was as corporate sales manager for Merchants Insurance Company in Buffalo, New York. I had an office and at that point spent less time on the road and more time in my office. When I took the job there was a white board on the wall behind my desk that had been left by the previous manager. The president came by one day and asked why I was not making use of the white board. I may have for a while written sales results on the white board; I do not remember. However, in time, I started writing my positive-thinking quotes and Bible verses on it.

Thus, what was begun in my company car continued in my work office. I was very non-threatening with what I wrote on the board. I never preached to anyone during my work time; however, hopefully, by the way I lived and worked people knew about my faith. I never got any hassle from anyone by doing this. Not sure you could do that today.

The last insurance company that I worked for was in Columbus, Ohio, Auto Club Insurance, and I was lucky enough to have an office for most of the time that I worked for them as a marketing manager. I did the same thing again—got a white board and placed it in my office and again wrote positive-thinking quotes and Bible verses on it. This time, more people who read these words began coming to me to share issues in their personal life and to communicate their faith stories. Here again, I did not seek to share anything, but was sought out as one who had a caring ear. I got to know people better, even those with whom I did not work on a daily basis. However, I believe what was written on the white board allowed people to trust me and to be willing to get to know me.

I remember one day that our marketing department was having a very bad day—everything that could go wrong did. One of my associates, Connie, said that maybe I should have a Bible verse up on my board rather than the positive saying that was there. Her feeling was that maybe we needed more spiritual help that day than some positive-thinking quote could give us. From that point on, I only placed Bible verses on my white board. Of course, that did not stop me from having problems and the normal work issues to deal with, because as human beings we are not immune from worldly struggles. However, in my car, from that time on, I only used Bible verses on my dash as well. Thus, a routine that I started in California was continued in New York and Ohio. As noted, that ritual has helped me be a support to those around me and has aided me on my own spiritual journey.

Another habit that I got into during these travel days was to listen to tapes (which are not used any more today). I started out with positive thinking tapes that could assist me with my low self-esteem and offer me encouragement and support while I was making my calls. Besides those I played Bible-based tapes and then later on branched out to a wide selection of faith-centered materials. When I had to make any long-distance trips by myself, the tapes helped the time pass more quickly. I normally kept a box or two of tapes, so that I could change off frequently, or choose a specific one depending upon what was going on in my life. Listening to those tapes did aid with my daily tasks. I think that they made me a better field rep and also allowed me to become more of the person God intended me to be.

## CONTINUED TOUGH TIMES AT ST. PAUL AND IN THE INSURANCE INDUSTRY

Sometime after beginning in my new territory and dealing with the changes that upper management at St. Paul made, more challenging decisions were made by them and throughout the insurance industry at large due to an ongoing hard insurance market. Many insurance companies began to restrict their insurance writings and tighten up their underwriting guidelines to be more selective about the type of accounts that they would write.

Right before I started in the Bay Area, St. Paul had written a wide range of professional coverages. They had liberally underwritten for lawyers, some doctors, and nurses malpractice insurance, but then they pulled out all together, or significantly reduced how much new business they were willing to underwrite in these lines. Having these products available was a unique benefit and also a wonderful source of income for the agencies that wrote insurance with St. Paul. There were not many companies that were willing to support such coverages. Thus, when St. Paul decided to pull out of these lines it really placed their agencies in a very difficult situation.

As a field representative I got the full force of the anger and disappointment coming from those agencies on my visits. I could not do anything about the decisions that were made; it was totally out of my hands. I could only listen and offer whatever suggestions or information of other markets that I knew about. Of course, I was not the only person going through that very frustrating time. Everyone from the field reps to the branch staff and the branch management were all getting an earful. It was tough to continue going out, but, thankfully, I knew that it was not directed at me personally; but it was still awkward! Again, having a spiritual foundation helped me get through that period.

What I learned later was that when the insurance market did loosen up a bit, the agencies that I had called on were more willing to listen to me than to other company reps who did not call on them at all while things were tight. Being able to be persistent and faithful in those tough times allowed me be a better rep for our agents and my company. Life is not always a bed of roses, but how we deal with those challenging moments, and whom we have our faith in about the future, helps us make it through. Knowing that God was with me, no matter what I was involved with, aided me each day.

For most of my time in the field, I enjoyed this job immensely. At that time in my life, I did not like having to be in an office on a daily basis. That situation would change over time, when I did have to show up in an office. However, back then, for three to four days a week, I would leave home in the morning to make my agency calls, do my paperwork in my car or somewhere else, and then go home in the evening. Once or twice a month I would have to travel overnight to visit the agencies that were farther away, but I also loved that as well.

I often said that my personality and the field rep job were made for each other. I knew that I was blessed to be doing what I did. It of course had its moments, but overall, I got to be good at fulfilling the role, and was able to be of help both to the company I worked for and the agencies called on. Most of the organizations called on became very comfortable in dealing with me. Here again, all of the skills that had been picked up in my life, plus my disposition, and my work knowledge, allowed me to be effective in my position. I loved being out on my own and working with people to get things done and thank God for that period in my life.

In time I became involved with the East Bay Field Club. This was made up of field reps from other insurance companies. We got together once a month to share concerns, learn about what was going on in the industry, and of course socialize. At one point I was elected to be president of the East Bay Field Club. The skills learned in Youngstown in church situations came in handy again. To my knowledge I was the only African-American field rep in the area and in this club. However, after they got to know me, they made me president for a year. (There were not any women field reps around that I knew about back then.)

## FAITH COMMUNITIES

Jude and I started attending an Assembly of God church that was in the Concord area where we first lived in California. Some of our friends went there, so we visited and then continued to go. They were a welcoming and warm group of Christians and a good support community. We attended their education classes as well as their worship services. It was a unique experience for us at the time and one we enjoyed for a while. As a family we always went somewhere for worship. However, this was the first time we ventured outside our Catholic/Baptist traditions.

In Youngstown I attended Jerusalem Baptist while growing up and then also attended Sacred Heart Catholic Church after Jude and I got married. In Denver we went to the Newman Center (Catholic) on the campus of Denver University. However, when we went to the Assembly of God church, Judy missed the Catholic Mass liturgy. Thus, when we later bought a home and moved to Suisun City, California, after living in Concord, we joined Holy Spirit Catholic Church and became active in that community.

As we made future corporate moves, we always found a Roman Catholic Church to attend as a family. Remember, we had promised to have our children raised in the Catholic faith; thus, we had Kevin baptized in that faith also, and then continued to worship in a Catholic church. I attended worship with our family in those Catholic communities and took part in various parts of the congregational life. But I never officially joined myself nor went to communion, because I did not believe as the Catholics did regarding communion. Therefore, after our children got older and were able to receive communion, I would sit in the pew while my family received it. It was hard to do sometimes, but I just could not get my head around their beliefs about communion. I did not personally join another church until we moved to Pickerington, Ohio, for the second time, and ended up joining Epiphany Lutheran Church; but more about that later.

## THE FIRST OF MANY HOMES

When we first moved to California, we lived in an apartment complex in Concord, California, on Adelaide Avenue. We were in a second-floor apartment for about a year and a half until we bought our first house. The complex had a pool, which our family often used; even got Kevin in it at a very young age. However, Jude grew tired of living in this small place. I could not blame her; she was home with two small children in an upstairs apartment. While I got to go out every work day to do something that most of the time I enjoyed very much, she was stuck at home. I give her a lot of credit for working to get us through all we had done: we moved close to her due date, she had Kevin after switching doctors, and we were a long ways from family. She had been through a lot and was in a small, confined space each day.

Needless to say, the cost of anything in the Bay Area was expensive and we were living on only my salary. It was very hard and next to impossible to save any money, and managing money was not one of our strong suits. However, she pushed us to do something, so we went into debt and also borrowed from her parents to buy a thirty-thousand-dollar, newly constructed twelve-hundred-square-foot ranch home in Suisun City, California. If it was not for her forcing us to do something, I do not think that we would have bought it. I was content where I was and willing to continue as is; but in the long run she was right. It turned out to be the best decision for us at that time, but it was one of those leaps of faith. Thank goodness, I had Judy to push us into making the changes that were needed.

Suisun City in the mid-1970s was a fairly new small city, next to Fairfield, which was larger, and both were near to the Travis Air Force Base. When we lived in Concord, I was about thirty to forty-five minutes from my office on a good day. Now we were nearly sixty to seventy minutes away. However, like many other people starting out and trying to find housing in a fast-growing area, we could not afford anything closer in the Bay Area. I nearly got into trouble with my company (St. Paul) because I was so far out. I did not realize it at the time but they wanted their field reps to live in the territory they worked in. They ended up giving me a few agents in that area. In time they also gave me some office furniture and set me up with a work office in my house. Therefore, I did not have to spent so much time on the road, unless I had to make my regular office trips into the branch office. Overall St. Paul was fair to me; however, I was a good employee whom they could trust when I was on the road and who could get the job done.

Because the house we purchased was brand new, we had to make a number of additions to the property. Most of the other homes in our neighborhood looked alike, a typical low-cost subdivision. We had to put in a lawn, which was a pain. But this became the first of many places where we had to do some major upgrades, which included dealing with a lawn. In time, we also installed a high wooden fence around our property, which was expected to keep anyone from looking into your property or, heaven forbid, walk across it. That was an expensive project to do, besides all of the other touches needed to make it our home. But, like all the places that we ended up living in over the years, Judy made this place a nice home to live in.

From a career standpoint, I wanted to advance with St. Paul and also improve my knowledge of the insurance industry. I had begun to take additional courses in Denver and continued after moving to the Bay Area. I started taking CPCU (Chartered Property and Casualty Underwriter) courses on my own, studying in the evenings and on weekends. In the property and casualty insurance industry, the CPCU is the highest designation one can earn. To me and others it is similar to the CPA designation one can earn in the accounting field.

These courses are tough and require a lot of effort to pass. I tried to apply myself with these courses, and also listened to tapes in the car as I was traveling to reinforce the course material. Initially, I was able to pass about one course a year, which was about normal. I say this because in my life journey I think that it is a good thing to be always learning something new, or challenging oneself to improve one's skill levels. However, as I have already mentioned and will continue to note later on, it is also important to keep the right perspective. For me, my focus should be on striving for God's kingdom first while taking courses or doing anything else in my daily life.

## LIFE IN CALIFORNIA

Living in California is different than residing in many other states. You have to remember that I had spent most of my life in Ohio, before moving out west and, therefore, saw California through a Midwestern lens. Thus, so many aspects of that area were really appealing to my family and me, despite the high cost of living, the traffic, and congestion. However, those things could be initially overlooked in order to be able to take advantage of the many features the state offered. The weather was very favorable most of the time and one could generally plan on doing outside activities. In northeastern Ohio winters could be challenging, and that is something one had to get used to dealing with. I remember making a big deal that I would not have to shovel snow again. I also remember reading about and seeing on TV scenes from the Midwest blizzard of 1978–79, and thinking, Why would anyone want to live in that area? I was definitely enamored with Northern California!

Those thoughts and comments were not very charitable on my part, for in looking back, I was being very short-sighted and self-absorbed. As humans we sometimes forget that changes will come down the road for all of us. Being on this spiritual pilgrimage carries with it many learning moments, when we are forced to grow even when we are not looking to do so. Having to eat one's words and becoming humbler in our walk comes to us all, no matter where we are on this journey. Because of future jobs and life moves, I did have to deal with winter storms again. In fact, since living there, I have only lived in areas that had some level of cold weather and snow. Looking back, it was foolish to make comments about people living in those winter conditions. But then, I was in this joyful space where I did not have to deal with it, and was a happy little camper for a while.

We had a number of people visiting us when we were there and I became a really good tour guide. Because of my job I had to drive around the region and thus got used to the freeways, bridges, and traffic flow. The amount of traffic did not annoy me, but that changed later. Thus, I was open to showing people around and was also willing and able to drive our family around for outings and to take advantage of the many wonderful sights the area had to offer.

One of the major highlights was San Francisco and the many unique attractions that it had to offer. Besides having very moderate weather it was surrounded by the Bay and all the beauty that it entails. We were so fortunate to live close to San Fran and would go there with our visitors and take advantage of the sights and sounds. We often got to see and visit the San Fran wharf, ride the cable cars, and tour the district. Even though I am afraid of heights, the Golden Gate and Bay Bridges are neat things to experience. Because my main office was in San Francisco, and I did have to go there on a regular basis, I got used to riding the BART (Bay Area Rapid Transit), and our visitors enjoyed riding it as well. At first, we also loved the downtown area, with all of its wonderful restaurants, stores, and energy. Looking at living there shortly after we moved through my Midwestern lens, I thought we had died and gone to heaven. But I also felt that way after we moved to Denver from Youngstown.

Besides being near the coast, the Bay Area is close to the mountains, and about eight hours from Los Angeles. The region and the state have a lot of wonderful things to do and see. While there, as a family we drove down to LA to visit Disneyland, while my son Kevin was very young. We were also able to visit Disneyworld in Florida later on. Judy was very good at planning family trips and activities that allowed us to take advantage of where we lived. I realize that was one of her gifts, which made me very lucky to have been married to her, and our children were also blessed to have her as their mother. Additionally, a couple of times my family traveled with me on my business trips, and that way they could see different parts of the state.

After we moved to Suisun City, we began going to Holy Spirit Catholic Church in Fairfield, the next town over. Holy Spirit was a good place for us to attend; it had a lot of young families like ours with a wide variety of ministries being carried out. My family joined Holy Spirit, but I never did, but we always attended worship as a family. Jude got real involved with the community there, and I took part in some of the activities when I wanted to. When Elizabeth was old enough to start school, she attended their school.

Through the Holy Spirit community, we got involved in Marriage Encounter and made one of their weekend events. It was a very emotional and moving experience for both of us. It helped us in our communications as a couple. As I noted before Jude was one of those persons who could very easily share her feelings and thoughts. On the other hand, I was just the opposite and getting me to relate how I felt was an ongoing challenge during the early years of our marriage. At times, I know that caused some pain for Jude, but she continued to love me and help me become a better communicator and better husband.

That Marriage Encounter experience and our daily writings afterwards did help us both and especially me. Being able to share one's concerns is one of the most important aspects in making any relationship become a better and more positive one. We became so involved in this movement that at one time our mentors asked us to take on a leadership role with the Marriage Encounter program. However, we never did take on a larger responsibility and over time we even stopped doing the daily letters. However, it was an important part of our individual spiritual growth as well as in the development of our marriage. I will always be grateful for having been a part of that.

We were lucky again to meet and get to know some really neat people. We became involved with people from the Holy Spirit community and in the lives of a number of folks around us. For the first few years we thought that we would always be in California. For many reasons we were comfortable and did not think about moving elsewhere. But isn't that how God wants us to live, to be in the moment, to daily strive for God's kingdom in our lives, and to not be so concerned about what tomorrow brings? Basically, bloom where you are planted, and I think that is what we tried to do.

One really neat thing we were able to do while in California was take a four-week vacation. This was a once-in-a-lifetime event, which we were very blessed to be able to do. At that time with St. Paul, you could save up a week's vacation from one year to the next. After five years of service with the company you received a total of three weeks' vacation, thus I was able to have four weeks to take at one time. I am sure that would not happen in many places. St. Paul was not a perfect company, as no place is, but overall, they treated their employees well. During this time the insurance industry and St. Paul were both in a very tight underwriting cycle, and no one was looking to write a lot of new business. Thus, I could be missed for that long of a period. We took four weeks of vacation during the summer of 1978.

We purchased a VW bus to give us the room to travel comfortably. Our children at seven and a half and three and a half were at a good age to do this and they had a great time on the trip. Jude was a wonderful organizer and made our trip as comfortable as possible for all of us. She got toys and games for Elizabeth and Kevin; however, she hid them and would take them out as we traveled to keep them busy during the trip. Remember this was before the age of all of the computer/electronic devices that we have today. All of us were able to see many of the great sights this country has to offer. We were also able to visit family and friends whom we had not seen in several years. It was a wonderful bonding experience for our family. I am also very mindful of the fact that we were fortunate enough to be healthy so we could do it, to have had the time to do it, to have the income to pay for it, and that we were willing to take that moment in time to do it. Of course, this is a good lesson for us all on this life journey about living in the present moment to the fullest extent!

Our main goal was to visit our family and friends in Ohio, most of whom we had not seen since we left Ohio in 1973. However, we also planned on taking in as many sightseeing spots as we could. Going back to Ohio we went the southern route, through Southern California, Arizona, New Mexico, etc., then up to Ohio. We spent two weeks in Ohio visiting family and friends, which made us a little homesick for the Midwest and our family. We did not know it at the time but this trip probably affected what we did a year or so later. On the way back to California we went via the northern route. We stopped and visited the Denver area, where we saw old friends, and also stopped into the St. Paul branch office where I had trained prior to moving. Everyone in Ohio and Denver got to see Kevin up close in person. He had been born in California and many had not seen him. During the entire four-week trip we saw so many neat sights, were able to renew old acquaintances, besides visiting our extended family. That was a time that I will always remember very fondly.

SEVEN

# Dealing with the Highs and Lows of this Life Pilgrimage

The Lord is near to the brokenhearted, and saves the crushed in spirit. Many are the afflictions of the righteous, but the Lord rescues them from them all.

—Ps 34:18–19

## ST. PAUL SERVICE ISSUES

EVEN THOUGH WE HAD a wonderful vacation during the summer of 1978, from a work standpoint, however, that period was not so great for me. Towards the middle to later parts of that year, things got increasing problematic for St. Paul as a company, and for me in my role as a field rep. The company developed some gigantic service problems. At that time, everything was mostly done manually. For many reasons, it was an issue that the people in charge could not remedy for many months. In my mind it grew increasing worse. In most cases, I loved doing what I did; however, for that period it was not any fun at all going out to call on agencies. All one heard was the same thing over and over again, "Where are our policies?" It took a lot of faith and positive thinking on my part to continue making the visits. Not a fun time for me and for others in our company.

That period became really frustrating for all of us. Besides asking for their policies, when we did call on the agencies, the visits turned into dumping sessions by the agencies on the other reps and me. Because the service was so bad, and things were not getting fixed in a timely manner, all we could do was listen to the complaining and try to help out where we could. After a while, the branch management told the marketing reps to stay in the office and help out with the service issues. The company did not want any new business at that point and we just got beat up whenever we went out.

However, since I lived so far out, it became an extremely long day for me to travel to and from work, and also, I did not like the idea of having to be forced to be in the office every day. Really disliked giving up my freedom of being in the field calling on agencies, which for most of the time was what I liked best about this job. Yes, I know that there are a lot of worse things that one has to do in this life; however, this was a real down period for me. It took a lot of physical and emotional energy to do what was required. This is one of those periods in life where on the one hand you know that God loves you and is with you; however, it appears that the Lord's presence is not as clear as in other times.

As the situation went on endlessly and was not getting any better, the tension between the various departments in the branch increased. At first the reps were told to stay in and help, but then they were ordered to stay out of the underwriting/service units. Apparently, some reps were going into these areas asking that their policies be issued, but they were very negative and hostile in their approach and attitude. Apparently, it got to be a very unhealthy situation and nothing was being settled. There were about four to five reps who worked out of that very large branch office. However, as I remember I was then the only rep who was allowed to physically go into those areas and try to resolve some of the service issues and ask about the status of certain polices. I tried to be helpful, supportive, and positive in my approach to the staff and was not looking to point blame at anyone, just wanted to get the problems solved. Even though that was a taxing period for all of us, I learned a lot about myself and continued to learn about how to work with a wide section of people. I believe that my time in the steel mill working with many types of individuals helped in my marketing role.

As we grow and mature, we all learn and acquire different skills and talents, that we may use later in life. We just may not know when that will happen or when they may be used. I believe that God helps prepare us for future situations and ministries as we go through certain periods in our lives. We are all called to do something different in our calls/vocations, and, thus, what we will need to fulfill that role is also distinct from someone else. That is why the faith journey is so unique for each individual person. Getting through that period at St. Paul required everything that I had learned and gone through up until that point in my life. However, with all that being said, this was still an unpleasant and painful time for me, and, yes, for those around me, including my family. I felt that the branch management was not doing enough to correct the problem, and over time I became very upset about their inability to remedy the service issues. I did not know it at the time, but this was the beginning of the end for my working with St. Paul and for us living in California; this was due to a number of different reasons besides the service issues.

Over time the Northern California way of living that I had embraced so enthusiastically in the beginning started to wear on me, and then on my family. Things like the traffic, the California lifestyle, the cost of living, and the fast pace started to get to Jude and me. Those factors got increasingly hard to take and live with. Initially those aspects could be dealt with; however, the longer we stayed there the harder it became to cope with them. Remember that both of us had grown up in the Midwest. Even though we had been gone for a few years, we still had that mindset at our very core. There were some things that we just could not get comfortable with, and those feelings surfaced about the same time that St. Paul's service problems were going on. Additionally, we did not know for sure that we wanted to raise our two children there. We were also so far away from our parents and that created a challenge for them to be a part of our children's lives.

The California lifestyle did not mesh with our Midwestern personality, and along with St. Paul's service issues, I was ready for some type of change, which led me to be open to leaving St. Paul. Overall, St. Paul had been good to my family and me; however, after five years with them, I was ready to move on. I contacted a headhunter and got a job in the area with CNA, another large insurance carrier and was hired as a senior sales rep and got a significant raise; I went for the money, which was a huge mistake! CNA was the total opposite of St. Paul. Whereas St. Paul treated their employees in a mostly humane/caring manner, CNA was more insensitive in their dealings. I started in January of 1979 and a week later the regional manager was let go without any notice. He had been there for years and had some major health problems. From my standpoint, it was rather cruel how that situation was handled. Shortly after that the marketing manager who hired me left as well. Not a good start for me. That organization definitely did not fit my personality, and shortly after getting there, I could see that. However, I was the first African-American senior sales rep for CNA at that time but I quit after six months, which is the shortest time frame that I ever worked full time for any company. One fun thing did come out of this: I got to spend a few weeks in Chicago for my training session and enjoyed that trip.

About the same time that I realized that CNA was not the best situation for me over the long run, Judy and I continued to grow in the knowledge that living in Northern California was not the best situation for us as a family as well. Living there seemed to become more of a strain for us; so, we prayed about it and reflected about what we wanted to do and she was willing to leave California.

Again, I contacted a headhunter and also mailed out resumes to insurance companies in the Midwest and Ohio. I would never suggest that anyone leave a major company after only six months, but at that time I felt it was best for us. I was fortunate enough to still be fairly young and had not bounced around too much yet in the insurance business, and thus was able to obtain a job in Columbus, Ohio. At that time neither of us had ever lived in that area, consequently it would be another new adventure for us. The Columbus area was within three to four hours of both of our families, who were in northeastern Ohio, which is better than being on the West Coast.

## BACK TO OHIO AND CRUM AND FORSTER

Being able to find a position with the Crum and Forster (C&F) Insurance Company as a service office manager in Columbus, Ohio, was a blessing. During the summer of 1979, we sold our home really fast, and made a nice profit from the three-and-a-half years in that house, but that was the California market at that time. Overall C&F was fair to us in helping us move. We ended up buying something in a suburb of Columbus, called Pickerington, in a brand-new sub-division, called Eastwood Village. We were the second or third family to move into it. The house was on Falmouth Avenue Northwest, the second of several new residences that we would buy over the years.

A service office manager would have up to three other people in this office when fully staffed. This was another learning curve for me as I had never directly managed people before. My office reported to the C&F's branch office in Cincinnati, Ohio. Right after starting there the branch manager that I had interviewed with, and was going to report to, was let go. Of course, no one saw that coming. But it really upset me, because the same thing had happened at CNA's office. That could have been a very nervous time for us, having just moved our family across the country, bought a house, and started a new job. At that time, it would have been easy to second guess if we had made the right move. However, I got over being angry and our family continued to walk in faith that we were doing what we thought we were supposed to be doing. We got through that period, and over time had some good experiences working for them, and we had some wonderful times living there.

Again, I was the only African-American who was a service office manager, and/or one who handled the marketing function for C&F. I traveled a little for C&F, not as much as while working at St. Paul. I called on agencies in central Ohio and down to Athens, Ohio, and enjoyed most of the parts of this position. Loved working in a small office where most of the time was left on my own to do my job. Once a month or so, I had to go to the Cincinnati branch office for meetings, which was not often a burden. However, C&F, like any number of companies, went through frequent transformations of various types during this time. They changed their name a few times, and changed the title and duties of the role that I fulfilled. It always got to me, however, about the cost and waste in making all of those modifications; some of them did not make sense to me for a number of reasons. But I learned a lot about change and being flexible in dealing with them, which can be a helpful skill to have on any journey.

Working and living in central Ohio overall was a very positive situation for both my family and me. Pickerington was a good place to raise a family and to put down roots for a while. Additionally, we were close enough to our extended family that we could visit each other on a regular basis. Thus, our parents could be more involved in our children's lives than when we lived out west. Yes, the pace of things, the lifestyle, the people we interacted with on a daily basis were something that we were better suited to deal with. We very much enjoyed being back in the Midwest.

Please know, however, that we also loved most of the time when we were out west. We were able to grow as a couple and family. Because we were so far away from our extended family, we had to develop our own traditions at holidays, all of which was a good thing. I also will always be thankful for being able to work and live in an area that allowed me to grow from a business, personal, and spiritual standpoint. What was learned and experienced there will be carried with me the rest of my life and in my family's lives. Also, we were blessed to have been able to visit and see so many wonderful sights, and so much of God's beautiful creation while there. With that being said, living in Ohio was also very rewarding for all of us.

Pickerington was a southeastern suburb of the Columbus/Central Ohio area. When we moved there in 1979 it was a growing area with lots of new families moving in. From our standpoint it became a great place to live and raise our children. The sub-division we lived in, Eastwood Village, grew to have seventy-nine homes, so we got to see most of the homes built and occupied. Most of the folks that moved in there were the result of corporate transfers, whereby they were moving in from somewhere other than central Ohio. Thus, most of those moving in did not have any family in the area and were open to making friends with those around them. Therefore, at that time Eastwood Village became an exceedingly welcoming place and one we enjoyed living in very much.

Both Elizabeth and Kevin were active in a lot of things at school and in the community. They were both involved in sports and Elizabeth did quite a bit of dancing when she was younger. I took classes and became a high school soccer referee and enjoyed doing that most of the time. We joined and became fairly active at Seton Parish Catholic Church in Pickerington. Seton also had a lot of young families that became involved in that community; thus, it became a very active parish. We all took part in activities at Seton, but I never officially joined. Again, I would attend worship with them but never received communion.

While we lived in Colorado and California, Jude did not work outside of the house. She did so many things to help our family out, and there are too many to reference. She also did other jobs where she could still be at home most of the time, such as selling Avon and Tupperware. However, when we moved to Pickerington and Kevin started school, she wanted to go to work outside of the home. Well, I had a really hard time getting my head around that. My mother never worked outside of the house when we were still at home, and Jude had done the same up until that point. I remember being rather stubborn about her wanting to do that. She had become really good friends with the Director of Religious Education at Seton, Sr. Chris Ritchey, O.S.F. Sr. Chris had a part-time secretary who left for another job and she wanted Jude to take over. Even though it was a part-time job at a church, I remember being a pain about it. Of course, Judy took it anyway, and enjoyed it and was great at it. Our family did fine with her working. I have a totally different view about those things today. But then, *oh brother*, I was not so open to the idea, and probably made things harder on her than they needed to be. So, I own it and admit that it was a huge learning experience for me.

She continued to work for Seton, and when Sr. Chris left to take another position, they hired Jude to be their Director of Religious Education (DRE). Sr. Chris became a lifelong friend of our family. She is one of the most outgoing and loving people I have ever met. For her life and God were always good.

Seton was a growing parish and had a lot of things going on in and around that community. Jude was their DRE for the last three years that we lived in Pickerington. She did a great job and was able to handle all of the challenges that came her way, and was well liked at Seton. At one point I agreed to teach a religious education class, which did not include teaching Catholic theology. I am probably one of the few people who can say he has taught religious education classes in an American Baptist church, a Roman Catholic church, and a Lutheran (ELCA) church. (Additionally, it can be stated that I am possibly one of the few individuals who have ushered in all three churches as well.)

Because of Judy's DRE role at Seton, I also helped form a youth group, called SPY (Seton Parish Youth). We were able to do a number of fun things with that group including taking them on ski trips. Being a part of that community, as well as taking an active role in almost every Christian community that I have been a part of, has helped me on my spiritual pilgrimage. Because of the Holy Spirit's guidance, I have been blessed to be part of others' spiritual growth and development, and in the process, mine has been enriched as well.

## CHARTERED PROPERTY CASUALTY UNDERWRITER (CPCU)

When I became a CPCU, it was an important part of my life from a business, personal, and spiritual standpoint, so I want to take a moment to discuss it. CPCU is a professional designation in the property-casualty insurance industry. The CPCU designation is held by a very limited percentage of those employed in this industry, and it was thought of as being the most significant designation one can earn.

Becoming a CPCU involves three different aspects that have to be met: education, ethics, and work experience. The education part involves passing several (some very demanding) national exams on a number of topics including insurance law, accounting, risk management, ethics, property insurance, and casualty insurance. CPCU designation holders must also abide by a specific code of professional ethics. They must additionally meet an experience requirement and have proven insurance expertise and knowledge. Bottom line, becoming a CPCU is not easy but is an important designation in that field.

Studying for these exams are generally done on one's own time. I would study for these courses in the mornings before going to work or in the evenings. I also would listen to CPCU course tapes in my car while driving between agency appointments, to reinforce the course material. Doing this took time away from my personal and family life. My family did suffer a bit in order for me to pass these exams. It took a huge amount of effort and persistence in order to prepare for the tests.

The manner in which these exams were passed and failed connects to how my spiritual life was changed in this process. When I started the tests were given once a year and had five parts. I passed CPCU I in June of 1975, CPCU 2 in 1976, and CPCU 3 in 1977. However, I failed CPCU 4 in 1978. After this the CPCU curriculum went from five parts to ten parts and the numbering method was changed. I took the above tests when we lived in California, and the remaining ones were taken in Ohio. Each year when a person completes all of the tests, there is a National CPCU Convention to honor those who have concluded the program. The company that I worked for would pay for the employee and their spouse to attend the convention. An upcoming convention was going to be in Hawaii, and I wanted to go there. Thus, thinking that I was better than I was, I took two tests at one time. In January of 1980 I passed CPCU 1, but failed CPCU 7. In June of 1980 I failed CPCU 6, but in January of 1981 I passed CPCU 7 on the second attempt. In June of 1981 I again failed CPCU 6, which was a really painful thing for me to go through. In June of 1982, after studying for nearly an entire year I finally passed CPCU 6. Thankfully, in June of 1983 I passed the final test, CPCU 8, and then was all done with taking CPCU national exams.

During this long process an aspect that had developed while a student at YSU had to be addressed. Basically, where was my focus in all of this? Was I trying to do my own thing, so to speak, or was my focus on striving for God's kingdom and God's will in my life? Was I attempting to do too much based on my own plans, or were my actions following the Holy Spirit's guidance?

In my case, it made me stop (*again*) and change my approach to what I was doing. This may be hard for some of you to understand, but until I could put those exams in the concept of striving for God's kingdom, they became a real struggle for me. You might ask, How did I pass the earlier ones? They were not as hard as the later ones were, and I tried to focus on them one at a time. When I tried to get in a hurry and not prepare in the right way, I had issues. Additionally, I do not have the greatest memory and in those later tests found that I was not retaining the material as well. As they got harder for me, I found that I had to go to extreme measures to pass them and began to write out longhand over and over the information that I thought would be on the tests. In those last few years, I spent hours upon hours writing out things of importance for the courses, so that I could better remember everything. It seems like a lot of work in order to get this done. But at that time, I felt that becoming a CPCU would be good for my insurance career. I did not know it at that time, but it also helped me develop skills that have been used throughout my life.

Again, the main point for me was getting my heart and soul to view what I was doing through the lens of striving for God's kingdom before anything else. I know that this may sound strange to many of you, but that is how I saw it then and continue to view it many years later. It did take a tremendous amount of energy, persistence, and patience on my part to become a CPCU; however, the fundamental driving force in doing this, and in all of my life is "*where was my focus?*" This entire phase became another learning period in my spiritual pilgrimage.

I completed the CPCU program in 1983, and that was a really big deal for me, for my family, and for the company I worked for. I was changed (again) in the process; my family was happy that I did not have to study as much anymore, and Crum and Forster had another CPCU in their ranks. The CPCU National Convention was in New York City that year, and Crum and Forster paid for Judy and me to attend so that I could be inducted into that professional organization. Since we did not have any family around, our very good friend, Sr. Chris, stayed with Elizabeth and Kevin while we attended the convention.

Jude and I had a great time there, and had fun visiting various sites around the city, besides taking part in the special activities for the attendees. One of the highlights was attending a dinner party hosted by my company on the top floor of the World Trade Center. Another wonderful feature was that the keynote speaker was Norman Vincent Peale. As I noted before, when I was younger, I read his books and used a lot of his teachings. I wrote him beforehand letting him know that I would be there and noted how much his writings had helped me in my life. He later wrote me back and said that his assistant had given him my letter right before he came to speak to us. But he missed me there, but was kind enough to write me afterwards. This was one of the most marvelous things that have had happened to me in my life.

When starting out in the property and casualty insurance business, it was mainly a Caucasian-male-dominated field. During my career, I was the first person of color to hold the positions that were held. Again, I was blessed to be in the right place at the precise moment, with a certain skill level and personality whereby I was able to function well in those areas. Becoming a CPCU was another special accomplishment. It was my understanding at that time that there were about eighteen thousand people who had the CPCU designation, out of the many thousands upon thousands who worked in the industry. Additionally, supposedly less than one hundred and fifty of these CPCUs were African-Americans; probably this number has grown since then.

My thought was that once becoming a CPCU it might get me noticed in the industry more or that I could receive offers from other companies to go to work for them; however, that did not happen. After not having to study for CPCU exams any longer I was looking for something else to do. One of the agents that I called on in Columbus, Saul Sokol (who was an agency owner) had written an insurance book and had had several insurance articles printed. One day while sharing my thoughts on this topic with him, he told me to think about writing articles for insurance magazines. He noted that periodicals were always looking for material to fill up their issues. It was good advice for me at that time.

After being turned down a few times, I eventually had articles published in several insurance publications. Not bad for a person who failed his first class at YSU, Communications 105. The articles published were in the *Best's Review*, February 1987; *Rough Notes*, August 1988; and in the *National Underwriter*, March 1988, June 1989, and November 1991. Again, I was fortunate to have these printed, one of the very few people of color who would have done so back then. Years later writing became a very significant part of my own spiritual pilgrimage and for others as well, as I was able to get things printed.

## ANOTHER MOVE

Living in central Ohio was by and large a positive experience for all of us. It was a good area to raise a family and it was within driving distance of both of our extended families. The Midwestern lifestyle was one we resonated with, and I mostly enjoyed what I was doing for C&F. We made a lot of wonderful friends and became involved in a number of activities revolving around our church, our children, and our neighborhood. We had a lot of fun times while living there and it is a period that I look back fondly on.

However, over time change continued to be a constant theme with C&F, some of it good, and some otherwise. In the service office, of which I was manager, in time the claims representative and the loss control representative left and neither were replaced. Their duties were then handled remotely from the Cincinnati branch office. I was told to move to a new location with just the secretary and myself. However, later on that new office was closed altogether and the secretary was let go. I often mention and write about how being on a spiritual pilgrimage often requires us to be open to making changes and then trusting God about the future. That also could be said about working for any corporation.

C&F asked me to move to the Cincinnati area because they wanted me to spend more time in the Cincinnati branch office, after they closed the Columbus service office. However, we wanted to stay in central Ohio; we all enjoyed living there and would have liked to stay. I tried really hard to find another job in my field. I mailed out resumes, contacted headhunters and other insurance companies, but nothing came up. I could not find anything in central Ohio and discussed it with my family about moving to Cincinnati. It was a hard decision to make because we had lived in Pickerington from 1979 until 1987, the longest period we had lived anywhere, up to that point. But now we were on the move again.

Sometimes in our life's journey we look back and say, *Why did we ever do that?* Well, that happened after we decided to move. Jude and I made the decision to build a house based on how we wanted it to be, versus buying an existing home. We settled on a lot on Lemontree Street in the Forest Park section of the greater Cincinnati area. From Columbus we got with a contractor and had the place built according to our specifications. It was a lot of work to do and we learned much from the experience. C&F was most helpful with the move and paid for our moving expenses, helped out with some of the closing costs of the new place, and even purchased our old house at a fair price when it did not sell right away. From that standpoint, things worked out well. However, I do not think that I will ever do that again, for a number of different reasons, including the big one, that we did not live in it very long!

One of the family issues that came out while we lived in the Cincinnati area was that our daughter, Elizabeth, age seventeen, started giving us major problems by her behavior. To me these problems started after we moved, but Jude said later that she had seen signs of these issues while we lived in Pickerington, but they were somewhat minor. After we moved, they became a big problem. She began to stay out past her curfew and disobeyed the rules of our household. I will cover more about this situation with Elizabeth in greater detail later on; however, she caused us increasingly more and more worry and anguish.

From a work standpoint, more time was spent in the branch office; however, I never liked to be forced to come into the office every day. The last few years in central Ohio and the year I was in Cincinnati, I thought a lot about starting my own insurance consulting business, to be on my own. In my mind I was really tired and fed up with working for companies and all of their hang-ups and constant changes. I prayed about it all the time and believed that was what I was supposed to do. In this case, it was more my wishful thinking, versus what God was directing me to do. I read information on the subject and even came up with a business plan about starting my own enterprise. I talked to other consultants and really went into depth with research in trying to find out how to do this. I even listed potential customers/clients in the Midwest and spent a lot of time on this. At one time I also thought about hooking up with vendors who gave short training sessions on various sales and marketing topics. I tried to figure out how to go it alone.

At this time some of my frustration with C&F was that I began to understand that I did not fit their image of someone who could be promoted to a higher level position. The company promoted a much younger in age and experience Caucasian male to a marketing manager job in their Pittsburgh branch; this person had previously worked alongside me. Additionally, they later promoted the Cincinnati branch loss control manager (another Caucasian male) to become the Cincinnati branch marketing manager, who did not have any background in marketing or working directly with the agencies. This person was to become my boss, even though I had more knowledge, experience, and skills in the field.

That really ticked me off, and I came to realize that I was not going anywhere with that company.

Over time I also came to understand that the local branch manager did not appear to want to promote anyone who did not resemble him. The branch manager and I had worked well together over the years, and he seemed to treat me well in most situations. To my knowledge I never gave him any problems and tried to do everything in a professional manner. However, when it came to picking a marketing manager for his branch, he did not choose me. Thus, I began to see the handwriting on the wall, and knew that I had to move on, *again*. Looking back now, that was probably okay for me, as I, more than likely, never would have *fit* within the company long term. I may not always agree with the statement that *everything works out for the best*, but in this instance over time it did; I just did not know it back then. On this spiritual pilgrimage, it sometimes takes months or years to understand how the past impacts our walk with the Lord.

In order to try and find another job, or to get into consulting work, I again began the routine of mailing out resumes to head hunters and other companies. The reality of moving again was becoming more apparent to my family and me. However, we had just had a home built to our specifications and had lived in it less than a year. For many different reasons moving again was not the wisest decision. But I was bent on climbing the corporate ladder. Additionally, we were also having behavior issues with Elizabeth, so there was a lot going on in my professional and personal life at that time. I did not know it then, but, for any number of reasons, I was about to enter a wilderness or desert period in my spiritual pilgrimage and life journey.

## BUFFALO, NEW YORK, AND MERCHANTS INSURANCE

From the resumes that had been sent out I was hoping to get some consulting work. I was instead contacted by a headhunter for a position with Merchants Insurance Group headquartered in Buffalo, New York. Merchants went after me and even though I so wanted to be on my own, or get into management somewhere, I accepted their offer without doing a lot of research on the company. I sort of followed the lead of the headhunter and the song and dance that was coming from Merchants.

It was my fault for not checking things out in more depth, but again it was a real learning experience for me, in many different ways. I started with them on August 8, 1988 (all eights). I got my big new title, corporate sales manager for Merchants Insurance Group. I was their first African-American manager, and the only one in marketing/sales. Merchants was a small regional company that sold insurance in the northeast portion of the country. I think things appeared to be fine early on, but the honeymoon was very short lived.

Jude and our children moved up to be with me shortly after I started working there. In retrospect, they should have stayed in our home until it sold. However, they wanted to be with me and we had no idea what was coming. We all lived in an apartment for a while, until we could figure out our next step. When we moved to Cincinnati, C&F bought our house when we could not sell it, but Merchants was not set up to do the same for us. Our home did not sell right away and we were left in a difficult financial situation.

The bottom line to all of this is that we (mostly me) really screwed up big time from a financial standpoint. We kept the price on the house in Forest Park up too high for too long of a period. Remember, we had only lived in it for a year and had built it based on our specifications. At that time, we thought we knew what we were doing. I, of course, prayed about it selling and thought all of the positive thinking things that I could come up with. As you know, even with prayer, things do not always work out how we want them to. Looking back, our realtor could have done more in consulting with us about what to do. However, this issue was more on me and wanting bigger and better things in my career. Because of that, our family took a huge financial hit, when the home did not sell as we had hoped it would.

Because my family moved there to be with me, we came up with the idea to buy a home in the Buffalo area even though the one in Forest Park/Cincinnati had not sold yet. Again, looking back, probably should not have done that, but we did. We went to Merchants for a bridge loan to buy the second house until the other one sold. The thought was to pay back the bridge loan when the first house sold. We ended up making two house payments for some time, *a disastrous move on our part*! We went through our savings and 401K funds that we had from C&F. It was not a very pretty sight. I thought that we would make it all up later when the house sold, but we never did. By the time the first house sold, we were fiscally in bad shape. This period put us into debt that would take us years to come out of. But yes, you live and learn and over time things do work out. I have always said that managing money is not one of my strong suits; but in this case, I really messed up on a grand scale. This was but one of three of the Buffalo wilderness periods in my life; the other two revolved around Elizabeth and Merchants.

During this time, problems with Elizabeth were increasing. These concerns were more than just her staying out too late. We started finding things missing around the house and asked our children about it, and no one admitted knowing anything. That was the beginning of many years of struggle dealing with Elizabeth and her challenges. In the beginning we were very naïve and trusted her, because she was our daughter and had been raised in our home. We did not think she would be capable of stealing from us and outright lying about it to our faces. We thought that if we tried to reason with her, her overall behavior would turn around. We thought that with love we had given her in the past, and continued giving her then, things would improve. However, they never did for very long, and she became a very polarizing person in our family for many years, in a number of different ways. I will share more of the stressful things we have had to deal with regarding Elizabeth later on. But for now, know that she was a very trying aspect of our life in Buffalo. Regrettably, her negative behavior increased with us at the same time as the move, the two-house situation, and my concerns about working for Merchants.

My time at Merchants started out fine; the first few months there I had a number of successes. I enjoyed being there and also leading the training of the sales force. I was able to develop a sales training program, that was used when we brought all of the marketing representations into the home office for training and was well received. I also was able to create marketing forms, call reports, etc., for the representatives to use. Initially things were going along in pretty good shape, and during this time I had another insurance article published. From a development standpoint I learned a lot of things during this period that are still with me today. One of the aspects of my current ministry is trying to stay focused on the main things that need to be dealt with (for example, striving for God's kingdom before anything else). Because Merchants had so much turnover in the marketing area, they were always emphasizing the point of keeping one's eye on the important goals and putting the minor things aside.

I also learned about working in a home office environment. Up until that time I had only worked in field type offices, but sometimes I had to deal directly with the president of Merchants, which was both good and bad. However, I became more aware of how to be a corporate thinker and strategic planner. In the home office, long-term goals were established for Merchants that had to be carried out by the people in the regional offices. That knowledge has been helpful at various times in my life and ministry. Of course, in order for me to have this position, I had to be in the office on a daily basis, much more than in any other previous role that I had. Thus, I gave up working out of a branch or service office where I had more independence regarding my comings and goings. But I thought I wanted to be in higher level management, and was willing to give this freedom up for that position.

With all of that being said, working for Merchants became the third wilderness or desert for me during that time along with the two-house situation and the issues with Elizabeth. It became apparent to me that the company's operating philosophy ran counter to my ethics and conscience. I became very uncomfortable with how the company did business and, more importantly, how their employees were treated. After I was there for a short while, I heard that people in the insurance agencies around the Merchants' home office would make bets as to how long the new home office marketing person would last. *That was me!* I eventually learned that Merchants had a horrifying track record from a turnover standpoint throughout the entire company, but especially in the marketing area. Home office marketing employees only stayed about six to twelve months for the very same reasons with which that I had issues.

It became a joke around the insurance industry about the high turnover rate at Merchants at that time. I did not know about that issue when hired. The people who I had interviewed with and reported to were soon leaving or being asked to leave. It became evident after only about six months that I did not have any long-term future with Merchants because of the culture of the company. If I was going to continue working for them, I would have to make some major changes in how I did my marketing job and interacted with those around me. Thankfully, I was able to recognize that I had to be true to who I was and would not be able to stay there long-term. Believe me, this was a huge learning period for me in my life journey and my spiritual pilgrimage.

I had put myself and my family into this position because of wanting to get into a higher-level management job and to further my career. That became a very stressful period for my family and me after they realized what I was thinking regarding Merchants. Jude and my family had always been very supportive about a move or change in positions if it meant taking advantage of a job opportunity, or if we thought that it was where we were being guided to go. However, this situation was totally different in that we had just moved. If we thought about relocating again that would be three moves in a period of about three to four years, and Kevin would have to adjust to yet another new school. That was besides the other issues of the financial strain of moving, buying and selling a house, not to mention the two-house issue we were coming out of, along with Elizabeth and her trials. Not a pretty sight to behold looking back on it now, but I bear the blame for putting us into that position.

Kevin and Jude were just getting comfortable being there and were not interested in leaving the area. Kevin was thirteen and liked his school environment and was hoping to settle down. Like most teens it could be tough having to adjust to a new school, and in his case, this was already the third school district in three years for him. Judy was normally the one who did all of the fixing up of whatever home we lived in. Now remember we had just had a home built to our specifications in Ohio, which we could not sell for a long time and we had a big house to care for that we just purchased in the Buffalo area. After concluding that Merchants was not what I thought it was, telling my family about my thoughts about another change so soon went over like a *lead balloon*! They were not open to listening to what I was telling them! But I could not blame them; they had been through a lot to allow me to fulfill my dream of climbing the corporate ladder, and now they just wanted to settle in and stay somewhere for a while. This was a tough situation for all of us to deal with.

I remember writing a note to Judy, explaining how I knew that I had put us into this situation, but also felt that I had to change jobs and move yet again. There was not anything in that area for me; Merchants was the only insurance company around that fit my skill set. Besides my issues with the company, I felt that Buffalo was somewhat closed to outsiders and never felt contented there. Maybe if I did not have the job stresses and could have stayed there longer, things would have improved, but at that moment, that is how I saw it. We had never really settled into a church community that we all felt comfortable with and where we could attend on a regular basis. Kevin did not attend any religion education classes at that time. Elizabeth was eighteen then and was causing us so much strain as she spread her wings going from a teenager to young adult. She continued to cause problems for us and herself, but she also wanted to stay there.

Going through a wilderness or desert period like this one can have a huge impact on anyone and it did for me. This caused me to make some major adjustments in my personal and prayer life. From that moment on I thought long and hard before making any important job changes in the future. I was in a very rough place in my life and was under a lot of strain. I did not know how to get out of it by myself, so I added some additional aspects to my prayer life, some of which are continued to this day.

## EXTRA PRAYERS NEEDED

Because of the stress that I was under, I went into a very concentrated prayer period expressing what I thought was needed in my life. Additionally, the hope was to renew my emotional energy and physical strength to navigate this taxing period in my life. I decided to try something different, and made a list of what I thought was required in my life and carried that list on me so that I could be as specific as possible during my prayer time. I read this, then handwrote my needs over and over so they would be reinforced in my prayer life plus remain in my subconscious mind. I am not sure if it had any impact on my prayers, but I thought at the time that it could not do any harm. I was pretty desperate for I had to convince my family that we needed to move, survive my time at Merchants, and eventually look for another new position. So, I prayed and prayed and looked for new ways to get the answers that I thought were needed and desired.

I might add that from my own experience, and from my readings of the ancient and current spiritual sages, prayer is more about changing oneself than getting something from God. When we are involved with sincere, Spirit-filled prayer as part of our spiritual pilgrimage, we are moved or altered on a daily basis. What transpires may be something that is gigantic and may forever change us. But most of the time it is some minor adjustment in one's life and environment that eventually becomes apparent. Primarily, prayer causes us to come into a closer relationship with our Lord and to become the person that God wants us to be. From my current viewpoint, that is the primary purpose of prayer. Do not get me wrong, I have maintained a really long list of people, situations, and things that I pray for on a daily basis. However, I try to remember that getting a specific result from our prayers is in second place to doing

God's will in our lives, and striving for God's kingdom wherever we find ourselves.

Something else that I eventually started during this time frame was to go into a church during my lunchtime to pray in general for my family, plus pray for the people and concerns on my list and for my need to find another job. This practice was started in Buffalo and has continued in some form or the other since then. Thus, what was a very trying and difficult period for my family and me caused me to begin a new prayer ritual. Most of the time church sanctuaries can be a quiet place to pray, think, and reflect. I found that this was also a way that enabled me to deal with the situation at Merchants for another day. It allowed me to prayerfully reflect on where I was and what steps were needed to improve my situation. It helped me to stay focused on what needed to be done for just one day at a time.

Probably the most important aspect that came out of this was the patience to live another day without knowing what each moment might bring. I have said countless times that I am not a very patient person and hate waiting. In this case, there was only so much I could do each day. I had to do my part and then quietly wait until something happened or until the circumstances evolved on their own. When you do not know how long matters will take, and you very desperately want things to occur quickly, waiting can become a wilderness time in life. Thus, this noonday prayer helped me daily with my patience. It also helped me to again realize that the future was in God's hands, and that the Holy Spirit would guide and comfort me, if I walked in faith and was open to this discernment.

Even with all of this praying (and, yes, also some pleading on my part) Jude and Kevin still were not too happy about the thought of moving again. There was a great deal of tension in our family during this time with everything we were dealing with. It was a struggle for me to know how to handle everything happening in our lives. However, thankfully, over a long and very difficult period Jude and Kevin began to be open to the thought of leaving the area. Prayer continued to help me on a daily basis, but it was not easy or without a lot of pain on everyone's part.

The prayers did guide me in the right direction regarding finding another job. Again, that took time and patience and was not easy, especially when I had to continue working at Merchants, without them knowing that I was seeking another job. Whenever Merchants got wind that someone might be looking for another job they would go ahead and hire a replacement and have them ready to start work before the current person even knew about it. Then the current employee would be met at the front door by the guard with all of their personal effects in a box and told that they were terminated. I did not want that to happen to me; therefore, I had to be very careful as to what I did on a daily basis. This entire situation seemed to last forever and was one of the most trying times in my adult life to that point.

In my mind, the best place to move back to was central Ohio where we had been for a number of years, and where the family seemed to enjoy living. Thus, that is where I looked for another position. One of the officers in a company called the Auto Club Insurance Company in Columbus, Ohio, to which I applied, had also worked at Merchants at one point. That officer had been one of the people who was met at the front door one day and told that they were done. Thus, he knew that working for Merchants was not easy. I think that helped me in the interview process. I ended up working for Merchants for a total of eighteen months, not a long time to stay at a company. However, it was longer than most marketing people lasted there. When I gave my notice, the management team was extremely surprised that I had been looking and had already found another job. They were not prepared for it, and allowed me to stay and work until I was ready to leave.

About nine months after moving to Buffalo, New York, we sold our house in Forest Park, Ohio and were able to pay back the bridge loan to Merchants, and could thus leave without owning anything. Finding another position in Columbus took some time and two interview trips. But thankfully, I was hired by the Auto Club Insurance Company (ACIC) and started with them in April of 1990. We were fortunate to sell our existing Buffalo home and then buy a new one in Ohio. I ended up staying with ACIC until leaving the insurance industry to attend the seminary in 2000.

Emma B. Coleman, my mom early 1940s.

Bennett N. Jones Sr., my dad early 1950s.

Madeline Murray (Nanny), my mom's mom 1920s.

John W. Coleman Sr. (Monk), my mom's dad 1960s.

Nellie McKay, my dad's mom 1950s.

Henry V. Jones, my dad's dad 1960s.

At Camp Fitch, with mom and two of my brothers,
Randolph and Bennett, I am on the left, 1950s.

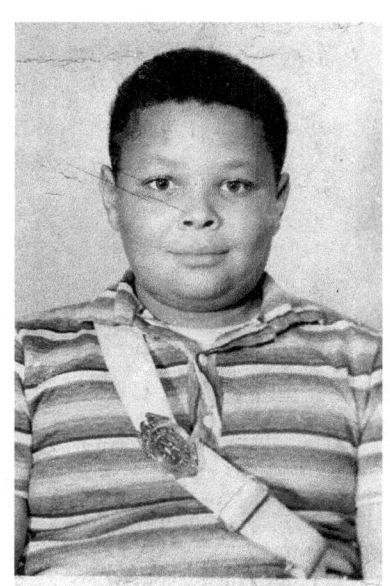

Sixth grade, as a patrol person.

My senior class picture, 1964.

Judy in a Humility of Mary, "Blue Nun" habit, 1967.

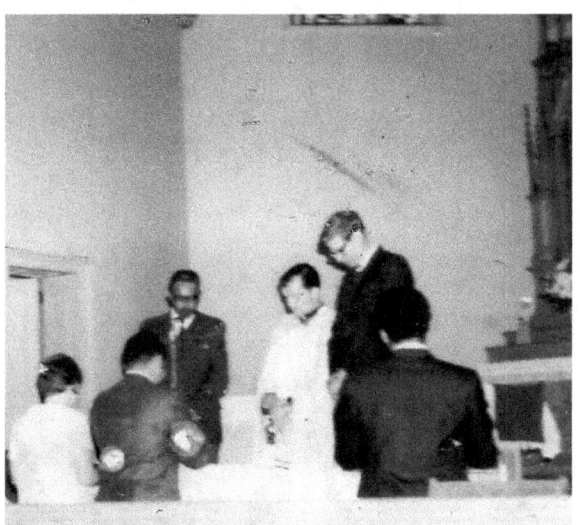

Judy and me on our wedding day, with a Baptist Pastor, Rev. Clyde Murray; a Catholic Priest, Fr. Bob Bonnot; and a future pastor, Steve Gifford, my brother, Bennett is on the right side, Marty Logan who stood up with Judy is not in this picture; wedding held at Sacred Heart Catholic Church, Youngstown, Ohio, June, 16, 1970.

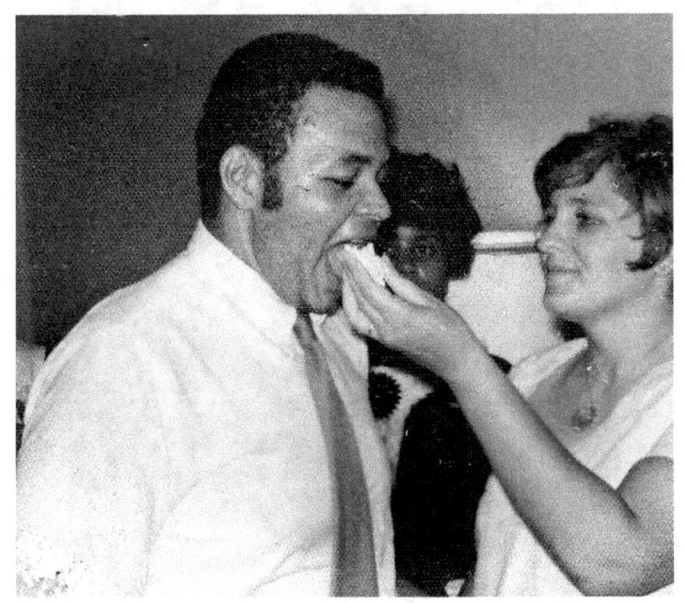

Our wedding day.

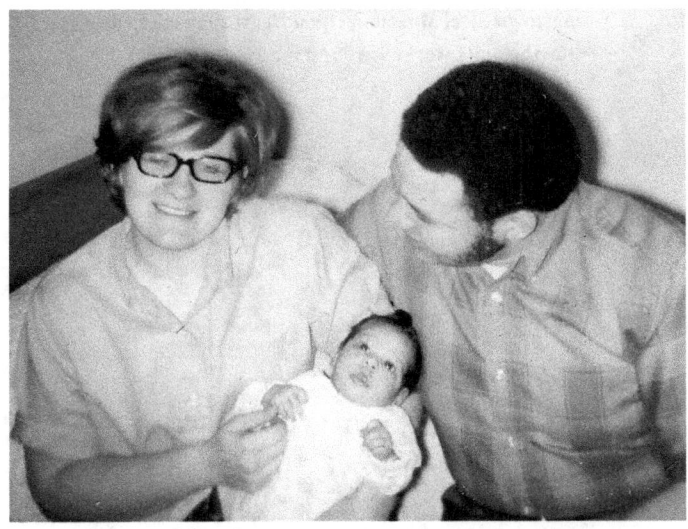

Elizabeth is one month old with Judy and me, January, 1971.

Youngstown Steel Museum, Open Hearth Furnace Door,
like the one I worked around for over eight years.

We both got our Bachelor degrees from Youngstown
State University on June 16, 1973,
which was also our wedding anniversary.

College graduation day, note the writing on cake.

Kevin's birth, I was in the delivery room when he was born and did not pass out, another miracle; Walnut Creek, California, February 25, 1975.

My mom around 1981.

Family trip to Walt Disney World, note matching tops, Summer of 1982.

Judy and me around 1983.

Elizabeth and Judy, early 1980s.

The four Jones' brothers, Randolph, Bennett, Brian, and me, mid—late1980s.

On a ACIC company team building adventure (Pecos River). I am very afraid of heights, but on this event, they got me to climb this tall pole and leap off and reach a cord with a bell on it, with nothing holding me up but some ropes and a harness held by my team mates; another miracle in my mind, October 1993.

Elizabeth at Walt Disney World, mid 1990s

The day I received my Master of Theological Studies Degree from Trinity Lutheran Seminary, with Kevin and Shirley, June 8, 2002.

Shirley and me on our wedding day, two pastors; Rev. Dave Shugert and Rev. Lori Carey and two future pastors; Shirley and Diane (Bareis) Greble, at Trinity Lutheran Seminary, Columbus, Ohio, July 13, 2002.

Our wedding day.

Shirley and me in Hawaii after our wedding, July 2002.

Shirley's Ordination, August 22, 2004.

Shirley and me in Venice, Italy, May 8, 2017.

Shirley and me at her Retirement Party from St. Paul Lutheran Church, Alpena, Michigan, August 12, 2018.

Kevin and me, September 2021.

Shirley and me, Easter, 2023.

EIGHT

# The Human Mind Plans the Way, but the Lord Directs the Steps

The plans of the mind belong to mortals, but the answer of the tongue is from the Lord. All one's ways may be pure in one's own eyes, but the Lord weighs the spirit. Commit your work to the Lord, and your plans will be established . . . . The human mind plans the way, but the Lord directs the steps.

—Prov 16:1–3, 9

## THIRD TIME IN OHIO

When we humans make plans about our future, we for the most part do what we think is best. We can reflect about what may be coming down the road and make our plans accordingly. However, what I have found out on this spiritual pilgrimage is that, most of the time, we are only able to see enough about the future to take the next step along the way. If we try to control too much of the direction we may be taking, from a long-range standpoint, it may take us to a place that may not be where God might want us to go.

We never know what may be coming our way in life and in most cases that is a good thing. If we knew for sure what lies ahead of us, it just might undo us. I had no way of knowing what was in store for us over the next few years when we moved back to live in Ohio for the third time. I know that if I could have seen what was ahead for our family over the next few years, I would not have wanted to face them. For sure we as humans can make the plans, but it is so much better when we allow the Lord to direct our steps, and pray that we will be able to see and feel God's Spirit alongside of us, for that is the only way we can make it. I know that if the Lord was not with me, I would have never made it through this next period in my life.

Thankfully, this move worked more smoothly than the one to Buffalo. When I started to work for ACIC in central Ohio, Kevin and I spent time living in a motel together, while he started school. Jude came later after taking care of our New York house. We were very fortunate to have sold our existing house fairly quickly and found one in Pickerington that we liked and that was ready to be occupied. We were also very blessed to have both closings go well and thus did not have any issues like our previous relocation. We were back in the Midwest, which I liked; however, we still had some challenges with Elizabeth, who had remained in Buffalo.

One of the first business trips that I took for ACIC was to Seattle, Washington. I had never been there before and was looking forward to the visit for a number of different reasons. However, after I had been there a short while, I got a call from Jude about Elizabeth. Apparently, Elizabeth had gotten into trouble together with another person back in Buffalo and had been arrested. Jude called and told me about what was going on and asked if I wanted my daughter to be in jail.

*What a shock!* So, I am on the road at the beginning stages of a new job, my family had just moved yet again, and we had to deal with our daughter being in jail. Looking back at that moment in time, I often wonder, If I had given Judy a different answer and let Elizabeth sit in jail, would things have changed for how Elizabeth acted over the following years? Those decisions are made quickly, and we make the best choice at that moment and hope it is the right one. But you never know and you have to move forward and trust the future to the Lord. I will never know if we would have left her in jail, if things would have turned out differently.

However, we talked about it and wanted to give her another chance to see if she could learn from this experience and make better choices in the future. We decided to get her out. Jude went back up there, picking up her father (Vito) along the way in Ashtabula, Ohio, and they bailed Elizabeth out. Unfortunately, and very sadly, that was the first of many times we did this, and ended up doing lots more to try and help her out over the years. At that point she came to live with us. Even though we can pray about something, and ask for guidance, and make what we think is the right choice, it does not mean that life will always be perfect and everything come out smelling like roses. God never said that we would not have struggles in our lives, just that the Lord would be with us through them. Having to deal with Elizabeth and her troubles would become an enormous problem for us and our family, in terms of time, emotional/physical energy, pain, and financial resources. Thus, this episode was only the beginning; we just did not know it at the time.

Even though we were beginning to have more difficulties with Elizabeth does not mean that we did not also have some fun times. I was very blessed to be married to Judy for many reasons, and one of them was that she made sure that we enjoyed life and had plenty of good times. When we lived out west far away from our extended relatives, we learned to do things with just the four of us to make the holidays special. In my mind we bonded, had fun times together, and our children seemed to enjoy being part of what we were all about. Because we thought we were a close-knit family we really struggled with what to do when Elizabeth's issues started and continued. With that being said, for a number of years, we grew together as a family unit, and had some great times together.

## EPIPHANY LUTHERAN CHURCH (ELCA) PICKERINGTON, OHIO

After we moved back to Pickerington for the second time, I began to reflect on my own spiritual needs and decided that it would be beneficial to find a Christian community that I could become a part of on my own. When we got married, I promised that I would allow Jude to raise our children in the Roman Catholic faith, which we did up to that point. However, the decision was made by me to not join the Catholic church, despite the fact that my family had joined, even though I had been active in every community that we were a part of. However, I did not become a member nor take communion all of the times that we worshiped together as a family. I had not joined any church myself over the years since belonging to Jerusalem Baptist Church in Youngstown, Ohio.

After we got settled into our new home and things were somewhat okay with my new job, Kevin and I went church shopping. Jude started going to Seton Parish again, and was welcomed very warmly by the people there, because of her past history with them. We, of course also attended with her, but at the same time started looking. Kevin and I visited several churches in the area for morning worship to check them out. I cannot remember much about most of them, but two churches stood out. One of them was not very hospitable and friendly; maybe because they did not know us, or because we did not look like them from a color standpoint; but their behavior toward us was not very Christian like. Obviously, we never went back.

The other community was Epiphany Lutheran Church, because of their acceptance of us and they were just the opposite of this other church. They were over the top warm and friendly and made Kevin and I feel that they were happy we were there. I remember one man who was older than we were made an extra effort to make us feel comfortable. Wayne Smith, a long-time member of the congregation, made a specific point to walk from the other side of the church to greet us the first time we visited there. Their welcome encouraged us to come back and in time we joined Epiphany.

I cannot tell you why I came to that conclusion, but I was led to do so. In my mind that is one of those crossroad moments that impact so many areas in one's life. Finding and joining Epiphany was a further step on the road to getting me where I am now. I think after my home congregation, Jerusalem, this faith community had the second greatest influence on my spiritual pilgrimage and life's journey. The senior pastor, Rev. Dave Shugert, the loving and caring people there, their spiritual-filled core beliefs, how they were always trying to be discerning where the Holy Spirit was guiding them, the ministries they were a part of, and the support they gave me in so many ways all drew me to that congregation and kept me there.

I did not know much about the Lutheran (ELCA) faith prior to this, but I attended new member classes, which helped in my understanding of their core beliefs. Pastor Dave, through those classes, was also able to help me feel comfortable about how they looked at communion. Because I had attended Catholic masses for years with my family, I was okay with the Lutheran liturgy, for the Catholic mass and the Lutheran worship format had some of the same elements. Had I tried to go from my Baptist church to a Lutheran church years earlier, that would have been more of a challenge. However, I was ready to make a change, and since Epiphany was who they were, the Holy Spirit led me to join and become a very active member of that congregation. After taking the new member classes, Kevin and I joined in December of 1990, and to my knowledge were the only African-Americans to attend on a steady basis. Yes, Jude also attended services with us, so she got to know the community there as well.

I am grateful for the people there who continued to make us feel welcome after we became members. Very soon after going there, Bill Wright Sr. and Jr. asked me to help them usher. They also always made sure that I did not have to sit alone during worship, if I was by myself. In time I team-taught junior high Sunday school classes for a number of years, and the students gave me as much as I gave them. I took part in a few committees, including a search committee for a new associate pastor. I am thankful for my time with that community, and they, like the other churches I have attended, will always be a part of who I am now.

## LIFE AT AUTO CLUB INSURANCE COMPANY (ACIC)

ACIC wrote personal lines insurance through AAA clubs in a number of states across the United States and were a small company headquartered in Columbus. Because they wrote insurance across the country, their marketing people had to travel in order to work with the clubs. Sometimes there could be a lot of trips involved by plane or car. But from my standpoint you got to visit some different parts of the country and work with a wide cross-section of people. As you know traveling can have its positive and less than positive aspects, like anything else in life. For me, I mostly enjoyed it, and feel very fortunate to have been able to do it. Being out of the office and calling on folks fit my personality and allowed me to use the skills that I had picked up over the years. Again, I was the first African-American manager for the company and the only one in the marketing department calling on the club agencies.

ACIC had a much friendlier culture than Merchants, and tried to be more patient with their staff. They had their structure and procedures, but they could be more flexible in their day-to-day operations. Because they only sold insurance through AAA clubs, they took on some of AAA's philosophy. They treated me well during my time with them. They were a huge support of my family and me, especially when we were going through all of the issues around Jude's cancer battle.

The job entailed both travel and being out and about, while at the same time being involved with planning and setting policy for the marketing department. I continued to improve on my time management skills, due to the pressure of being in a home-office position and having to meet certain deadlines. I also was able to train the sales agents who sold our insurance and wrote some training materials similar to what was done for Merchants. Some of the aspects of that sales training and my time management experiences have been included in my discipleship writings and presentations that are done today. Interesting how something that was done back then is still with me today and being used in my current ministry.

The stress felt at ACIC was nowhere near the strain that was experienced working for Merchants. Even though situations could have a fast and hectic pace on occasion, I generally was able to keep up with them. During that period, I lost interest in writing any more insurance articles and no longer had a desire to start my own business or go into any consulting work. I continued to change and evolve in my personal and business life. I tried to maintain my prayer life and continued going into churches once or twice a week during my lunch time to pray and reflect. I also lit a candle weekly and prayed for our family members. At work I kept a white board behind my desk, and used it to write a weekly Bible verse on it. Because of the culture at ACIC I was able to do that, as long as it did not impact my work. Like any job, it had its high and low points, but overall, it was a good experience being employed with them.

As you can tell I have had my share of new jobs and physical moves. However, in all cases, it appears that one main choice or path always arose above all others. That is, when looking for a new position one specific company stood out as the way to go. Some of the choices did not turn out perfectly, like my time with CNA and Merchants, but I always seemed to be led in just one direction. This aspect continued to play out while I was working for ACIC.

State Auto Insurance Company, also headquartered in Columbus, was a fairly large regional insurance carrier. A couple of times I interviewed with them, while I was with ACIC. The second time this happened, they actually offered me a position as a territory manager/underwriter with the same pay as ACIC, however, without a company car, which I had at ACIC. After some reflection, I turned them down, because even after spending time talking to them, I did not feel that it was a good fit for me. I did not know it at that time but that was a really wise decision on my part, because of how well ACIC worked with me around Jude's illnesses. I would have had less time with State Auto and they may have not been as understanding. I also applied for a vice president position at ACIC at one point. However, I did not get it, but later on I was glad of it for a number of different reasons. The bottom line for me and my business career: I have been given one path to follow whenever a change was needed.

## JUDY'S FIRST OPERATION

Having to deal with Jude and her cancer issues became an extensive part of my life during this period. It began after being with ACIC for a few years, while on a business trip in Helena, Montana, in January of 1993. I had planned to be there most of that week when Judy called me. We normally would talk in the evenings after my work day was done and could catch up on things that had gone on for both of us. She called to inform me that she was going to see a surgeon the following day because she had seen her family doctor due to having pain in her head. The doctor saw pressure in Jude's eyes and thankfully did not waste any time and made an appointment with this surgeon. I will always be indebted to her doctor who was on top of things. I did not know if it was serious or not, but I called my boss and told him what was going on. He told me to get home, no matter what it took, so I could be there with her. Again, I am so grateful for not staying in Montana as scheduled. I was able to rearrange my flights and get home by midnight, traveling from Helena, to Salt Lake City, to Atlanta, and then home; what a way to do it, but I made it.

By the time I got home, my son, Kevin, was sitting in the kitchen waiting for me and he explained what had happened. Judy's pain had gotten worse and he had driven her to the hospital and I could not see her until the next morning. The hospital medical staff gave her medicine, which relieved the headaches. She felt better than she had in a long time. After an examination we were told that she had a tumor about the size of a lemon, and surgery was planned in a few days. They wanted to have time for the medicine to work to make things better for the operation. We called her family and some of them came down to be with us. Judy was remarkably calm during this time, and believed that everything would be okay. Have to love her faith and trust, especially not knowing how things would turn out. She was even willing to have her head shaved so the surgery could go more smoothly.

The following Monday they operated on her to remove the tumor. The surgery was mostly successful in that we were told that 90 percent of the tumor was removed. Apparently, the remaining part had to be left in because removing all of it would have caused brain damage (several years later, that happened anyway). The name of the tumor was *Oligodendroglioma* and it was malignant. It was not known what caused the tumor to grow or if it was due to heredity. Jude had not smoked and had lived a pretty heathy lifestyle. At that time, I had no clue what was coming later on for us, because of this tumor. It is a very good thing that we cannot see into the future, because in some situations, it could scare us to death. In this situation that would have been the case. However, I was just happy that she came through it as well as she did. To me it only took a few days for her to recover and she had very little if any side effects from it and came home and was doing fine rather quickly.

I did not fully realize it then, but, as time went on, I came to appreciate again and again about living each day to its fullest. There are plenty of Bible verses to explain how we ought to regularly live and to trust God about the future. However, sometimes, life can be a better coach than the Bible; for life can give us a critical lesson, no matter if we are ready for it or not. Jude's journey with cancer was another important teacher to me about this subject. It is a message I continue to relearn every day. But the time with her during this period caused me to be more completely aware of daily enjoying each moment in a more focused manner.

Besides having to deal with Judy's health issues, we tried to get into some kind of normal life routine, whatever that means. As noted before, I really enjoyed living in central Ohio, and most of the time liked what I did for ACIC. In 1993, Kevin entered Wright State University in Dayton, Ohio. However, Elizabeth was in and out of our house and continued to be in trouble with the law. We also struggled with how best to support her; we went from helping her with her issues to using tough love. It was so hard to keep a good balance regarding the best way to assist her long-term.

However, after Kevin was off to college, we were empty nesters for most of the time, and did some traveling together. We were so fortunate to have done that when we did while Judy was well enough to travel. In a few more years that would not be the case. She began going on business trips with me. Once we went to the Seattle area and then to Vermont and Maine. For a number of years as part of my job in marketing, I was the point person/main planner for an agency council meeting that ACIC held every year in the late spring in the Scottsdale/Phoenix, Arizona, area. It was a major event for ACIC, and we stayed at some really wonderful places. After all of the hard work in planning the event was done, it was a fun time. ACIC treated us well at those events and Judy loved attending them with me.

Probably the best personal jaunt we took was for our twenty-fifth wedding anniversary in 1995. We went on an Alaskan cruise, which was an awesome vacation. I had saved up my frequent-flyer miles and we were able to fly first class going and coming, which added to the pleasure of the trip. In hindsight, I am so glad we were able to go when we did. Because after her second operation in 1996, it probably would not have happened. It is so important to enjoy each day.

We also were thinking about matters that most people our age are concerned about. We began being more intentional about building up our savings and getting out of our long debt. We reflected more on retirement and what we could be doing down the road, even though I still tried to learn to enjoy each day as it came. But little did we know what was coming! At this time, I submitted some articles to *Guideposts Magazine* and their *Plus* publication, but they were all rejected. One area that I will always be grateful for, even with Judy's health challenges, and our issues with Elizabeth, is that I have had really excellent heath most of my life. I generally do not get sick and very seldom have had to go to the hospital overnight for any illness. I could credit my family genes, trying to eat right and exercise, and taking care of my body for this. But I know many people who can also say the same thing and still have problems. Therefore, I will only say that I have been truly blessed to have been so healthy thus far.

## NINE

# Judy's Second Operation

O Lord, all my longing is known to you; my sighing is not hidden from you.
—Ps 38:9

### THE TUMOR CAME BACK

IN MAY OF 1996 I was totally unaware that I would be entering into a prolonged period of prayer, moaning, begging, and yes sighing to the Lord. This was a time when my prayer life became unceasing and when I would break new ground in my spiritual pilgrimage. But this change came about because of the pain and loss that was experienced. I was forced to do something bolder than what had been done before, and some of those prayer habits and routines are still with me today. We were entering another wilderness/desert time for my family and me. It was far worse than the one we experienced during our time in Buffalo, or any other period prior to this time. This would last for several years and would take us down a road that I hope and pray never has to be traveled again, *ever*!

About this time, I observed Judy having difficulty when she tried to talk or eat. It was gradual at first, but then got worse in a very short time frame. After several exams, the surgeon said that the tumor was back and was an extremely fast-growing one, and we had to deal with it quickly. After some prayer and thinking about it, we gave the approval to have another operation, which was our only option at that point.

She had surgery toward the end of May and we had no clue what would be coming next. This operation was much longer than the first one, and, as the hours ticked away, we became more and more concerned. After what seemed to be an eternity, we were allowed to see her. Elizabeth was with us then, so she, Kevin, and I were led into the recovery room to visit Jude and were *shocked*. She looked so much worse than after the first surgery. The nurse on duty said that was because of the extensive operation, and in trying to remove as much of the tumor as possible brain damage occurred.

*We were told that she could not talk, walk, or move her right side.* She was also in a coma-like state. Later on, the surgeon called the tumor a nasty one, which was very difficult to remove. It had bled a lot and had entangled itself deeply into parts of Judy's brain, and thus was hard to cut out and had caused the extensive damage. We were all depressed, afraid, and worried. I for one, had been spoiled by how well things went with the first operation three years earlier. That tumor was easier for the surgeon to deal with and caused very little damage. She had recovered quickly from the first surgery, and I was looking for speedy improvements this time. But we were not prepared for what was in front of us. It hit all of us like a ton of bricks!

Trying to describe the mood we were in is so hard to do. Words cannot express what we had to face. Some of you may have been in a similar situation and you may have some small idea of what we were going through. However, each person's crises are unique to themselves, and cannot be compared to ours, or ours to yours, only that there is pain, a sense of loss, and despair in each. Judy's personality was always so upbeat, loving, caring, and outgoing. Seeing her in that hospital bed in the condition she was in was so overwhelming for all of us. It took so much for us to just get through that day. But, thankfully, somehow, we did make it.

The day after the operation she improved ever so slightly. On the third day we saw even more progress with a little movement on her right side, and she was transferred from the intensive care unit, causing me to become more hopeful. Thankfully, she seemed to be getting better. However, I think they made a change with her medicine, and she suddenly slipped into a coma-like condition again. I hit rock bottom once more for I had allowed myself to think in more positive terms, only to be crushed by this change. I had not gone into work since the operation and spent the entire day with her and dealt with all of the circumstances that came up daily. Very shortly I became like a zombie just trying to get through each day the best that I could.

I was as low as one could get, with seemingly nowhere to go. So, I did the only thing I could at that point, besides being sure that Jude was getting the best care that she could; I started to pray even more than had been done up to that point. I could not deal with the idea of not having my Judy back, the one who I loved and who loved me. I could not get my head around the fact that with all that we had been through together, that we might not make it through this. So, I practiced my very best positive-thinking prayers and asked that Judy would be healed to the point that she was before this last surgery. (*Yes, I know that may have not been very realistic; but that is what I prayed for!*) I started praying this request when getting dressed in the morning, while driving in my car, while eating, working, basically all the time. For years I had written Bible verses on business cards and had placed them on my car dash, so that I could see them to help with my attitude while driving to meet with my agents. So now I wrote a prayer on another card for my car asking God to heal Judy back to be who she used to be. I totally believed that God would answer that prayer, for I reasoned that if I prayed hard and often enough that it would come to pass. I never prayed so much as was done for months after her second operation. I was so down and that was all I could do; so, I prayed, and prayed, and prayed for Judy to be completely restored to her former self.

Looking back on this time and based on what I know now, prayer may be less about getting something from our prayers, but rather is more about deepening our relationship with our loving Lord. I truly believe that God can and does answer prayers, and hears all of them, even when we do not get the answer we want. Additionally, when they are not fulfilled in the manner, timing, or fashion that we want, I know that God still loves and cares about us. God is love and cannot help but love us. However, that does not mean that God has to give us everything we want or ask for. But, from my understanding, God does want to be in relationship with us, to walk with us, and be in and through all we do on this earthly journey, and to welcome us home when we leave earth. Thus, prayer can be thought of as strengthening our trust and helping us to become the person that God wants us to be, more loving and closer to the Lord, versus prayer being just a way to get what we think we want. However, back in the summer of 1996, I prayed for Judy to be healed and restored to where she was before.

## MORE PRAYER

In addition to praying that Judy would be completely healed and restored, I also had to find support for myself to just make it through each day. I cannot begin to relate how hard it was for me to get up every morning, not knowing what we had to face that day. I came up with a prayer that was used to help me make it. I so needed to feel God's presence with me and had to continue to pray and reinforce that the Lord was walking with me. I of course knew that intellectually, but was emotionally and spiritually struggling with Why her? Why us? Why this? and What does this all mean? Thus, I needed to express verbally what was known and needed to hear it over and over again.

While getting dressed in front of my bathroom mirror, I repeated this prayer that I came up with: *Lord help me get through this day, give me the wisdom that I need for this day (help me to enjoy this day), help me to love and be loved, and keep me from all spiritual and physical harm.* It was so hard to get through each day and I had to keep asking for help to make it. So much of what I was doing I had never done before, and there was no road map for what we were going through. Even for those who had various cancer diagnoses, Jude's situation was different from that of anyone else, so wisdom and support were definitely needed by our family and me. Jude was the love of my life and I missed her love. Yes, I got love from God through other people. We had lots of people praying for us, visiting us, mailing us cards, and providing us meals. However, I still felt the need to be loved. I have continued to use this prayer today. Again, a number of prayer routines that I still do today came about because of this wilderness period during Jude's cancer battles. I do not know if I would have started them without going through what we did.

## DAILY HOSPITAL VISITS

For the first ten days after that surgery, I was at the hospital daily. I took leave from my job and would go there just to be with Judy, and deal with all of the decisions that had to be made. I might add that I very much dislike being in any type of medical facility and had been known to get queasy in them prior to this. Therefore, having to spend some part of each day in a hospital was a gigantic challenge for me. It took a lot of emotional and physical energy and prayers to get me to show up and be with her.

Over a twelve-week period Judy ended being in two different hospitals and a nursing home before she was able to come home. That was a long, trying, and tiring period for all of us. But we were very thankful for all of the prayers, the medical staff, friends, family, and our church communities who helped us get through it all. This first hospital was Mount Carmel East, on the east side of Columbus, where the operation was performed.

After that first ten days, she was moved to the Mount Carmel Hospital in downtown Columbus. While there she healed from the surgery, and she also began doing rehabilitation to help relearn all of the functions that were damaged. During this time, she had to relearn basic skills such as walking, talking, reading, and bathing. She took cognitive training to help with her speech and reasoning abilities. She also started radiation treatments to get rid of any remaining cancer cells. Before we started those treatments, I was concerned if we were doing the right thing for her. I took her to have a second opinion at the James Cancer Center in Columbus. They agreed with Mount Carmel's plan, so she began radiation treatments while she was downtown. She was there for about four weeks and was then moved into a nursing home on the east side of Columbus to continue her rehab and to recover some of her strength.

After using up my ten days of leave, I went back to work. However, I would go into the office in the morning, stay until the middle of the afternoon, then leave to go back to be with Judy for the rest of the day. The next day, I would start all over again. On the weekends, I would do chores around the house, then go and stay with Judy. This routine was done while she was at both Mount Carmel locations and the nursing home, until she came home. Kevin, who had dropped out of college to help us out, would go and be with Judy during the morning, until I got there in the afternoon. So, during her stay, one of us was around during the daylight hours. We found out that she got better care if one of us was physically there to be her advocate. I am so grateful that Kevin was willing and able to do what he did. It was certainly a God-send for him to be around. Something else that I am most thankful for is that I was working for ACIC at the time. If I would have been employed with some other company, I am not sure if they would have let me do what I did. Until she came home, I did not do any business traveling, which was a huge plus.

Needless to say, there were a lot of new things that all of us had to get used to during this period. We all had been fairly healthy for most of our lives and only had minor medical issues to confront, but this experience took dealing with stressful medical conditions to a whole new level! Nothing we had ever faced before prepared us for what we were now encountering.

It was a long time until we were able to see some small improvements in Judy's overall behavior. We did not know how long it would take for her to get back all of the abilities that she had lost, or even if they would ever come back. Looking back at it all, sometimes things happen that you do not pay much attention to until later on. After this operation, the surgeon said something about giving her a little while longer to live. It was one of those things that you hear, but do not really hear. I was so intent on praying and working to get the old Judy back that I put on my blinders and just dealt with what was needed to get her to where she was before. Thus, I just focused on that goal and his words did not come back to me until much later on.

We just kept going to be with Judy day after day to deal with what had to be handled. We definitely hoped for the best down the road, even when we had no clue how it would turn out. I guess that is how we should all walk this earthly journey and spiritual pilgrimage, taking it one step at a time, and leaving the future to God. However, in this case, we had absolutely no other choice; that was definitely all we could do.

When she was at the nursing home the staff still worked with her on her rehab and she continued to slowly make progress. She also became more aware of what was going on around her. I began to get really concerned and troubled about going home and leaving her at night to be cared for by the nursing home staff. That feeling led me to begin another prayer routine. I got a *Christ in our Home* devotional booklet and used it for an evening reflection before heading home. At first, I would do everything, then, when she got better, we would share the duties. One of us would read the scripture for the day, and the other one would do the reading from the booklet, and then I prayed. By doing this I felt somewhat better about leaving her for the evening. We continued that practice until she left the nursing home and then kept it going when she came home. Much later, after she went under hospice care and could not read any longer, I once again did it all until she passed away. However, from that period on, I have continued to do an evening prayer time on my own, with a number of additions added over the years. Thus, this was another spiritual practice that was begun because of going through this wilderness period with Judy.

## HOME AGAIN

Judy finally came back to our home on August 17, 1996. We all were so glad for this after everything we had been through over those many months. However, we had to again adjust to a new set of problems with her returning. It was a struggle to deal with keeping her safe while she was in our home environment. Because of the brain damage she had lost some of her higher-level thinking. Even though she became much better than she was right after the surgery, she would eventually only come back so far, from a brain functioning standpoint. In this case, the brain damage was permanent. From that point on, she was not ever able to drive nor work outside of the home again. We had to watch her carefully near the stove and anything else dangerous around the house. She could handle basic things but did not have the mental ability to make any in-depth decisions, or deal with any involved issues. We could not leave her overnight by herself, which meant, when I began traveling for work again, someone had to be with her at night. I continued doing the majority of the household chores, such as cleaning, washing, shopping, and taking care of the lawn, etc.

We continued to work on her daily living skills and tried to make her life as stress free and comfortable as humanly possible. Even if she made improvements with her physical abilities, she was not the same outgoing person that she was before this second operation. Even though Judy was alive, we lost the Judy that we all loved and enjoyed being around. That in essence was another death for us, in losing bits and pieces of our Judy. She remained fairly stable and had a moderate quality of life, until we once again began seeing signs of neurological difficulties.

Besides the spiritual practices that came out of this wilderness period because of Judy's surgery, this time also changed me in a number of other ways, more than I have the space to mention here. However, one way this experience impacted me was to make me more compassionate toward people with disabilities and, overall, more caring for folks who are struggling in any manner. For example, now I go out of my way to help individuals by holding the door for those who need help. I am also more aware of those who cannot move as well as some others. At various phases Judy was in a wheelchair or would be walking more slowly than normal. Thus, getting in and out of cars or going in and out of buildings, etc., could take more effort. I like to think that I was always an empathetic individual; however, I know that after dealing with Judy and her challenges, it greatly opened me to be more aware of those around me who had physical limitations. Yes, all of this made me a more caring and considerate person.

My outlook on life was changed by all of this, and especially my respect for the human mind and body. I was always grateful for my good health and the overall well-being of my family. However, I became more thankful for how awesome the human mind and body are, and how amazingly they function together. I became even more grateful for my health then and now. The good Lord in creating humans made us so unique and different, that as humans we cannot totally explain or understand how we function. Human words cannot begin to describe how all of our parts work so wonderfully well together. ("I praise you, for I am fearfully and wonderfully made," Ps 139:14.) The simple fact of moving our hands and arms, walking, and talking, is really astonishing. I came to be more mindful of this when witnessing firsthand, up close, and personal, what Judy went through after this second surgery. How she could not do certain things right after it, and then somehow the brain sort of fixed itself; in a limited fashion and for a short period it was repaired. It was retrained to regain some of what she had lost.

Because of this I became more interested in how newborn babies function and normally can learn how to do so much in a very short period of time. I have always loved being around babies, but this took my interest to a new level. Also, God's creation, new life, rebirth in any form, became miraculous to me. I came to appreciate how the good Lord has created all of us to live, move, and have our being (Acts 17:28). That all of life is a gift that is easy to take for granted and not give thanks for. Every day that we wake up and open our eyes is a reason to say, *Thank you Lord for the gift of life!*

About this same time, my son, Kevin, was also going through some soul searching in trying to determine if college was really the best thing for him. He had been thinking of leaving school because he was not sure if that is what he really wanted to do. He dropped out after he finished the spring quarter in 1996. Thus, he came home to lend a hand in caring for Judy, to help out around the house, and also to reflect about what he wanted to do next with his life. He was a really great help for us in dealing with our situation. He stayed with us most of that time, except for when he took a few short-term jobs on some movie projects. In college he was a film major. He went back to Wright State University in Dayton, Ohio, for the 1999 spring quarter. He was able to earn his college degree in June of 2002. I will always be grateful for how much he aided and supported us during those years.

Our daughter, Elizabeth, continued to cause us and herself problems with her behavior. She persisted to get into trouble with the law and seemed to be always one step away from being in jail again. During this time, she also gave birth to our granddaughter, Anna, born May 7, 1997. Kevin ended up being Elizabeth's coach for her delivery, and all of us were there for the event, including Judy. At this point, Judy's improvements had peaked, and she was not going to get any better from then on. Thus, to a certain extent, she was able to enjoy being part of Anna's birth. Elizabeth came home to live with us for a while with Anna until her legal issues surfaced again.

TEN

# A Dark Valley

> Even though I walk through the darkest valley, I fear no evil; for you are with me; your rod and your staff—they comfort me.
>
> —Ps 23:4

### THE BEGINNING OF THE END

OUR LIVES CONTINUED FOR a while in a somewhat daily routine, with Judy eventually reaching a plateau where she would not get any better. She was with us physically but never as she was before. We appreciated the additional stretch of time that we were given to have her with us, even if she was not the same person as before. Looking back, I do not regret what we had to go through with her after the second surgery, for one never knows how things will eventually turn out. If the operation would have done less damage, that would have made that time a little better, but it did not and we had to deal with it.

However, going through that phase allowed us to be able to make the very painful decisions that would soon be facing us. Often prior experiences that we have give us a little insight into how to best make future choices, and that was the case for our family. The dark valley that was awaiting us would require a lot of wisdom, courage, and faith. We had hoped that we would have Judy forever, even with her condition being what it was. That is the way we lived, and what I continued to pray for every day; but it was not to be. Trying to live one day at a time and leave the future to God was how I struggled to daily function. Believe me, it was a strain and very tiring to get through each day; but that was all I could do at that moment. Life during that period took on a pattern that is hard to describe and to understand unless someone has been through something similar. With all this being said, the bottom line is that I feel very blessed to have had those extra months with Judy, even with all of the side effects that came with it.

Unfortunately, in the spring of 1998, some of the same cognitive and physical problems reappeared. We were of course upset and worried about seeing these signs reoccurring, but we had no choice but to head to the doctors once again. After all of the tests and our consultation with the specialist, it was determined that her tumor was probably back. But this time our options were very limited. She had already had two surgeries and a third one was not feasible. Radiation treatments had been done and she could not have any more.

We were told that she could receive chemotherapy, but it would only slow the tumor down and would cause side effects. Also, one of the treatments was to drill holes into her skull and place chemo tablets directly into her brain. That did not sound like something that we wanted to do. I remember sitting in our car outside of the doctor's office after we had heard all of this, when Kevin, our son, came up with one of those great all-time statements. "You hate to see someone that you love suffer." That was so true, and in that moment, we knew that we could not ask her to do any more treatments to stay alive. Basically, even if the chemotherapy could buy Judy some more time, she would suffer from it.

That was a very painful and stressful decision that we were forced to make. Judy's higher-level thinking was not there at that time, so we had to decide for her. However, we all knew what she would have wanted, and to just keep her alive at that point, by any means, was not the path she would have chosen. All of us had been through so much over the past few years because of this, and those experiences helped us choose the direction we took. After our discussions and some heavy prayers, we decided to make her as comfortable as possible for her remaining days, and not do any more treatments. We were told that she had about six months to live.

## HOSPICE CARE

As we started out on this new journey, we placed her under hospice care and decided to keep her at home instead of placing her in a nursing home.

Because we had experience with a nursing home after her second surgery, and knew what they had to offer, we were going to try to take care of Judy at home. I am very glad we made that choice, but had no idea what was ahead of us. Probably if some of the hospice staff and other medical people would have told us how tiring it would get, we more than likely would have still made the same selection. We wanted to give Judy the best care that we could, and at the same time let her know that she was loved by us, her friends, and of course loved abundantly by God.

Little did we know that our decision would cause us to walk through a very dark valley in our life. Yes, the Lord walked with me through it; however, as a fallible human being, I became worn out with the load that I was carrying. I just did not know how overwhelmingly demanding and emotionally draining all of that would become. However, I loved Judy and knew that she would have done the same for me, and that we had been through a lot of life challenges together up to that point. I tried to believe that we would get through this one as well. As time moved on, I just did not know how awful it would get.

We decided to set up the hospice bed and other supplies in our dining room. We did not use our formal dining room that often and it was right off of our kitchen. We found out that she could stay connected to what was going on in our home by being there. It also had a large picture window that she could look out of. It was convenient for those who came in to visit her and for those taking care of her. I am glad we made that decision, instead of putting her in our second-floor bedroom. Later on, trying to get her up and down the stairs would have been next to impossible. As time went on people who came by to see us commented on how well that choice worked out for all of us.

Initially, Judy was pretty much able to take care of herself. Getting in and out of bed, coming to the kitchen table for meals, or going into the living room to watch TV or just hang out were all things that she could do on her own. However, over time she was able to do less and less by herself as the tumor grew. What I am about to say may sound unsympathetic and I do not mean to be disrespectful to those of you who may have a loved one who is dying in somewhat the same manner that Judy did. But the best way I can describe what she was going through was like a watch that was winding down. The watch gets slower and slower, it is not able to tell the correct time, and eventually it just stops all together. Over time, Judy was able to do fewer things and we all had to do increasingly more for her.

I had never been through something like that before, and did not fully know what was coming next, only that in time she would die. So, every day was a learning curve about what was needed to be done for her. Eventually she could not get out of bed by herself. We then had to use a Hoyer lift to get her in and out of bed and place her in our easy chair or her wheelchair so she did not have to stay in the bed all the time. Using the Hoyer lift was a blessing in some ways but could be a challenge to get it to work, especially when you were alone. Then over time we began to feed her, wash, change her, etc. One thing that I am very proud of and was told by the hospice staff was that through this entire time Judy never got any bed sores. Bed sores are common when people are in the latter stages of life and cannot move around much. But I pray that I never have to go through something like that again, *ever*!

A hospice aid came in three mornings a week to help care for Judy. They would give her a bath, get her up, and basically be sure her basic needs were taken care of. A hospice nurse would come in to help with Judy's medicine, check on her physical status, and offer support and guidance to us about what was happening with her. They also sent a hospice chaplain who was available to help. I am so grateful for the hospice staff who came in during this time. For the most part they were great and very helpful to Judy and my family. I know that I would not have been able to do what they did. It takes a very special person to work in that field knowing that everyone they deal with will in time die. That is a very unique calling and vocation and I give thanks to anyone who was and is willing to do hospice work. They were certainly a God-send to us; *God bless them*!

Even though a hospice aid came in three mornings a week, the rest of the time it was up to me to take care of her. At first that was not so hard as Judy was able to care for herself, but as time went along that became more of a burden. Thus, I looked into some private pay firms that could fill in when the hospice person was not there, but none of them worked out. Thus, when hospice was not there, it was basically up to me to care for Judy during the evenings, weekends, and the other mornings.

My employer, ACIC, allowed me to work out of my home so that I could care for her. One of our upstairs extra bedrooms was turned into my office. Thus, I could still try and manage to get some work done for the company. I did not make any business road trips during this stretch. However, a couple of times a week, I would go into ACIC's main office about thirty minutes away. Of course, if I wanted to go to that office or to the store, church, or run errands, someone had to be found to be with her.

It was a stressful situation to keep all of these things balanced, to have everything taken care of, and to coordinate all aspects of our life at that time. Every day, I had to think about what was needed to be done on that day, be sure Judy was taken care of, get some work done for ACIC, be sure things were taken care of around the house, and also try to take care of myself in the process. Everyone kept telling me that I, as the primary caretaker, had to take care of myself, both physically and emotionally, but that was so very hard to do. I realized later that I did not do a very good job in that regard.

But all that being said, I will always be so grateful that ACIC allowed me to care for Jude in the manner that I did. The leadership of that company was so supportive and willing to bend the rules to let me do what was needed. Granted, in my mind, I had always been a good employee, had very seldom been off sick, and always tried to give them my best effort in an honest and professional manner. Also, I believe that I had a very good working relationship with the company staff and the agency sales force. However, ACIC was not required to do what they did, and I image that very few places would have bent over backwards for me back then like they did. Thankfully, I was with them at that time and not with another company. I firmly believe that I was divinely guided to be with ACIC during that period.

## HITTING THE WALL

For about three months I cared for Judy, together with hospice, Kevin, and a few friends. People offered to help, but at that point I did not know how they could. Friends and many from our two churches provided meals. Because we were involved with Epiphany Lutheran Church and Seton Parish Catholic Church, both in Pickerington, we were able to get meals from each. That was a real blessing for us. I of course continued to handle all of the previously mentioned aspects of dealing with Judy's condition.

As the days went on, it became tougher and tougher for me to get up every morning to face another day. The strain kept piling up on me, but I did not realize its full impact on me. Then, out of the blue, one Wednesday, after three months of the constant care of Judy, I hit an emotional/

physical *wall*. The dark valley that I had been in got even worse, and the wilderness/desert area that I had been trying to walk through totally stopped me. Suddenly felt like I was in quicksand and could not do any more.

When I woke up that morning, I was totally and completely exhausted, spiritually, mentally, physically, and emotionally; and had nothing left to give to Judy, myself, or anyone or anything else. These words cannot begin to describe what I was going through at that moment. Yes, in my mind, I knew that God loved us, and that many people were praying for us, supporting us, and sending us love. But at that moment, I was so low that none of that mattered and I was drained, completely empty and had nothing left to give. Up to that point, I apparently had not done nearly enough for my selfcare and was now paying the price for it. I hit that brick wall and could not see my way around or over it; it had me completely blocked.

Deb Schmidt, Epiphany's parish nurse at the time, had offered help before, but I never took her up on it. I called on that Wednesday and told her I could not do it anymore. I also called Epiphany's associate pastor, Mike Walters, and left a message for him about Judy's eventual funeral service. Bless their hearts, they both showed up at my door later that morning. They came to comfort and to again offer support. I told Debbie my condition. This time I was open to the help and willingly accepted it. In hindsight I should have asked for help a lot sooner, but did not. Judy and I had generally been able to work together to handle whatever had come our way in the past. But we never had a challenge like this one. I also should note that I am one of those people who hate to ask others for help and always try to work things out on my own. Thus, because of my hard-headedness, I caused some of my own problems. However, I could not do any more on my own, and was now very open to asking for and accepting the help that was needed.

## ANGELS

I still remember sitting around our kitchen table talking to Deb and Pastor Mike about what was going on. Deb heard my despair and immediately offered support. She said that she would get some assistance from Epiphany's Health and Wellness Committee. She very quickly got some women from that committee to offer to come over day or night, whenever I needed them. I also got volunteers from Judy's church (Seton Parish) to pitch in, as well as a few close friends to come over, plus a neighbor who was a nurse to fill in as well. A schedule was set up and those wonderful women came by to assist me in taking care of Judy on a weekly basis. Some came in the morning, to help me get her up, dressed, etc., when the hospice aid was not there. Some came by in the evening, to assist in getting Judy ready for the night. They stayed about half an hour and sometimes longer in caring for Judy.

They very much eased the burden of taking care of Judy, but they also helped me emotionally, for they were able to share what I was going through. Since I worked at home, I did not always have a lot of human interaction during the day. Over time Judy also lost her ability to talk. So, these visits helped me in two ways: the care of Judy plus conversation for me. Their chats were one of the reasons I made it through that period. That made what was happening less stressful and overwhelming.

The love they showed by taking part in that journey was love that filled our home. There was no way I would have been able to continue without their love, support, kindness, and help. When they came in, I could feel their love and that love renewed me and fed my hungry soul. In my mind they were angels sent by God to walk with us through those dark days. Yes, they were humans, but when they walked into our home to bathe and care for Judy, they were bringing God's love with them, and in my book, they were angels. This was the third time God's angels (human or otherwise) had come into our lives. They continued helping out for the remaining *four months* of Judy's life.

None of them ever complained to me about what they did. I think that some of them must have felt that it was an honor and privilege to walk with us through this wilderness/desert part of our lives. Much later I wrote an article about these angels. The story was published in the March/April 2001 issue of *Angels on Earth* (a *Guideposts* magazine). Even with their help, we still had our struggles making it through this period, but we made it. We never placed Judy in a nursing home and she passed away at home.

## OUR LIFE AROUND THE HOSPICE CARE

Life around our house continued to function despite all of the hospice care that went on during Judy's last days. Somehow, I kept things going, for our family and me. My scaled-down work load, household details and duties that could not be put off, and dealing with family issues that could at times be as concerning as Judy's struggles all needed to be handled. Over the years I had become fairly organized and during this time that quality was essential.

I also tried to maintain my prayer routine and spiritual practices as much as possible. However, many times that could not be done because of more pressing matters. My prayers were changed regarding Judy's health. After her second surgery, I was really focused on asking God to heal Judy to where she was before and I prayed for that with all my heart, mind, and soul. I truly believed that if I fervently prayed for it that it would come to pass. After we went under hospice, I still prayed for Judy, but now was asking that she pass away without any additional suffering. In my heart I believe that prayer was answered. Supposedly at the end of life there sometimes is pain involved as the tumor grows and takes up more space in the brain; then medicine has to be given to relieve the discomfort. In Judy's case we never gave her any additional drugs toward the end. I do not think she ever experienced any pain, and she was able to die as peacefully as possible, for which I am most thankful!

As I have noted before and as has been written about by many spiritual authors, prayer is more about changing us to become the person that God wants us to be and to enhance our relationship with the Lord, than for us to always get what we request. Our petitions may or may not be answered in the manner in which want. However, God is love and cannot help but love us and only wants the best for us. When we go through dark valleys, it can be especially tough if we think God is not listening. Even if we do not clearly hear an answer and the Lord seems far away, we should keep pleading anyway; for it continues to change us and brings us closer to God. I kept praying but changed what was being asked for; that was all that I could do at that point. I know that those years did significantly transform me and helped me to see God's hand more clearly in my life, and of the lives around me. But I will always be grateful that Judy passed away without any apparent pain.

Over the years I have held up family members, friends, people in our communities, and various worldwide situations in my daily prayers. Our daughter, Elizabeth, has always been included. The prayers have mostly centered around her being able to turn her life around and to make better life choices, which, as she got older, seemed to become more challenging for her to do. By her actions she caused herself, our family, and society at large immeasurable damage. Her struggles continued while Judy was under hospice care and our family had to expend additional time and energy in dealing with what she created.

During part of this time Elizabeth was under house arrest, so we also had to deal with her and Anna, her daughter, as well. Then things got worse when Elizabeth had to spend some time in jail during the summer of 1998 while Judy was under hospice. Thus, Kevin and I had to take care of Anna as well as continuing to care for Judy. Anna would have been about fourteen to fifteen months old at that time. That was a real challenge for all of us. I believed that things could not get any worse, *but they did*! For a few weeks during that time, Kevin was hired to work on a film in Kentucky. He was a film major in college, and loved working on film locations as a grip. He took the job so he could get away for a while and make some money. The only way I was able to make it through that period was by the grace of God, and the power of all the prayers and love coming our way.

Losing someone you love is certainly a very difficult and heartbreaking situation for anyone; no matter the age, sex, ethnic background, or color. Death does not care who you are or where you came from; it comes when it comes. During this phase, my family and I experienced many slow deaths relating to Judy as we continued to lose bits and pieces of the person we knew and loved. It started after the second operation and accelerated after we went under hospice care.

At some point during this period, I joined a grief support group at Epiphany Lutheran Church that Pastor Mike had started. The group helped me to better understand what I was going through. Even though Judy was physically with us, I lost more of her each day and my grieving process had already begun. That sorrow and sense of loss continued until well after she passed way. Mourning is a long, drawn-out process and very painful. However, it is also one of those things in life that one cannot go around or try to disregard. Grief takes ahold of you and will not go away until you have gone through the valley. I might add that everyone's valley is unique to themselves. What I went through is totally different from anyone else, but is generally very agonizing no matter who you are.

Shirley lost her late husband, Bob, in an unexpected accident. When he left on that Saturday morning, he was well and healthy, but by the afternoon he was gone. That impacted her so profoundly that she has described that period as if she were torn in half, like she had lost half of herself. We have since had many discussions about the deaths of our late spouses and how painful they were; Judy's was over a period of time, and Bob's was sudden. Shirley and I agree that they both were dreadful and we would not want to go through anything like that—*ever again*!

## JUDY'S DEATH AND FUNERAL

During her last few weeks, Judy ate less and less until she stopped eating all together. When she did this, there was a reduced amount of care needed as her body kept slowing down, until it stopped. We all knew that her time was getting shorter on a daily basis. However, we tried as best as we could to keep up our routines. Supposedly, the hearing is the last thing to go, so we tried to be around her and talk to each other and her so that our voices could be heard. Of course, during those last days, we do not know for sure what she could hear, but we continued to show our love for her. I also carried on our evening devotional practice with her until near the end.

Much later after Judy died Kevin remembered that the last movie that we took Judy to while she was able to get out was a James Bond movie, *Tomorrow Never Dies*. It came out in December of 1997. He recalled that on January 23, 1999, the Saturday night she finally passed away, he and I watched the same movie on TV. That was amazing in my book. Equally as incredible was that, about six months after she died, and I began traveling again for work, I was sleeping in a motel room in Salt Lake City, Utah, and I heard Judy's voice as clear as day, saying that *she was alive*. That was all I recollect her saying. Now, up to that time, I had never heard anyone's voice like that before, or since, but it was definitely hers. For those of us on this side of God's kingdom it is hard to fully understand what our eternal life will be like. But sometimes we get a very small glimpse into how things will turn out. I do not know what will be coming next but truly believe that Judy is alive in some form or the other. The life that we know now will end, but our new one will live on into eternity because of Jesus' life, death, and resurrection.

We knew that Jude was going to die, but it was still hard on all of us when it actually happened. On that Saturday evening she died around 10:00 p.m. I had put her to bed and was getting ready to go to sleep myself. However, upstairs through our baby monitor I could hear her breathing very strenuously and loudly. Kevin and I were the only ones there at that time. I came downstairs and stood by her, watching her body completely shut down and take her last breaths, and I was able to be next to her when she passed away.

I called Elizabeth, who by this time had moved into an apartment in the area and told her to get Anna and come over. I did not tell her that Judy had died at that point. I then phoned hospice and asked them to send over their on-call nurse, so that they could verify her death, and then call the undertaker. I had been told earlier by the staff at Epiphany that I did not have to go through this period alone, and to call if I wanted their support. I called Pastor Dave Shugert from Epiphany and told him about Jude's passing. He asked if I wanted him to come over; I told him yes, and that was one of the best decisions that I have ever made.

Pastor Dave came over and stayed with us a while and his presence made a huge impact on me. I saw him in the role of a loving pastor revealing God's love to us just by his presence. For a while he did not say much, just took it all in, and he spent time looking at Judy's body. After some time, he started asking us questions. Just by him being with us in that moment and how loving and caring he was with our emotions told me a lot about how he viewed his ministry and the role that he felt he needed to fulfill. What he did that night also influenced how I viewed various aspects about ministry in general, and then much later how my own ministry would develop.

He was with us in that very raw moment, but his kindness helped us through what we were experiencing, and that was his gift in being there. He walked with us through that very dark valley. After a bit he got us telling stories about Judy. Elizabeth and Kevin related memories about how Jude would keep information from me, in order to get things done for our family. They were details that I had never heard previously. Before he left, we were all laughing with the telling of these accounts. We were still grieving the loss of Judy, but our tears were turned into joy by recalling some wonderful moments about a past that we all shared, even though some of them were new to me. I will always be grateful for Pastor Dave's presence on that evening. He was a vessel of God's love for all of us. I began to realize that pastors, and those in certain other roles in life, have an opportunity to walk with folks on holy ground and be in very sacred moments. Doing this requires trust by all parties, and a willingness to be vulnerable to each other in that moment in time.

This is something that I have learned more about since being married to a pastor. Shirley does not share with me any of the details of those moments that she has been privileged enough to be a part of. However, she has noted that she feels honored to have been able to have walked with people through their holy journeys, and to have stood with them in their sacred moments of joy or pain/sorrow. That is what Pastor Dave did for us that evening. What he said was fine, but his loving-caring presence, and him just being there was the more comforting part. Pastor Dave is no longer on this side of God's kingdom with us, but his loving spirit is still a part of our family's life experiences.

Judy died on January 23, 1999, which was not on any important date for our family. Afterward I was told by Sr. Chris Ritchey, our very dear friend, that she had been praying that Judy would not pass away over the Christmas holidays. She knew that if she did, that every Christmas holiday after that would carry with it the memory of Jude's passing and thus be more of a challenge. I honestly did not think about it at the time. But looking back, it probably was a blessing to all of us that it happened the way it did. I understand that many people have to concern themselves with this issue, having loved ones dying around major holidays or other important dates. In this case, we did not have to deal with that situation. However, a couple of years later, my mom died on December 23.

I knew that having a funeral Catholic Mass would be important for Jude and also knew that there would be folks who came to the funeral who would not be able to take communion at a Catholic Mass. Previously I had asked my associate pastor at Epiphany, Pastor Mike Walters, to ask the Catholic priest at Seton Parish, Father Steve Hawkins, if we could have two communion stations, one for Catholics and one for non-Catholics. He said we could not do that because it was a Catholic Mass. But that got me to thinking about some other things. We asked and it was agreed that Pastor Dave would deliver the homily at Jude's funeral. It ended up being quite an ecumenical event. In addition to Pastor Dave and Father Hawkins, we also had Pastor Mike do a prayer, and the other Catholic priest, Father Dennis Kigozi, took part in it as well.

Because of my concern about the non-Catholics being at the funeral service and not being able to take communion, I had this printed up in the funeral bulletin:

> Thank you for coming to this going home celebration for Judy.
> Our marriage was somewhat unique, because of differences in our background. However, these differences did not stop us from becoming one, as Paul noted in Ephesians 5:31.
> We were a Christian couple first, before being a Catholic or Protestant couple. The Catholic Mass was very essential for Judy

and held a special meaning for her. Therefore, it is important for us to celebrate her going home with this Mass.

Judy and I attended service here many times together. Because of the differences in how communion is offered during Mass, compared to other denominations, I never took communion here. Thus, communion today is limited to those of the Catholic Faith.

However, all are welcome to participate in the rest of the celebration. Please, take part in singing, in hearing God's word from the scriptures, in the prayers, and in saying the Lord's Prayer together. By praying and singing together we can all join in and be one Christian Community. When Christ comes back, he will not care about any differences, he will come for his Christian Community.

Besides taking part in this celebration, you are also welcome to come back after we visit the cemetery, to break bread together in Bishop Herrmann Hall; directly behind the worship space. The meal has been prepared by the Helping Hands Committees from Seton Parish and Epiphany Lutheran Church. God Bless You: Vernon T.

People told me later that they felt that her funeral service was very beautiful and moving. There was a cross-section of people there, since folks from both sides of our families were present and we had individuals from different faith communities as well. I was told that there was a lot of love in and through the service, and the love could be especially felt in the meal afterwards where everyone could eat together and share stories and memories. I recall more about the dinner and walking around and greeting many of those who were there than about the service itself. That meal and time together was a joyful time for me. She was buried on January 27, and we were blessed to have mild weather for everything.

I was also told later on that Pastor Dave did a really wonderful job with the homily. I did not hear much of what was going during on the service, so later I asked for his outline; here are a few of his comments. He talked about what Kevin had written about Judy. Kevin wrote, "Her life was a seed that planted a mighty tree, whose branches were love. As we love each other these branches grow, moving onward, living forever." Pastor Dave noted that Kevin spoke of Judy's love in the present tense, that her love is still with us and is unending. The Gospel was from John 17:9–11, and he outlined the unity element of those verses and how unity was an important aspect of our marriage and of our lives. That we had interracial unity, interfaith unity, and intercongregational unity. He also mentioned that Judy was now in God's kingdom without a tumor, and without any of the side effects of it. That is something that I will always remember, and I am so grateful and thankful that Pastor Dave could deliver Judy's funeral service sermon. The entire event was a wonderful example of God's love and grace pulling people of different faiths and backgrounds together to celebrate the life of someone who loved life and those around her.

Something that Judy and I had talked about long before this period was funding a scholarship in the name of her parents at their home parish. Education was important to us and we thought that establishing a scholarship was a positive thing to do. That gave me the idea of setting one up in Jude's name. The Judith A. Jones Memorial Scholarship Fund, for college-bound students at Seton Parish in Pickerington, Ohio, was created. Thus, when she passed away, if people or companies wanted to donate funds in her name, they could contribute to that scholarship. I was so wonderfully surprised by the number of people who gave, and the amounts given to this fund in her name. That fund is still ongoing today.

With some of the life insurance monies received on Judy I also set up the Vito A. and Stella V. Buonavolonta Memorial Scholarship Fund for college-bound students at Mount Carmel Parish in Ashtabula, Ohio. That was Judy's parents' home congregation. That parish is now closed and those funds were added into Jude's scholarship. Additionally, the Emma B. Jones Scholarship was established at Youngstown State University in my mom's name for YSU students who came from the east side of Youngstown. Both Judy and I received our degrees from YSU and I also grew up on the east side. That fund is still ongoing as well. Those were set up many years ago, and I think that doing something like that is a good way to give back in some small way to honor all those who have helped us over the years.

## GRIEF

After the funeral, even though many things that had to be done, the grief and pain became overwhelming. I remember wanting to get flowers and gifts for the many people who had helped us out over those months prior to Jude's death. I did not feel that I could focus on the tasks at hand and drive myself. Since Kevin was at home, I remember him driving me, getting these errands done. I am so glad he was there then. In time I went back to work full time, but I also was carrying a heavy load from Jude's death and what had happened over the prior few years.

The emptiness felt was agonizing and I struggled to make it through every day. I would cry at the drop of a hat, for almost any reason. I remember being in a grocery store shopping by myself when I saw a couple about my age. I thought it was not fair that they got to be a couple and I could not be and got very sad about that. Yes, I knew it was not logical, but grieving does not always come with a clear, logical mind. That period made me rethink the importance of my life and where I was going. I knew that I was not the kind of person that would be able to live by myself forever. Of course, over a very long time the pain and sorrow eased a bit, but I was very lonely and missed the companionship, friendship, and intimacy that I had with Judy. Even though I knew that God loved me as well as my family and friends, I still missed Judy's love, hugs, and just being with her.

Many an evening after working, I would be sitting in my easy chair, just crying, with seemingly no positive thoughts about what lay ahead. It did not help that it was wintertime and the days were short and the evenings long and dark. Also, I did not realize how physically and emotionally exhausted I had gotten caring for her. She died in January and I noticed that I did not get totally renewed energy until that July. She was under hospice for about seven months and it took seven months to regain my strength.

On top of what I was going through, about a month after Judy died Elizabeth took Anna and left town. Kevin and I knew something was up with Elizabeth during Judy's last days. She was acting like she did whenever she was about to get into trouble again. I even wrote her a letter and asked to her to straighten up or she would be in danger of missing out on Judy's last days and her funeral. We generally knew when something was up with her because she began to act squirrelly and behaved nervously whenever she was around.

It was about a month later because we all got together to celebrate Kevin's birthday, which is February 22. She left town shortly after that, and we did not know where she went. Basically, she had gotten into trouble again, and she decided to leave town, rather than go to jail. Thus, I continued grieving the loss of Judy and was still extremely worn down from caring for her and now was also worried and concerned about my daughter and granddaughter. Saying that I was depressed and really low is an understatement. It is amazing that I did not have a total breakdown from all of that. However, thankfully the prayers of my family and friends kept me going. At some level I must have felt God's presence being with me and will always be grateful for the support of Kevin and those around me. Nonetheless that winter and spring were a dreadful and trying time for me. But thankfully I made it to the summer.

In the spring quarter Kevin went back to Wright State University in Dayton, Ohio, to finish his degree. He had been home to support us and help out with Judy when he was needed. I am sure he also had an opportunity to reflect on what he wanted to do with his life at that time. I am also certain that what he went through with Jude's illness and death changed him. It appeared that he went back to college with a new sense of purpose and direction. That experience drastically changed me in more ways than can be counted. I also began to look at my life through a different lens as well.

## LOVE AND RELATIONSHIPS

I had to cope with my grief and having to live alone for the first time in over twenty-eight years. Occasionally, during this entire ordeal, I began thinking about what I wanted to do for the rest of my life and came to realize that what was important to me before was not as significant anymore. I had less drive at work, and found it really tough to focus on getting anything done. Even after that summer and getting fully rested, my concentration level was not what it used to be. When first starting out in the insurance industry, my goal was to be the president of St. Paul Insurance Company. I wanted to advance as far as possible with any company that I worked for. Over the years that goal was dropped, but I was still fairly determined. At one point in my career, I thought long and hard about starting my own business of some type.

Those desires were now less important in my life. Going through those years of struggles with Jude drastically changed me. During that winter and spring, I had lots of time to think, reflect, pray, and then listen to what was coming to me. At the same time, I continued to grieve and deal with the pain and sorrow of that period, a dark valley for sure for me. However, I had a wonderful epiphany out of that desert time; I came to realize that the things that were most important to me were *love* and *relationships*. Those were the things that should be first and foremost on this side of God's kingdom.

Over time I recognized that anything else that we might strive for or work toward were all temporal, and would fade away at some point. If we did not have love and relationships, whatever else we obtained in our life would be empty. Thus, what I thought I wanted to work for before in the business world changed so much from my experience of walking with Judy during those last few years. I thought that I had been striving for God's kingdom on a daily basis before, but my direction took a sharp turn after her death. Love and relationships were what my heart, soul, and mind wanted to embrace even more, besides the seeking of God's kingdom; or maybe they were one and the same. I just looked at them a bit differently now. Hence, what would be done over the next few years would be driven by those thoughts and emotions, sometimes even without me realizing it. When we are on this pilgrimage and engaged in our spiritual practices, we are in fact asking for and expecting the Holy Spirit to comfort and guide us. In this case, that direction was aided by my desire to leave many of my past ambitions behind and focus instead on embracing my yearning for love and loving relationships in my life.

## ELIZABETH

During this time, we continued to have difficulties dealing with Elizabeth and her problems. She got into trouble because of her misuse of other people's credit cards, checks, and credit information. Since she was about eighteen to twenty she had been in and out of trouble with the law due to these fraudulent acts of identity theft. She had also spent time in jail and had been on probation a number of times. She had stolen from us and used our credit cards without our permission. It took us a long time to figure out what was going on because we trusted her and never believed that she would do anything like that. She also got into trouble at her places of employment. If she was around money or other people's credit information, it was like an addiction. She would use that information in an illegal manner.

As a family we bailed her out of jail many times and paid off her debts a bunch of times because she told us that she would not steal again, which was what we had hoped and prayed for. I began writing down rules for her to follow and goals for her, in the hopes that she would do better. Over the years we spent tens of thousands of dollars because of her crimes. We tried tough love, but sometimes Judy and I were not always in agreement on what to do. Elizabeth kept promising us that she would turn around and do better so we tried to get her help and get her involved with groups that could assist her. We helped her get established in an apartment after she was released from jail.

Besides the financial cost, she also caused us many heartaches, much emotional stress, and lots of energy, time, and worry. Sadly, none of our efforts ever seemed to make any lasting improvements, and heartbreakingly for us her behavior never permanently changed while she was still in our lives. She could be a very loving and caring person who we all enjoyed being around at certain times. However, her actions impacted our family environment in many negative ways over the years. Judy and I raised her and Kevin to the best of our ability, and of course we made our share of mistakes. However, we loved them and did what we thought was best for both. We were not perfect and had our share of challenges within our marriage, partly because of our different backgrounds. I am sure it was not easy being a biracial child and we probably should have gotten professional help for her earlier than we did.

Elizabeth was an attractive woman with a wonderful personality, who could get along with almost anyone. When she walked into a room, she filled it up and could charm those she around her. I have often said that she was a really smart person, and could do pretty much anything that she wanted to in life. Both Kevin and Elizabeth would tell you that one of the many things that I did in trying to get them to live the right way was when I would give them "dad's sermon" about using the gifts that God gave them. I believe that all of us have been given certain gifts that should be used for God's kingdom and that those talents should be developed, enhanced, and nurtured as indicated by Jesus' parable in Matt 25:14–30. This is the story of the landlord going on a journey and leaving talents with his workers, expecting them to use and multiply them, and not bury them. One could say that Elizabeth did not use her talents as God intended them to be used. The bottom line is that having to deal with Elizabeth and her challenges over the years had been extremely trying for my family, especially during the time shortly before and after Judy's death.

## ELIZABETH AND ANNA IN NEW JERSEY

In February 1999 after Jude died, Elizabeth took her daughter, Anna, and left town, in violation of her probation. She left because the company she was working for was about to discover that she had written company checks that she should not have. She ran and, at first, I did not know where she was, or what or how she was doing. I was still very much grieving the loss of Jude, who had died only a month earlier, plus dealing with the long winter days, also being so tired from all that I had been through; and now she and Anna were gone. Elizabeth called a couple of times to ask for money. She told me that she would come home and face the consequences awaiting her. However, those promises were empty ones. She headed south of Ohio, then east and ended up in New Jersey. She somehow came into contact with a wonderful Christian family who ended up helping Anna and her out. This family had met Elizabeth and Anna when they got to New Jersey and fell in love with Anna. In my mind that was a miracle that this family came into the picture when they did.

Eventually, Elizabeth did something illegal in New Jersey and ended up in jail. This family ran a daycare and remarkably were able to have Anna turned over to their custody rather than the custody of New Jersey's Social Services. If that had occurred, no telling how difficult it would have been to get Anna out of that system and back to Ohio. After this family took Anna in, they kept her safe and treated her like their own. They even gave her a party for her second birthday in May and loved her and cared for her while her mother was in jail.

The family called me and explained what was going on. During this period, I sent money to help out with Anna's care. However, I will always be indebted to this family for what they did. Even with all of the challenges that Elizabeth caused herself—Anna having this family come into their lives was a God-send. They were God's human angels showing love and compassion to my family when it was needed. I do not know how it can be explained any other way.

We all knew that, at some point, Elizabeth would have to come back to the central Ohio area and face her charges there. Jude's family and my extended family were about three or four hours away and did not know what was going on at that time. I was working full time and my job required me to travel fairly often. Additionally, I was still grieving Jude's death and regaining my energy from having taken care of Judy. I was not in a very good position to handle any more strenuous family situations, but God sent yet more angels our way.

While talking to my neighbor about all of this, she said that she would help us out when Elizabeth and Anna got back to Ohio. She knew Elizabeth and Anna and had a little knowledge about what was going on. She had two children around Anna's age, was a social worker herself, and did not want Anna to go into any social services arrangement. She volunteered to keep Anna, when they came back. This woman, who was not a relative, just a good neighbor, offers to help out! She had someone who provided childcare for her children while she worked, and the sitter agreed to keep Anna as well. That was utterly amazing in my book.

Over the 1999 Memorial Day weekend I drove up to New Jersey by myself. Elizabeth had been released from jail, and I was able to bring them both back to Ohio. I met the family who had taken care of Elizabeth and Anna for those few months. We drove back the next day. That entire weekend was both a relief to have them back, and very stressful because of what was yet to come. Elizabeth had to turn herself in to the police in central Ohio and start serving her time. Additionally, *she was also pregnant again*!

Think about what must have been going through the mind of little two-year-old Anna. Her mother and she had basically been on the road for four months. She was separated from her mother while Elizabeth was in jail. She had lived with some loving people that she had not known for very long, and now she would have to lose her mother again. She would begin living in someone's house and start an entirely new routine again. That was an awful lot for anyone so young to have to deal with and understand. No telling how all of this impacted her life.

However, at that point, I did not see anything else that could have been done. I know sometimes life just stinks, even when God's angels are all around trying to help out. Nonetheless, we started on a journey of which we could not know the end, and so we literally had to take it one day at a time, for we had no clue what would be coming next. We did what we thought was the best for Elizabeth and Anna at that time. Maybe something else ought to have been done back then. But remember that it was less than six months since Judy had died, and my emotional state only allowed me to deal with the next moment, instead of thinking of the long-term ramifications of our decision.

When we got back into town Elizabeth turned herself in to the police and started serving her time. This new routine that started for all of us began around May 31, 1999, and continued until September 25, 2000, when Elizabeth was released from jail, and she was able to care for Anna. My neighbor and her sitter watched Anna during the weekdays, and I kept her from Friday evenings until Sunday evenings. All of this is another miracle that happened in the midst of the pain and sorrow that surrounded what Elizabeth had done, and the terrible conditions that Anna had to deal with at such a very young age. Because of this I became a parent again, and learned how to comb Anna's hair, made sure she was clothed and fed, and tried to love her while setting up boundaries for her at the same time. I, of course, continued to go to worship at Epiphany, and Anna went with me.

I did not see all of this coming after Judy died. I could not help thinking that things would have been a lot different if Judy were still around at that point; there would have been two of us to deal with what was happening. However, she was not, so I tried to do what was right and fair for everyone. I loved Anna and only wanted the best for her. However, sometimes you wonder about how much one person can take before they say, that is enough, I am out of here. The last few years of caring for Judy and then her death would seem to be enough right there for one person to deal with. Thankfully, I did not walk away and just say the heck to all of this and let someone else handle it. Nevertheless, for any number of reasons, the struggles of life, as it pertains to Elizabeth and her family, would continue for me for some time.

Taking care of Anna gave me something else to focus on instead of my grief, tiredness, job, etc. During that period there is no telling what unwise choices I might have made, or harmful things I may have gotten myself into, while going through the pain of all of this. At times I am not very strong and can be subject to making decisions that may take me down the wrong path. I realize that my spiritual practices and the prayers of others helped me out, but I am subject to my weak periods coupled with raw emotions that can lead me astray.

However, having to prepare for and think about keeping Anna every weekend kept me focused on all the things that needed to be done. Sometimes I could do household tasks with her, but other jobs were best done during the weekday after work. I did not know it at the time but God had plans for me to start another chapter in my life, within the next year, and I did not need any detours in the meanwhile. Thus, in some ways taking care of Anna focused me on her care, versus my own hurt and needs. That dark valley eventually ended and the next stage of my spiritual pilgrimage, one that I did not know existed at that time, began.

Beside taking care of Anna, grieving, and working, I was also continuing to support Elizabeth in jail. I was her only living parent and Kevin was away at college. At that time, I still believed that she could turn herself around and do what was best for her and her family for the long run. Thus, when she needed small amounts of cash for stuff, or new socks or underwear, I supplied them for her. This was not the first time she was in jail, but, if I remember correctly, that was her longest sentence up to that point.

I also still felt that it was important for Elizabeth to continue to bond with Anna and maintain their mother and daughter relationship. Thus, after doing the research about jail visits, I started visiting her in jail with Anna. Once I began going, I kept the visits up until she got out. Again, I do not know how all this impacted Anna, for she was just past two years old. But I wanted her to physically see and hug her mom so she knew that she was loved by her. Therefore, most every Saturday morning when I kept Anna on the weekends, we would get up and go over to the jail and spend a couple of hours with Elizabeth. That can be a very humbling experience having to go through jail security to visit someone. It was hard at first to psych myself up to go there, but I felt it was so vital for them so that, when Elizabeth got out, they could once again be a family.

Going into a jail situation nearly every weekend of course changed me in more ways than I can write here. Many spiritual writers have noted that being on this spiritual pilgrimage will transform us. It will also take us to places that we might not have chosen to go on our own as well as taking us way out of our comfort zone. Making weekly trips to jail to visit my daughter definitely took me to a place I would have not have elected to go, physically or emotionally. Taking care of my granddaughter and supporting and loving my daughter certainly changed me.

As mentioned earlier Elizabeth was expecting when we brought her back to Ohio. In November of 1999 she gave birth to Judah. The sitter who had been taking care of Anna while my neighbor was at work apparently was contacted by Elizabeth. Somehow, not sure how it was done, but the sitter went to the hospital and was allowed to bring Judah to her home. She kept him, took care of him, and loved him deeply until Elizabeth was released, in September of 2000. Another miracle in my book!

When Elizabeth was released, Epiphany Lutheran gave her a great amount of help. They organized a drive and asked their members for supplies for someone wanting to make a fresh start without naming Elizabeth. The appeal was set up for people to donate items that Elizabeth would need to begin living on her own. They put up a board with notes on it of the things they were looking for. Those who were willing to help out would take a note, purchase the article, then bring it back and place it in a basket at church. They were very creative in pulling this together.

The good people at Epiphany generously furnished an apartment for Elizabeth and gave her a great opportunity to begin her life over, without the burden of buying a lot of things that were needed. They provided kitchen supplies, furniture, clothes and toys for Anna and Judah, a lot of wonderful items. She could basically move into an apartment and start living as a family. I helped get her a used car. I will always be greatly indebted to Epiphany for what they did for my family at that point, and many other times as well. In my mind, they are a wonderful example of what a loving, Spirit-filled community should be about. They will always have a special place in my heart.

She told me that my mom, Emma Jones, was an inspiration to her about how to live as a single parent and raise a family. My prayer was that, with the help from Epiphany, others and myself, and my mom's example, she could turn herself around, raise her children, and do what was right for herself and her family for the long term. However, that was not to be. I just did not know it at the time and, therefore, continued to hope for the best.

Like most of life, and especially that of the spiritual pilgrimage, the majority of the time all we can see is the next step in our journey. We have to trust the future to God and put our hope in that trust and the fact that we cannot always control what is to come next. That is most surely the case here; I *so* wanted Elizabeth to do what she needed to do to have a better life for herself and her family, and kept hoping for that to happen. I did not have a crystal ball where I could see into the future, for if I would have, I would have acted differently at that point. However, I had to go through that period before I was able to make the really difficult decisions later on. But that was down the road; for now I hoped, continued to pray, and helped out as much as possible.

## ELEVEN

# A Hopeful but Unknown Future

> For surely, I know the plans I have for you, says the Lord, plans for your welfare and not for harm, to give you a future with hope.
>
> —JER 29:11

### TRINITY LUTHERAN SEMINARY

AS HAS BEEN NOTED the time around Jude's death guided me to change my focus in life, from the career in the insurance business to placing more interest in the love and relationships in my life. All of the things that I had to deal with, mostly around Jude's condition and her passing, really caused me to reflect and ponder about what was really important in my life and in the world around me. I still tried to do my job as best as I could, but over time my desire to do something else continued to grow, and I began thinking about going in a different direction in my life.

At some point during Jude's hospice period, I got information about various area graduate programs, and also obtained information from Trinity Lutheran Seminary in Columbus, Ohio. It is hard to explain, but, as I looked at the materials that were received from a number of different places, the packet from Trinity was the only one that I was interested in filling out. Looking back, I know it was God, through the Holy Spirit, who was directing me. However, it seems odd that I would have requested a lot of information from numerous schools, but only picked one out to pursue.

Now, I had never thought about going to a seminary before this period, nor did I know much about Trinity. However, I did have some awareness of them, because of all the pastors from Trinity that Epiphany had while I was a member there. We also had a number of people at Epiphany who were working for or had been employed at Trinity. Because we were close to Trinity, Epiphany always had Trinity students around who filled a role as Ministry In Context (MIC) students and who did some work at Epiphany as part of their course requirements to become a pastor. Of course, I did not know it at the time, but by joining Epiphany in 1990 that had put me into a better position to end up at Trinity than if I had belonged somewhere else. But the main point here is that Trinity's packet is the only one I seriously read and completed.

Even thinking of leaving Auto Club Insurance Company after nearly ten years, and the insurance industry itself after nearly twenty-eight years, was a really huge deal for me. That business was the only kind of work I had done since leaving Youngstown. I was doing okay with ACIC, and to my knowledge could have continued working there as long as I wanted. I had a good salary and a decent benefits package; I enjoyed most of the travel that was done, had an expense account, and continued to get along with those I worked with inside and outside of the company. I knew what I was doing and needed to do to continue adding value to the organization. However, my heart just was not there as much as it had been previously because the Lord was leading elsewhere.

Jude was not around to walk through this decision with me. Mostly I did the reflecting, praying, and visioning on my own. Further down the road, I shared my thoughts with some people around me who were close to me. I did not have enough company time in to actually retire from ACIC and so would be leaving them cold. Thus, it would be a really big leap of faith in a number of ways if I left them to go to Trinity. One of the biggest issues would be the financial concerns, in leaving ACIC; how would I pay for the education and my living expenses? As noted in the past, I am not that great of a money manager; therefore, I did not have lots of savings to live on. Also, what would I do, once finished? However, this was where I was being led, and could not stop the guidance and direction from coming. The drive to go became stronger as time went along.

The verse from Jer 29:11 refers to the plans that God has for us; they are plans that are for our welfare, and not for harm; but to give us a future with hope. For me the issue was that I was being positively guided to think about going to Trinity; however, for a long time, I did not know why. It was an act of faith on my part to continue moving along that track, because I did not have a clue what was coming or that it would be a future with hope; and also, a future with a new love and companion, and a completely different life direction. For I would enter into a totally new ministry and did not know where it would lead me. This is another excellent example of taking it one step at a time and trusting the future to our loving Lord. Additionally, like so many times in my life when it came to major decisions, it seemed that one path stood out above the rest, and became very clear to me as the way to go.

It became increasing obvious to me that I should leave ACIC by way of some small signs and one really large signal. Some of the smaller clues were based around my new life direction; that is, having less drive for the things of the business world, and having more focus on the spiritual aspects of my life journey, especially around the love and relationship areas of my life. They also came, believe it or not, from my job. Most of the companies that I had worked for generally provided the marketing staff with a company car because of the travel involved. Well, at some point in this reflecting period that I was going through, ACIC decided to stop providing company cars. For those existing employees, they gave us the cars that we were using and began paying us for using that car on company business. That was great for me. They also made changes to our savings plan, which was beneficial for me and allowed me more financial freedom in the future. There were other small changes they did that were indications for me that now was a good time to leave, especially since being guided in a totally new direction.

The really enormous signpost revolved around my pastor, Dave Shugert of Epiphany Lutheran Church, who has been mentioned before. Also, God put two more human angels into my life to aid in this endeavor. I took a week's vacation that summer to see if I would be okay taking a seminary course and to further determine if I was on the right path. I took a summer class and nothing told me to stop going toward Trinity. At some point during this time, I spoke to Pastor Dave and filled him in on all of my past signs and direction. I told him that I was led to go to Trinity, again not sure why, only that I felt like that is what should be done. My initial thought was to go part time, taking classes in the evening and continuing to work at ACIC and then maybe starting full time in 2001. That is how I earned my college degree, taking classes part time, and it seemed like the practical thing to do this time. *However, God had other plans.*

He asked how much it would cost; I told him about ten thousand dollars a year, just for the classes, books, and fees, if I stayed in my own home and handled my own daily living expenses. After speaking to him, he said to let him pray about it and he would get back to me at some point. Later on, he told me what had happened. His initial thought was to go to various people at Epiphany, and tell them who I was and what my plans were, and ask for those persons to contribute to my expenses. He had hoped that he would get enough individuals who would eventually kick in the full amount. Pastor Dave said that he had never done anything like that before, but that is what he was led to do. Now while he was engaged in a period of prayer, a couple's name came to him, and they are who he called on first. The thinking was that if they gave something, that he could then use their gift as a sort of seed money to encourage others to give until he got the full amount. After talking to that first couple, they told Pastor Dave that they wanted to pray about it and would get back to him.

This couple were members of Epiphany, but did not know me at that point. When they called him back, they told him that they had prayed about it and that they would cover the entire first year's cost of ten thousand dollars. *Yes, that's right*, people who did not know me directly were led by God to step out in faith and were guided to help me! Talk about people who walk by faith knowing that what they have are gifts from God, to be used by God. What a great witness for those of us on this spiritual pilgrimage! Please note all of the praying being done at this point; I was praying for guidance about what to do next, Pastor Dave prayed about how he should move forward, and the couple also prayed about what they should do.

That was the really big sign that I was meant to go full time, and right away; no waiting!! Bless their hearts, this generous couple also paid the second year's cost of ten thousand dollars as well. I ended up working on a Masters of Theological Studies Degree (MTS), which took about two years to earn going full time. I, of course, eventually met the couple, and will always be indebted to these two human angels who God placed in my life. I did not know it at the time, but the main reason why it was so important that I enter Trinity in the fall of 2000, as a full-time student, was to meet and fall in love with Shirley Ross, and eventually marry her after completing my degree.

Had I gone part time in the evenings starting that fall in 2000, I would not have been in the classes with her, and we never would have met. That first quarter we were in three of our four classes with each other, and got to know one another in those classes, as well as being in study groups together. Shirley enrolled at Trinity when she did because the Holy Spirit had guided her steps as well.

Shirley's pastor, Lori Carey, who had encouraged Shirley to think about becoming a pastor, wanted her to begin earlier than she did. Pastor Lori wanted Shirley to get her paperwork in so she could start in 1999 on the track to become an ordained pastor. However, because one of Shirley's best friends had recently lost her sister, Shirley did not want to leave her at that point. Thus, she started classes in 2000. If Shirley would have started in 1999, or if I would have started part time in the evenings in 2000, we would not have met each other. We had to start at the same time, each going full time. Yes, in my mind that was a *miracle* for us to end up there together. We did not know each other before going to Trinity, but God wanted us there at the same time and it worked out that way. Even with all of the issues with Elizabeth and her family, God still had a future filled with hope for me, which included a new love and a new relationship; I just could not see it coming, until it arrived. Taking it one step at a time was what I was doing and trusting the future to God. *Wow!*—what a journey to get to that point.

## SEMINARY CLASSES

On August 4, 2000, I left ACIC and the insurance business to attend Trinity Lutheran Seminary that next fall. Even though I knew that it was what I should be doing, it was very difficult leaving a career that had been known for so many years. A lot of energy and effort was put into my business life and I had my share of great moments and not so good ones. Because of the companies I worked for, I was able to either live in a wide range of wonderful places or visit some neat locations on my business trips or vacations. I was blessed to have a good salary and benefits that allowed us to enjoy a decent level of living and was also fortunate to have been able to work with an equally wide range of great people, from whom much was learned. Additionally, many of the skills that were developed during that time have been used and reused in my current ministry and life experiences and I will always be grateful for them. Those experiences, individuals, and places are still a part of me now.

I am also aware that many have not had the opportunities that I was able to have. Thus, I am very grateful for what I have been given. In every position held in the insurance field, I became the first person of color to hold that job. I may have been the first, but since then many others have followed and also broken barriers that were even more important than what I was blessed to take on. So, leaving that field was done with some measure of sadness and trepidation. I was sad for leaving the great people at ACIC and the industry that I knew so well and all of my experiences that I had while there. My anxiety came because I knew that God wanted me to leave, but I had no idea what was coming down the road. However, I guess my faith in God won out over my fear about the unknown.

One of the good things I did for myself was to take off a month from work to get ready for the new adventure that God had for me. I did not fully grasp what was coming, but wanted to be prepared as much as possible for this new life. I cannot tell you how hard it was for me to know that I was meant to do this, without knowing for sure why I was going, only that I knew God wanted me there. This was explained to all of my family, friends, and work associates, but it was still difficult to understand, for them and for me.

In my mind, a person has to be specifically called by God in order to become a pastor. This calling is not something that a person wakes up one day and simply declares: I think I will be a pastor. We are called to do something for God's kingdom, and what I am called to do is different than others. Most of the people who go to a seminary are doing so to become a pastor. Thus, many who first heard that I was going thought that was also the case for me. Therefore, I spent a lot of time telling people, "Yes, I am going to Trinity Lutheran Seminary but am not called to be a pastor, and don't know why I am going; however, I know I am meant to go." These words were repeated over and over again, before going, and after I got there. Once my classmates got to know me, they would say, "Vernon, with your faith and skills you would make a great pastor." I just repeated my answer, which never changed the entire time at Trinity.

During Trinity's orientation and welcome for the new students we met some of the staff and heard about seminary life there. I cannot remember most of the things that were presented at that time; however, one aspect stood out to me, for it has been used in my ministry. We were told that if we were looking forward to finding new ways to enhance our spiritual growth, that we would not find it by just being there. Yes, our journey could be enriched; however, we had to do something above and beyond to make it happen. Just being a student there and taking the required courses would not necessarily provide us with these gifts. So, unless we came to Trinity with some spiritual practices, we might not find them there. Shirley and I and some other students did come with some rituals already in place, but most did not. Because of the work load and time restraints it was very difficult to begin anything new there. Basically, we were told that just because a person went to a seminary did not mean that they were on a spiritual journey and had a spiritual core about them. If I had not gone to Trinity, I may have not been aware of that aspect about some church leaders.

I have used that point in my ministry by understanding that my calling is to work with individuals and groups on their spiritual pilgrimage to assist them in starting or enhancing the spiritual practices of prayer, Bible study, and reflection. People in congregations who want to begin these habits often look to their pastors or their church leadership for help, or as examples when starting on this path. However, if pastors and the church leadership are not actually engaged in these rituals, it is difficult for them to be good role models for their members. One would be very surprised about the number of church leaders who do not have any regular prayer, Bible study, and reflection habits. Thus, my ministry was developed to aid church leadership, individuals, and congregations in their spiritual pilgrimage by assisting them in starting or enhancing their spiritual routines.

It has often been noted by spiritual writers and me that being on this spiritual pilgrimage will possibly change you and take you to new and often different places that you did not know anything about. Going to Trinity was a new adventure, of course, but it also significantly transformed me. The first quarter there drastically altered me in a lot of different ways, and it also caused me plenty of pain and anguish. One of my initial classes was on the Old Testament, taught by a first time professor at Trinity, who was very demanding and, in my mind, not very flexible or caring. Besides the very heavy work load for that class and the other three classes that I took, that OT class shook the very foundation of my faith and my knowledge of the Bible.

I had always thought I knew the Bible fairly well and was firm in my faith beliefs. However, I was devastated to my very core by what I learned. Things I thought were true literally about the Bible and my faith were not necessarily true, or only half correct. I actually got a little down and depressed because of all that I had to reconsider about my faith and my Bible knowledge. The entire seminary experience changed me and caused to rethink a lot of things; however, that first quarter was off the charts in that respect.

It is a good thing that it was very certain that God wanted me there, for I am surprised that I did not leave. However, I had been through a lot in my life and generally do not give up very easily; but that period transformed me and challenged me greatly. Thank goodness, my classmates helped me make it through that, and was I able to continue and finish my degree. Some of them were also having concerns and doubts, and we would cry on each other's shoulders. But it was still a challenge and it was something that I hope I never have to go through again. I might add here again that just because God leads us to something new and different does not mean it will be a bed of roses. There may be some pain and discomfort along the way. In this case there was plenty of agony and anxiety for me.

Another stressful class that first quarter was "Person in Ministry." Today I cannot completely tell you what it was all about; however, it did a couple things for me. First of all, we did a lot of writing and reflecting about our personal and family history. Thus, I wrote plenty about Judy and her life and death and how she affected me. I can remember sitting there crying and typing at the same thing, as I wrote and reflected on my life. This was both good and sad for me. It gave me time to work through some of my feelings about all that I had been through with her. It was also difficult, because I missed her and was still grieving her death. That class and the writing and reading done for it ended up being very good therapy for me.

One of the other aspects about that class was that it made you examine your family tree and its history. We needed to recognize that there are no perfect families or individuals, that all of us have some faults, hangups, or shortcomings, in ourselves and/or in our family. If we were going to be doing ministry work of some type, it was important for all of us to not think that we were holier than others, just because we went to the seminary. Thus, we had to confront our negative past, so to speak. Therefore, I had to acknowledge my faults, and those of Elizabeth and others in my family. Again, this was very good for me to reflect and ponder about how I got to where I was at that point. This class and the OT class and many of the others taken had a huge influence on me.

Yes, that first quarter at Trinity was very stressful, and of course there were parts of the entire two years that had its moments. But isn't that part of being on the spiritual pilgrimage and our life journey, times of the good and the not so good? I did have phases that were enjoyable and less traumatic. After getting into a flow of reading countless books and writing numerous papers, I mostly did okay as long as I stayed on top of the work load. Skills learned in my former career and in the mill came in handy during that time. Time management, doing the vital things first, not sweating the small stuff, and trying not to let problems get me down were abilities and traits that were used daily in this specific journey.

One of the neat events that went on weekly back then was the Wednesday worship service. During the school year this was a full Lutheran service with the Eucharist. This Wednesday service was normally attended by the vast majority of the faculty, staff, and students, and anyone else that was around. It was also a training ground for those who were being educated as pastors, musicians, worship leaders, etc. Thus, we got to see a number of different people preaching, leading worship, and singing. I enjoyed being part of those services and tried to go whenever possible.

## SHIRLEY ROSS

Shirley and I started at Trinity as full-time students during the fall of 2000, and that was a wonderful gift from God to both of us. We had never met before coming to Trinity. She had lived most of her adult life in Michigan, and I had moved around the country, but kept coming back to central Ohio. She lost her late husband, Bob, in an accident in 1991, and Judy passed away in early 1999. We were both blessed to have had very caring and loving spouses, who no doubt we would both still be married to if they had not passed away. We also had two adult children, a son and daughter each, who were near the same ages. She was coming to Trinity to be a pastor, something that she knew she had been called to do for many years. However, in her mind the time was right for her to formally answer that call when she did. I came to Trinity not knowing why, only that I knew I was supposed to come.

We likewise had been on our own faith journeys and tried to allow the Holy Spirit to direct our daily steps. Our spiritual travels had some similar traits, but, of course, they were individually structured, based on our own personality and path. We had additionally been active members of various faith communities that we had belonged to over the years. Over time, we discovered that we had other things in common, such as our political views, and how God's love and compassion were for *all* people, and not just a select few. Subsequently, we discovered that we loved and were both huge Notre Dame football fans. All of these aspects are sort of amazing in a way, for we had a number of things in common, besides losing our spouses.

During the first quarter at Trinity, Shirley and I were in three of the same classes together (out of four). We got to know each other as we both struggled with the class work and the new routine that was required of us. It is hard to explain how demanding the first months there were. We were both hard workers and had done other things in life that had prepared us for handling the work there. However, it was still overwhelming and took a lot of effort, patience, and energy to make it. Thus, we needed the support and empathy of other classmates to make it. Shirley and I also settled into one or two study groups together and got to know each other that way as well.

As mentioned, we were told that if a person did not have established spiritual practices before coming to Trinity, they should not expect to start them while there. That statement was mostly true. However, after that first fall quarter ended, a wide range of classes were offered where one could earn several credits during the three-week December period. Some of the offerings were off campus and involved some traveling and additional expenses. One of the classes offered was a three-day "Spirituality and Prayer Retreat" in Columbus at a retreat center. That course did offer some assistance regarding one's spiritual pilgrimage.

I signed up for it and was pleasantly surprised about how much I received from being a part of it. We were asked to get a number of books for the short course. Two authors I had never read before, but since that time have become a wonderful part of my spiritual pilgrimage, were Dietrich Bonhoeffer and Thomas Merton. Both authors have been a wonderful source of spiritual direction and support to me, as they have been to countless others. Also, we were asked to purchase the *Book of Common Worship: Daily Prayer* published by Westminster/John Knox Press. I call it the Red Book, and it has been used regularly by me since then. It is a fantastic resource and marvelous tool, which has been an aid in my spiritual growth. We were also asked to purchase a journal and try to journal while there. I did so and continue to practice journaling to this very day. In my case being at Trinity did aid in my spiritual pilgrimage. The class was very beneficial for me and also helped me to know Shirley a bit better because of it. So, I was extremely thankful to attend it.

Shirley had thought about taking part in some of the other offerings that December. Later on, she told me that she waited too late to make her decision and supposedly this course had filled up and they were not taking any more students. Well, in any case she applied after the deadline and somehow, someway, her name got on the class list. Thus, it was a miracle that she got in and we were there together with about twenty-five other students. However, like us starting Trinity at the same time, we both needed to be at there, to continue on the path that God had intended for us to be on. From our viewpoint, that is what occurred and why it ended up in the manner that it did.

We were asked to reflect on the worship services that we were doing out of the Red Book, and on the many authors that we were asked to read. We were encouraged to jot down in our journals anything that the Holy Spirit had given to us. Of course, we were able to meditate on whatever else that we might like to. Thus, during the first part of the retreat my focus was on wanting a companion who could share aspects of my life with. I still very much missed being married and deep down knew that it was very difficult for me to be alone. Even though having lots of family and friends who loved, prayed for, and supported me, I longed for the intimacy, closeness, and affection that I had before. However, I did not come to Trinity looking for another close relationship, but came because it was clear to me that was what I was supposed to do. However, on that retreat it was what I took time to ponder and pray over.

Toward the end of the retreat and after much contemplation about this, it came to me that it was better for me to not try to focus on this in particular. Instead, I would attempt to just trust God about what was upcoming. I wrote in my journal on the last day of the retreat that I would not do anything to find a companion, but would just leave it up to God. I had not done anything up to that point and felt that it was best to leave it that way, even though I really wanted companionship. However, I decided to not do anything proactively unless God led someone else to take the first step. Thus, I was going to let go and let God handle it, when it came to seeking someone to share my life and walk along on this journey with me. That was very difficult to do, to let go and, on faith, continue to put my future into God's hands rather than my own.

It is sometimes very amazing how seemingly small things that occur can turn into something more significant as matters evolve. During this time, we had some discussion about the psalms of lament as prayers for help. There was some debate about how anyone could ever feel as forsaken as was described in a number of these psalms. I noted that I felt that way and had undergone similar thoughts because of the loss of my wife. I also commented that maybe those who were unable to connect with those writings had never lost anyone close to them. Later on, Shirley told me that my comments around that topic really touched her, and she could understand where I was coming from.

An additional small incident that made an impression on Shirley happened on the last full day of the class when a group of us went out to dinner together. Shirley was near me at the dinner table, but I was directly across from another person. That other person kept talking and talking about themself and about their successful prior life for most of the entire evening. Shirley again related to me at some point that she was impressed with how much patience I had showed while listening to the other person who kept going on and on. Apparently, with these two small occurrences, she began to see me in a totally different light than just another classmate.

This new and evolving view that Shirley had about me continued to expand even more during the following day. That next day we gathered together as a class to do a short debriefing about the retreat. After that meeting, a group of us were standing around and Shirley was looking for someone to hang out with for a few hours. She was going back to Michigan to spend the Christmas holiday and also work for a few weeks. On her way back, she was going to visit her former pastor in Ann Arbor; however she had to wait a few hours before she left and was looking for someone to hang out with. She asked me and I was available and said yes. We went to a nearby Starbucks for coffee and talked until she had to leave. One of humorous things about that is that I do not drink coffee, but went anyway.

We ended up conversing for a couple of hours about our lives, our marriages, our spouses' deaths, and how we got to Trinity. Later on, she told me that during that discussion, *something like scales fell from her eyes*, and that she saw me in a totally different light. What got to her apparently was how I related about how my relationship was with Judy, and that I really loved her and how much Judy had meant to me. Shirley said that she had never heard any male talk like that before, and it really moved her.

When Shirley came back to Trinity after the Christmas break, we started seeing one another as more than just classmates. In time we fell in love, became engaged, and eventually got married. Because of starting Trinity at the same time, being in classes together, going to this same retreat, and then finding the time to share each other's life experiences, we were blessed to be given a second opportunity to once again be part of a loving relationship—that is more than either one of us could have ever imaged.

After the Christmas holiday Trinity's winter quarter started; our class work continued to have its stressful moments, but nothing was as challenging as that first quarter. For the remaining time at Trinity, I continued to learn and grow as an individual and in my spiritual pilgrimage. Writing all of those papers and reading countless books impacted and stretched me. Besides my class work, Elizabeth had gotten out of jail that previous September, and started to try to once again lead a "normal life," and I endeavored to help her do so. That could be both rewarding and frustrating at the same time. Besides these other things, I also started spending time with and "seeing" Shirley whenever we could. Because of our age and we both had lost spouses, we did not think of ourselves as young people and "dating." We thought that because of our situations, we were at a unique stage in our lives and saw things from a different viewpoint than many others would.

We tried to spend time with one another without our classmates knowing about it. This ended up being a really big deal. Trinity seemed to us to be a community where too many people got overly involved in each other's lives. A person could not do much around there without people finding out about it, and then having that information freely shared. Of course, as the news moved along the true facts often became distorted. Thus, we kept our relationship from the Trinity community until we were ready to share it. We did not want those around us to start talking about us, and then trying to put the cart before the horse and attempt to get us to move along faster than we wanted to. We knew that it was important for us to take things one day at a time and trust the future to God.

Over time we did tell our immediate family, and we also took into our confidence one person on campus, Diane Bareis (now Pastor Diane Greble). Diane started at Trinity when we did, was in the initial three of four classes that we were in together, and was a part of the study groups that we were in. We felt that we could trust her. Diane ended up being a wonderful support for both of us. We were blessed to have her walk along with us on that early journey, and still feel very fortunate to have her as a trusted friend.

Thus, until we were ready to tell everyone on campus about us, no one else knew about our relationship, and looking back that was the best decision for us at that time. Doing that allowed us to continue our class work, and see each other, without the gossip mill there causing us any stress. We enjoyed a number of the same things and seemed for the most part to like each other's company. We also began praying with each other over the phone at night after we shared our day with each other. That is a practice we continue today, praying together in the morning before starting our day. Thus, besides growing together in our personal relationship, we also shared some common spiritual practices. We announced our relationship after we were engaged in September of 2001 and people were amazed that we were a couple. A number of people were disappointed that they had not figured it out, and wondered how they had missed it!

The summer of 2001 Shirley returned to Michigan to fulfill her CPE requirement, which took most of that summer. CPE (Clinical Pastoral Education) is set up to give future pastors the experience of handling crisis situations that they might someday encounter in their congregations. She worked in a hospital as an intern chaplain and experienced a wide range of human emotions and struggles. This included the deaths of a number of people, including the passing of some very young children, which was extremely hard for her to deal with.

Meanwhile, that summer I had an extended period of contemplation time, plus taking summer classes. At that point, I still did not fully know why I was called to go to Trinity, from a ministry standpoint. There was a lot of uncertainty about what was going to happen when I graduated in the spring of 2002. However, one big reason was to be there when Shirley arrived so that we would be there together, and in time get to know each other. So that summer, I did a lot of praying for discernment and reflecting. I can remember spending a lot of time on the swing on my back patio, just thinking and pondering where I was and what was to come next. I asked Shirley for some help concerning a good book to read during that time and she suggested two books: *Seeds of Hope*, a compilation of Henri Nouwen writings, and *Prayer—Finding the Heart's True Home*, by Richard Foster. I used those two books throughout the summer and continued journaling, which I had begun during Trinity's winter retreat. I meditated and thought a lot and just sort of waited until an answer came.

After a while, it slowly came to me that whatever I was going to do and what was needed down the road was already in me. I did not have to reinvent or greatly change who I had become at that point. The funny thing about that summer reflection was that I still did not exactly know what I was to be doing in the future, but came to realize that I had or would be given what was needed for the path ahead. I just had to trust the good Lord about the future and continue in the direction that I was currently going, and things would be revealed in God's timing. However, that time was beneficial for me, because it gave me the encouragement and drive to finish my course work.

## OUR SECOND WEDDINGS

Additionally, that summer I reflected on my relationship with Shirley, which was continuing to grow. We spent time together whenever we could and grew as couple as we shared our histories and issues that we went through before we met. We both kept up with our class work and seminary duties, while at the same time beginning to think more about our future. We both had great first marriages, had lost our spouses at a fairly young age, and knew that Judy and Bob would always be a part of our spirit and soul, no matter what we did. We knew that we would never try to replace them, but could use their love for us as a means to enter into another loving marriage.

Thus, at some point that summer we started to talk about getting married and how that could impact our mutual ministries and individual lives. It was definitely a walk of faith to go down that path, because of our age and knowing that we both had gotten set in some of our ways. We knew that when we got married the first time, we were both much younger and less rigid in our habits, and more flexible about putting two lives together. Therefore, at some level we realized that this time it could be more challenging adjusting to married life.

Obviously, we did not know how tough it would be; however, we felt that with God in our marriage somehow things would work out. Therefore, after many discussions and prayers, we continued our thinking about getting married. From where we were at that time in our lives and because of what we had been through, deciding on that path was definitely a leap of faith. Looking back, we are glad that choice was made, but of course we had our ups and downs along the way. However, thankfully we continue to be a couple, walking this journey together and, we celebrated our twentieth anniversary in 2022!

The way I proposed was somewhat unique. It was done on her birthday, September 29, 2001. For the week leading up to that day, I mailed her several cards and notes. Each had another word of this sentence: "Shirley will you marry me?" The first time we were together for an evening of "seeing each other," after our December Starbucks conversation, was in January. We got together to watch a Notre Dame football bowl game. So, on her birthday eight months later I picked up the same food that we had eaten during that bowl game. After that meal I drove us to Trinity's parking lot and for a moment waited and asked her if she still wanted to continue with our relationship. Good thing she said *yes*! I then drove her to the same Starbucks where we had spent several hours talking back in December of 2000, when she asked me to have coffee with her, before she drove back to Michigan for the Christmas holiday.

Earlier I had gone to Starbucks and put flowers and a folder on the same table that we had sat at that previous December. She was surprised to see them there. The Starbucks staff had worked with me to pull this off. In the folder was an outline of all of the major events that had taken place since we had gotten together as a couple. We went over all of the events again; it was neat to review how far we had come in eight or nine months. At the bottom of this listing, I had typed "Shirley will you . . ." On the next page I wrote, "Shirley will you marry me?" Thankfully she said yes, and I gave her a ring. I am glad that I put that much effort into doing it this way; it made everything very special for us.

That fall and winter of 2001, in addition to our seminary work, our daily life routines, and my dealing with Elizabeth and her family, we began to work out the plans for our wedding. Also, at that point we announced our engagement to the Trinity community. We had some definite ideas about how we wanted things to flow on that day. We wanted it to be a worship service first and a wedding second. Additionally, we wanted to invite as many of our family and friends as possible within our budget. So many people had been through the pain with us of losing our late spouses and had been with us during the many ups and downs of our lives. Therefore, we wanted them to also share in the celebration of us coming together as a newly married couple. Early on we asked them to save the July 13, 2002, date, after we had determined that was the best time for us to get married.

When we had time, we also tried to meet each other's family members and close friends, so that they could get to know Shirley or me. For the most part that went along great, except for a very few who had a hard time with our being together. I might add that our own children were very supportive and were on board right away. We will always be very grateful for how open and willing they were to accept us. With that being said, as our wedding date came closer, Elizabeth found herself in trouble with the law again. Thus, she was not able to take part in the wedding. We were moving ahead with our plans, and the vast majority of our friends and family were delighted to join us in this new journey. We were and are very fortunate and blessed to have such a wonderful, supportive community.

My last year at Trinity was full of the many ups and downs that life has to offer for all of us at times. I was learning about doing ministry in my courses, enjoying the new life I had been given in my relationship with Shirley, while at the same time dealing with Elizabeth and her issues. However, thankfully I was able to finish my work toward a degree and received my Masters of Theological Studies Degree from Trinity Lutheran Seminary on June 8, 2002. It had been a very trying but rewarding experience for me. I had the support and prayers of many people, including the couple who paid my two years tuition and fees, my pastor and congregation, family, friends, and, of course, Shirley.

I went to Trinity not fully knowing why, and never got a call from God to become a pastor, nor has that call come even now. But it was very clear that I was meant to go. I was glad about going when I went; however, it was not something that I would have decided to do on my own. It was a totally Spirit-led decision. It was not a very practicable choice to make for anyone; however, walking on this spiritual pilgrimage often takes us to places that go against one's logic and common sense.

Shirley and I were married on July 13, 2002, at Trinity Lutheran Seminary in Columbus, Ohio. We had met at Trinity and wanted to get married there, rather than in either of our home parishes. We did a lot of planning for the wedding and, since we had been involved in worship at Trinity and many other places, we tried to personalize parts of it. We used the "Now is the Feast" liturgy and wrote all of the prayers ourselves. We were very blessed to have each of our Lutheran pastors participate in the service, for both had been important people in helping to get us to where we were at that point.

Pastor Lori Carey, from Michigan, who was Shirley's former home pastor and had encouraged Shirley to go to the seminary, delivered the sermon during the service. Pastor Dave Shugert, from Epiphany, who had preached at Judy's funeral and who had also helped get me to Trinity, did the pre-marital counseling and performed the wedding vows during the service. During his counseling, he had us write a marriage statement that we had to work on together, and that along with the wedding vows we wrote were read at the wedding.

At the beginning of the service, Pastor Dave gave some opening announcements and read the message that Shirley and I had written. We wanted to set the tone for the service and wanted everyone to know that we were glad that they could join us.

> All of you are very important to Shirley and Vernon and are part of who they are today. You, plus many other people who are not here, have helped, supported, prayed for, and loved them over the years. They are also who they are today because of their marriages with Bob and Judy. They are and will always be a part of them. Shirley and Vernon recognize that they have been blessed by God's love through all of you.

Because we had friends and family from both sides, many people did not know each other. We had students and staff from Trinity, former work colleagues, and those of many different faith traditions; and we wanted everyone to feel comfortable in being there. From the comments afterwards, apparently this was achieved by the above statement, the worship service, and the reception afterwards. Those who were there felt loved and very welcomed. One person noted that he had never felt so much love in one place, like he felt at our wedding. We were blessed to be surrounded by so many people who had loved us over the years and loved us and prayed for us on that day.

We were also fortunate to have some friends assemble a worship bulletin for us. Since we had people from such diverse worship styles it was helpful to have most of the service printed in the bulletin. We also included our statement of marriage in it.

> Our marriage, a gift from God, will be a sacred lifelong commitment. This unique relationship will be new each day and will provide a sanctuary for us. Our response to this gift will be to communicate with and cherish each other, and to daily act as channels of Christ's love . . . Shirley and Vernon

This statement was one that we worked on jointly and it meant a lot to us back then and continues to be meaningful to us even today. We are so grateful to Pastor Dave for making us write it. The day before our wedding we had a rehearsal and dinner, and Pastor Lori, who would be preaching, asked us questions about how we ended up at Trinity together. During her sermon she included things she had discovered and outlined how everything had worked out for us from starting at the same time to ending up being married on that day.

The couple who had provided the funds for me to attend Trinity had never heard all of those details before. At the reception the wife of the couple expressed how excited she was to hear how things had worked out. She and her husband had both lost spouses and had remarried and were so happy in their second marriage. She was overjoyed that we also had found each other, and that they had had a hand in making that happen. If Pastor Lori had not included those details in her sermon, it is doubtful if that information would ever have been completely known by everyone. She did a wonderful sermon, which was enjoyed by many. We were so blessed to have both Pastors Dave and Lori take part in the entire event. Like many others there that day, they had been a part of our life stories, and now joined with us to celebrate the new adventure that we were starting together.

As you may remember, when we had Judy's funeral Mass, I was concerned that some people might not know that communion there was only for people of the Catholic faith. I had that information printed in the funeral bulletin so that no one would be hurt. Again, I had that same concern that there would be people who may not have felt comfortable taking communion at our wedding service, because of their faith tradition. In the bulletin we noted that all were welcome to participate in taking communion. However, we also mentioned that those not choosing to commune were invited to come forward for an "Exchange of God's Peace" with Shirley and Vernon. We were the ones distributing the communion, instead of the pastors, and we had our children Amy and Kevin helping us out.

We did not know when we planned everything how it would turn out. However, by doing it this way, the entire communion process turned out to be one really big love feast. Many people who did not take communion came up anyway and just wanted to share a greeting and give us a hug. Because Shirley and I had the communion elements in our hands, we had to give them to Amy and Kevin to hold while we hugged everyone. As more people came up for mainly a hug, it spread to nearly everyone. Thus, some of those who did take communion also wanted a hug, which caused us to have to pass the elements between us more frequently. It was a really loving and Spirit-filled, but a rather lengthy, experience for all.

However, I might add that it was a really big challenge for the two people who were providing the music for us. We only had two songs picked out as the communion hymns. But, as this process went on and on, Terry McCandless and Tim Storca, who provided our music, kept playing and playing and improvised what they were doing. They were wonderful about it and kept playing anyway, so there was some music in the background for this long love celebration. After it was all over, we got very positive feedback from people about this; however, we felt terrible for Terry and Tim, for they had no clue, nor did we, how this would turn out. Expressions of love do not always operate in the fashion and manner that we expect. In this case Shirley and I were definitely blown away by the love shown to us and those in attendance over the entire day, and especially during the communion part of the worship service.

We had a lot of love shown to us as well during the reception, which everyone seemed to enjoy. Shirley and I had a great time walking around and greeting everyone and letting them know how much we appreciated them coming and sharing the experience. One of the really neat things about this, as noted before, was that we had a wonderful cross-section of people of different faith traditions and backgrounds who came. Later on, we heard some great comments from two of my aunts regarding this.

My mother had already died, but two of her sisters attended, along with a number of other people from my extended family. My aunts, Ruby and Julia, told me about how graciously people had interacted with them. Apparently, once people found out that they were my aunts, our friends went overboard in making them feel loved. They were so pleased about the way they had been treated there. I might add that, because they were women of color and of a certain age, in other places where there were people of different races and backgrounds together, that may not have always been the way they would have been treated. My aunts' acceptance is a very small example of how God's love should be shared with all those we meet. I, of course, was too busy to notice this aspect at the reception, but they told me afterwards about how much love they felt from our friends. Shirley and I will always be so grateful for the love of our family and friends that made that day so special.

A few days after the wedding we went on a wedding trip to Maui for nine days. Neither of us had been there before, and it was a vacation of a lifetime! That was a wonderful time and we were able to get to know each other so much better while on it. We started this new adventure from the high of the wedding and the trip, but of course, we could never remain that high and had to come back down at some point, and we did. But the joyful period was glorious while it lasted, and we are so thankful for that time.

## A FAMILY SPLIT

Even with the joyful time we had planning our wedding, and taking part in the wedding itself, and my finishing the work for my degree, we continued to deal with Elizabeth and her issues. A lot of support had been given to her so that she could take care of her two children, stay out of trouble, and start a new life. However, our prayers and the help she received were not enough. She went back into jail in August of 2001, after being out less than a year. The two families that had kept Anna and Judah previously agreed to care for them again, another miracle in the life of the Jones family. Even though that assistance would not last forever, it was very welcomed at that time.

During this time, how I saw Elizabeth began to change. My hope and prayer had always been that she would turn around and be able to take of herself and her family and stay out of trouble. But she was not moving in the direction to make that happen. I did not even think of bailing her out this time, as I had done in the past. At first, I did drop off the clothes that she needed, and would give her spending money. However, I took a really major step in that I did not visit her as had been previously done. I also decided to *not* take Anna and Judah to visit her, unlike the last time when I took Anna almost every weekend to see her mother. I began to realize that Elizabeth was not going to turn around, even with all of the help given her; and I started to pull away from her.

That was a very painful decision to make, for a father to start removing himself from his daughter; but that was what I was being led to do. Believe me, this position was taken after a lot of prayer, thought, and reflection. I was going through a lot of emotions at that time, with the love of Shirley and the new life we were planning together, my seminary class work, the spiritual journey that I was on, plus not fully knowing what was to come next, along with the pain of dealing with Elizabeth. Additionally, the families who were taking care of Anna and Judah were letting me know that they could not continue to do that forever, for it was taking way too long for things to improve in Elizabeth's life. Thankfully, I made it through that period, but not without some very difficult choices that had to be made.

During these very challenging periods, I began to realize that unless she drastically changed, Elizabeth did not have the capability to raise her children. She was not able to handle her issues that kept getting her in trouble with the law, for it appeared that she was not making any progress in dealing with her money addiction. Thus, she could not be a responsible mother to her children, if she was always running from the law or in jail. Slowly, and maybe too slowly, I realized that something had to be done, and I was the only one who could do anything. Basically, I was being guided to split up my family in order to try and help my grandchildren. My relationship with Elizabeth was never the same after that time. I had to mourn that loss of my daughter even though she was still very much alive, a couple years after grieving the loss of my late wife. That is a situation that I would not wish on anyone. The bottom line was that I could not continue to try to support Elizabeth while at the same time attempting to do what I was being led to do, to help Anna and Judah so that they could be given the opportunity for a better life.

## ANNA AND JUDAH

On our life journey, we are often asked to take a path that is hard to follow, which more than likely will have an unknown ending. That is how it was with what we were being guided to do for my grandchildren. When we started this process, there was no way we knew how things would turn out. However, I had been very hurt by what Elizabeth had done to my family and me over the years. There were many others who had been hurt by her from a financial standpoint, including members of our extended family. I was also in pain by having to watch what Anna and Judah had been through because of Elizabeth's actions, and at a very young age. I felt especially sad about all of the many changes and adjustments that they endured, and in my mind it was not fair to put anyone through that. It would take me a long time to start feeling better about all of this. However, those emotions guided me to take legal action against Elizabeth.

We contacted an attorney and began the very long and expensive procedure of removing Anna and Judah from Elizabeth's custody. Think of that for a moment: I was going to take my daughter, who I loved, to court and have her parental rights removed. I would be saying that she was not a fit mother unless she drastically turned her life around. I had felt that many of us had given her enough chances to change; however, she had not. Now I was forced to do what was best long-term for my grandchildren. This process was very painful for me and those around me. I always felt that dealing with Judy's cancer issues and her death was the hardest thing that I had ever done. However, this entire ordeal was just as trying and emotionally draining as dealing with Jude's issues. Talk about going down a path where you could not see the ending; that was certainly the case in this situation! This required a lot of prayers and walking by faith for Shirley and me, who was also very involved in this entire journey.

In December of 2002, five short months after Shirley and I were married, and after many meetings, court dates, letters, and legal expenses, we were able to rescind Elizabeth's parental rights, in the hope that Anna and Judah might have a better life. However, things do not always work out as hoped for. In my heart, I feel that their lives ended up being healthier in the long run than if they would have stayed with Elizabeth. But there were many road bumps ahead that they had to endure over the course of their growing-up years.

Unfortunately, several couples who had initially offered help in raising Anna and Judah over time all fell short in coming to their aid and becoming a long-term solution. Thus, Anna and Judah's story had a few highs and far too many low points in the years to come. They continued to be a part of our lives and my spiritual pilgrimage, and caused me to endure things that I would not wish on anyone. But these moments are part of who I am now, and part of who they are as individuals. There are many details that could be shared with you about this period relating to Anna and Judah and other persons who were in and out of their lives. However, noting these many particulars could cause pain to some, and the story maybe best told by Anna and Judah. At some point they may want to share their lives with others, after they have had time to reflect back on their past. Also, in another setting and time I may be more willing to share what I experienced firsthand during this time. However, at this point, I want to move on to other areas relating to my life journey.

TWELVE

# The Beginning of Our Mutual Ministries

> And Jesus came and said to them, "All authority in heaven and on earth has been given to me. Go therefore and make disciples of all nations, baptizing them in the name of the Father and of the Son and of the Holy Spirit, and teaching them to obey everything that I have commanded you. And remember I am with you always, to the end of the age."
>
> —MATT 28:18–20

## SHIRLEY'S INTERNSHIP

IN THIS PASSAGE FROM Matthew Jesus is giving what seems to be the last set of instructions for his inner circle of supporters. They were to go out and make disciples of all nations, to baptize, and to teach, and Jesus assured them he would be with them forever as this mission was carried out. As you know, most of Jesus' supporters could not handle his death and left him. Only a few close followers, mainly women, stayed near him while he hung on the cross. Thus, to carry out this new command given after Christ's resurrection, it would take courage and faith that most had not shown during the time of his crucifixion. Therefore, Jesus had to reassure them that he would be with them in this commission.

Probably most of us today are no different than the majority of Jesus' followers; we all doubt and have our fears, no matter how faithful we strive to be. Shirley and I have always tried to believe that, on our spiritual journey, God, through the Holy Spirit, would be with us and comfort us when we tried to listen to the Spirit's voice. But we like others are also impacted by the same emotions and shortcomings that we all have. It is a daily challenge to turn toward God's kingdom and strive for that kingdom on a regular basis.

Shirley and I were called to ministries that were different but compatible. As an ordained Lutheran (ELCA) pastor her role became more of baptizing and making disciples and mine was more of a teaching/supportive process. Over the years I have come to refer to what we have been called to do as our *mutual ministries.* While Shirley was working on her requirements to become an ordained Lutheran pastor, she had to fulfill a year serving as an intern in a congregation, which was to begin in the fall of 2002. Internship is meant to give a seminary student hands-on experience in dealing with the daily duties of a parish pastor. Today, in some Lutheran seminaries, that format has changed, but back then internship was compulsory.

The spring of 2002 was a bit stressful on all of us, I was trying to finish up my course work in order to earn my Masters of Theological Studies Degree (MTS); we were planning our wedding in July; we were also dealing with Anna and Judah and their situation. Besides all of that Shirley was awaiting a place to do her internship. Often in obtaining an internship site, the seminary student was required to move to another location, even in another state. If that happened to Shirley, it would have created a lot of additional strain for us because of Anna and Judah. However, Shirley asked to be restricted to the central Ohio area, even though she was not sure the request would be granted. She had heard stories about how the student had very little influence in choosing the location of the year-long internship. But thankfully, she was restricted to the central Ohio area; thus we did not have to move and could continue to deal with Anna and Judah and their challenges. We still had lots of things to work through, but I will always be grateful that we did not have to move for that year.

Shirley was able to fulfill her internship requirement by serving Saint Jacobs Lutheran Church, a small congregation in Tarlton, Ohio. It was about forty-five minutes south of us, a bit of a drive, but we did not have to move for that year. Shirley got to preach every Sunday, and was able to learn a lot about parish ministry. Her internship supervisor was the pastor of a Lutheran church in Circleville, Ohio, where she attended weekly staff meetings and met with this supervisor. She functioned as a pastor to the Saint Jacobs community. I attended all of the worship services and activities that she led while there and became involved with that community. I got to know the people there and they welcomed both of us very warmly. I think it was a good experience for both of us. The area had been a farming community at one time, but had changed over the years. The church and the entire area had struggled as people left the region to find jobs. They could not afford a full-time pastor, but were open to trying new things, and Shirley enjoyed her time there.

Even with all of our challenges before and during Shirley's internship year, it was overall a time of spiritual growth for everyone, us individually, and with our mutual ministries, and for the people of Saint Jacobs. Because the Saint Jacobs congregation was open to new ideas, Shirley was able to do things there that had not been done before. The one major event was having a special community Thanksgiving service the Tuesday before Thanksgiving during her year of internship. Saint Jacobs invited people from the surrounding area, and even from the much larger Lutheran church where her internship supervisor was. She and the members had no clue how many and who would show up. It was a risk on their part, but they were willing to step out in faith to do the worship service.

We became somewhat disheartened on that Tuesday for there was a fairly major snowstorm, which was very unusual for that part of the country and for that time of the year. Traveling in that area meant driving on two lane roads that could be quite hilly in certain spots. Thus, just getting to the service was a pain on that evening. The church made about seventy-five bulletins and amazingly we counted about seventy-five who came. Most of the people who arrived were not from Saint Jacobs but from the wider area, including a number from Shirley's supervisor's church.

That was a miracle, that so many came out to a small country church in the middle of a snowstorm. Apparently, there was a need in that neighborhood to have a Thanksgiving service, where people from different faith traditions could worship and give thanks together. However, no one knew for sure how many would show up beforehand. Remarkably, Saint Jacobs continued hosting a community Thanksgiving service with the interns that followed Shirley, until they had to close, a number of years later. We never know what lasting legacy we leave behind when we follow the guidance of the Holy Spirit on our spiritual journey. We felt very blessed to have been a part of that worshiping body during that time.

## VERNON'S WITNESS MINISTRY

After finishing with my course work at Trinity and earning my MTS degree, I did a lot reflecting and praying as to how best to use my education and to determine where God wanted me to go next. As has been noted, I went to the seminary not fully knowing why, only that it was very clear that that was what I was meant to do. Of course, I met Shirley Ross and we eventually got married, and that was one big reason for going there. Also, I grew in the certainty that I was not called to become an ordained pastor. I was faced with the question, now that I was finished with the seminary, "What next?" One thing for sure, I wanted to support Shirley's ministry, and thus became involved in her internship site.

Besides supporting Shirley, I was led to develop a program that I titled my "Witness Ministry." I wrote materials that outlined my own personal life story, and included aspects of my spiritual journey and background information that had been learned during my seminary training. I tried to base it on scripture that related to my own spiritual walk. I wrote and created a small booklet that outlined my program. Over time copies were printed, using a logo and faith statement. I also created up business cards, stationary, envelopes, and a flyer that explained this ministry. I used these materials to try and get the word out about this ministry, with hope that there would be groups willing to use my services and allow me to do presentations to their congregations. That is what I thought I was called to do at that point.

I wrote to local Lutheran churches and explained my background and what I had to offer. I wrote the ELCA Southern Ohio Synod about my Witness Ministry. I even wrote the central Ohio Catholic headquarters and had an appointment with someone from their office. Pastor Dave from Epiphany helped me out by calling Lutheran pastors in central Ohio, and that led to a number of interviews with those pastors. During this time, I also got on the Synod supply preaching list, and was able to supply preach for a few churches.

From all of that effort, I did not as get many speaking engagements concerning the Witness Ministry program as I had hoped. Shirley, however, was able to arrange for me to do a couple workshops at Saint Jacobs. I was somewhat disappointed that more activities did not come out of all of the effort I had been put into this program and the materials that I spent hours writing, developing, and printing. However, I did not know how they would be used later on. For all of these materials would be the basis of the next program that would be developed into more presentation materials and eventually into published books. Yes, this spiritual pilgrimage is normally not a straight line, with easy-to-read road signs. In my case here, these initial Witness Ministry materials were not used as I had envisioned, but they were what was needed to get me to the next step in my ministry.

## SHIRLEY'S LAST YEAR AT TRINITY

During Shirley's last year at Trinity after her internship year, we had a number of things that we had to handle. Becoming an ordained pastor in the Lutheran (ELCA) church requires that a number of processes have to be fulfilled. Shirley had to complete those requirements and finish her course work for her degree. We were in the second year of our marriage, and even though, overall, we were doing fine, we still had issues. Being married a second time at our age, after being in really good first marriages, and after being single for a while, presented challenges at times. I was still trying to get my Witness Ministry going and, on top of all this, we had another major crisis regarding Anna and Judah.

After Elizabeth's parental rights were terminated by the court we began working with an agency in the hope of Anna and Judah eventually being adopted into a loving, stable family. However, arrangements to that end that had been made suddenly fell apart. So, we got them back to care for them full time on March 1, 2004, the spring of Shirley's last year at Trinity. Thus, we had to deal with being full-time parents and grandparents to them. Needless to say, it was a very stressful time for all of us. Besides the daily care for them, we continued to work with the legal system in regard to their future. Looking back, I am glad we had the time with them, but at that point it was not always a blessing, because of everything else that was going on in our lives. That period certainly tried our faith, patience, and persistence, in order to be able to deal with all of it and not have a major meltdown. This issue put an additional strain on our marriage; however, we were able to come through it.

The Lutheran (ELCA) has a unique method by which its pastors become ordained. Any prospective pastor has to pass all of the required seminary courses as well as meet the candidacy committee for its approval. Following that their names are placed into an assignment process, whereby the national church assigns them to a region. A candidate cannot become ordained until they are actually called by an ELCA congregation, which can be a very lengthy and stressful period. This is mentioned because Shirley was assigned to the Southern Ohio Synod of the ELCA for her first call. However, the bishop of that synod at that time said that all first call pastors (which Shirley was) would be assigned to rural churches and, in Shirley's case, to Appalachia. That would have been a horrible situation for Shirley and me as an interracial couple. Additionally, being an interracial couple carried with it some challenges besides all of the other factors.

Thus, this situation caused both of us more worry, and Shirley was extremely anxious about how everything would work out. She was very concerned about the possible problems if she got a call to Appalachia. This, along with the other items, mainly the situation with Judah and Anna, stressed her to the limit. We also knew that at some point we would have to move; we just did not know when. Consequently, we began to get my house ready to sell, which included removing some wallpaper and doing other items around the place. What a time for us while all of this was going on!

We spent the spring and early summer of 2004, not knowing how any of these situations would turn out. Talk about walking in faith, taking it one day and step at a time, or doing what we thought we were supposed to do for the moment, and leaving the future in the good Lord's hands. Any way you want to phrase it, that was all we could do during that time. We just had to wait, pray, and hope about what was coming next and continue doing what we were led to do on a daily basis.

Sometimes on this spiritual journey things unfold that come totally out of the blue, when we had no clue that they could work out as they did. We believe that is what happened for Shirley during this call process, which definitely fits into this unbelievable category. Shirley was from the North/West Lower Michigan Synod (normally called the Mitten Synod), and she had hoped to return there if she could, but was assigned to the Southern Ohio Synod. Through a few conversions between the bishops of the Mitten Synod and the Indiana/Kentucky Synod, they arranged to help Shirley out. They got the Southern Ohio Synod to release her, which in our minds was a God-sent miracle; and she was then assigned to the Indiana/Kentucky Synod.

I will always remember that we were having Shirley's graduation party, on June 5, 2004, and I answered the phone, and it was the chairperson of the call committee from Saint Paul Lutheran Church in Louisville,

Kentucky. He wanted to set a date for an interview with her in Louisville. That phone call was *so* welcome for all of us, because we had renewed hope that all of our worry and concern would be relieved if things moved forward from that point. We will always be very grateful for those two bishops stepping forward to help Shirley get this call. After that phone call, we went down to Louisville in July for an interview, Shirley led worship and preached, and they then voted to call her as their pastor. *Wow*, sometimes things work out better than you could ever imagine, for that definitely was the case in this situation!

## SAINT PAUL LUTHERAN CHURCH
## LOUISVILLE, KENTUCKY

Needless to say, the remaining summer weeks were extremely busy. We had to get the house ready to sell, get prepared for the move, and manage the long-range care of Judah and Anna. When Judy was alive, we had lived in a number of different places, but neither Shirley nor I had lived in a Southern state before. I had visited Louisville on business previously, but had never spent much time there. It would be a new adventure for both of us, but we knew if that was where Shirley was being called as a pastor, then that was where we were meant to be. Because Shirley had a definite call, she was able to be ordained as a Lutheran pastor during the summer. That took place in her former home congregation, Prince of Peace Lutheran Church in Kalamazoo, Michigan, which had helped her while she was at the seminary. In late August of that year we moved to Louisville, to start the next new adventure on our life journey and spiritual pilgrimage. She started as pastor of Saint Paul Lutheran Church on September 1.

Even though Saint Paul was a small and struggling congregation, it was in a metro area and Louisville had many of the amenities of a larger city. There were a lot of wonderful things to do in that region. However, because Saint Paul had recently had some hard times and had been without a full-time pastor for four years, they noted that they only had enough money for two years. Thus, it was a leap of faith for Shirley to take that call. She ended staying for eight years, and we felt that a lot of good ministries were carried on during that time.

She was really looking forward to fulfilling God's call to be a pastor. This was something that she felt called to for most of her adult life but did not follow the call until much later. But she had many experiences prior to attending seminary working in various roles in the church and in the secular world, which gave her the great tools to function in her role as a parish pastor. Thus, all of the skills learned in her life roles, like being a wife, mother, Sunday school teacher; leading women's groups; serving on the church council and on the township boards; working in insurance; being a financial planner; etc., would be used in some form or the other by her moving forward in this new call.

I began in my role as the spouse of a pastor. It is a function that one cannot prepare for or read a book about; one just has to live it daily, and pray for the wisdom to not make too many mistakes. During this time, I was led to continue working toward getting Anna and Judah into a more stable, loving, and permanent family. There was a lot of stress around dealing with their future, but over time things settled down for a bit. But I hope and pray that we never have to go through that again.

## VERNON'S MINISTRY

After we settled into our lives in the Louisville area, I started taking steps to become more involved with my own ministry. Because I had a background in marketing during my time in the insurance industry, I initiated my own marketing campaign and started writing local churches and letting them know about the Witness Ministry. I also started attending various worship services at some of the local churches that I had written to in order to be visible. I would often follow up the marketing letter with a phone call. One of the few pastors who actually answered my phone call was a United Church of Christ pastor close to where we lived. That pastor was very open and welcoming, and over the course of the following few years I was able to supply preach for him, when he was away.

Since we were in a large metro area, there were many churches to contact. If Shirley had been sent to a rural Ohio community, my options for doing ministry would have been very few. In many ways, we were blessed to have landed in Louisville. In time I was able to get on the local Lutheran supply preaching list. I supply preached at Saint Mark Lutheran Church in September of 2005. A member of that congregation, who had been a member of Bethany Lutheran Church, told the council chairperson of Bethany that they ought to give me a call. Bethany could not afford a full-time pastor and was looking for someone to supply preach on a steady basis.

After some prayerful discussions together, I agreed to become their primary worship leader each week, with one Sunday off every month. Thus, with the approval of the Indiana/Kentucky Synod, I was able to lead worship there, even though I was not an ordained pastor. Because they were trying to discern their long-range future, I also acted as a spiritual consultant for them. They had lost members over the years and had not been able to grow and had some financial challenges. They wanted to prayerfully seek where God was leading them, and over time consider whether they should continue at all. From January 2006 until November 2007, I was their main worship leader and a spiritual consultant for them. In November of 2007, they got an intern to preach for them on a regular basis. After that person left, I came back and led worship for them once or twice a month until they closed.

The really neat part that I liked, while with them, was my role as a spiritual consultant and when I did a number of midweek sessions with them. In these discussions I helped them look at where they had been, where they felt they were at the present moment, and where they thought God was leading them in the future. In doing this I did a number of Bible studies related to this discernment process, and included a lot of input about my own spiritual pilgrimage, and how that background would be beneficial to what they wanted to learn. I tried to help them come up with some ideas to help in growing their ministry, while at the same time listening to the voice of the Holy Spirit, as to where they should go next. Overall, I became very involved in the activities at Bethany; I was even able to take part in a first communion service and lead an Easter service. Preaching most every Sunday gave me the chance to study and write sermons on a frequent basis, which was also helpful with my own spiritual growth.

I coordinated the working agreement between Bethany and myself with the dean of the Lutheran conference that Shirley and I were in. The dean was pastor of Christ Lutheran Church, in Jeffersontown, Kentucky, which was in the greater Louisville area. The conference dean initiated various activities between the Lutheran churches in the area and represented those churches to the Indiana/Kentucky Synod office. I also kept the Synod aware of what I was doing with Bethany. Regarding the old saying, "One thing leads to another," when Christ Lutheran Church was looking a staff person, that pastor came to me to help fill a specific role for them.

Consequently, I was able to have another part-time position, helping another congregation with their spiritual pilgrimage. From November of 2006 until February of 2009, I was their director of small group ministries, and also preached there once a month. The pastor had started small groups before, but was not able to keep them going due to his other duties. The hope was that if someone could deal with the small groups on a more consistent basis the groups would continue or at least be renewed as time went on. This congregation was much larger than Bethany Lutheran, and thus I was able to do more hands-on programs for them. That position ended when the church voted to call an associate pastor, who would oversee the small groups plus assist the lead pastor in other duties. However, my time at Christ Lutheran was enjoyable and very beneficial, for it allowed me to grow in my own ministry and develop programs that are still being used.

Always in my preaching and teaching, the concept of one's faith journey was focused on as well as how the Holy Spirit can help one with that walk. I wrote the materials for and taught several discipleship classes that raised the basic issues of being a disciple of Jesus Christ. I helped teach new member classes, where my focus was on the spiritual practices of Bible study and prayer, and also on the small group programs that Christ Lutheran was developing. I wrote a small group facilitator manual, which was used in my training of small group facilitators. Small groups were started and assistance was offered in finding discussion topics, and other support was given as needed. Additionally, I helped in coordinating the establishment of a men's fellowship group that met twice a month and was centered in faith conversations and service projects. As part of my role there I was able to act as a consultant who assisted the church staff in finding different methods to aid in the spiritual life and growth of the congregation.

My responsibilities at both Bethany and Christ further helped in my own spiritual growth through my preparation in preaching, teaching, and working with the small groups. Another revelation for me was seeing that even though people went to worship, and were involved in various activities within the church, they wanted to learn more about enhancing their own personal spiritual growth. They had a need that was not being fulfilled by simply showing up at church; they wanted to grow in their own personal faith, and I was able to assist them in a small way to help that happen. What I developed during that time was later incorporated into the program "Discipleship, A Spiritual Pilgrimage." Over time those systems and practices were used in the writing of my first book, *Discipleship—A Lifelong Spiritual Pilgrimage*. My time with both of these churches established the foundation of my ministry today.

THIRTEEN

# A Message

*Give ear, O my people, to my teaching;
incline your ears to the words of my mouth.*

—Ps 78:1

## BLENDED FAMILY VACATION

When Shirley and I were at the seminary and beginning to get serious in our relationship, we made a point of getting to know each other's families and close friends. One thing that we will always be grateful for is that our adult children were very open and loving to each of us after they got to know us. We can all think of situations where that is not the case. When one parent is deceased and the other parent meets someone new, there could be some concerns on the part of the children in accepting the new person. Of course, the parent who died can never be replaced, but often there can be resentment and/or an unwillingness to receive the new person. We never had those issues. We were also fortunate that the adult children also got along with each other, which was a double blessing!

All of our adult children, expect for Elizabeth who was not included in any of our plans, were extremely supportive of our wanting to become a couple. When we were married in 2002, they were all very much involved with us prior to the wedding, and then took part in the ceremony. As Shirley and I finished our seminary work and she then received her first call, and we moved to Louisville, we made a point of visiting our family and close friends whenever we had the time. However, our children were never all together again after our wedding. Once driving back to Louisville, after visiting Shirley's son, Matt, and his wife, Angie, in northern Michigan, I got the idea of trying to get our adult children and grandchildren together for a family vacation. Of course, Shirley thought it was a great idea, and we started planning to make that happen.

Getting very busy people to all show up at the same place at the same time certainly can be a challenge. Amazingly, they all thought the idea was great and plans were made. We got together from July 5–12, 2008, at a large house we rented close to the beach near Saugatuck, Michigan, which is a wonderful place to have a vacation. My son, Kevin, and his friend Ellen came from California; Shirley's daughter, Amy, and her husband, Kevin, came from Denver; Shirley's son, Matt, and his wife, Angie, came from northern Michigan; Shirley and I drove up from Louisville; and we had hoped Judah and Anna could come from Ohio, but more about them later. Nonetheless, bringing us all together took a lot of work, but it was mostly a great time and, ultimately, I was glad we could pull it off. (Elizabeth was not in the picture, for she was still dealing with legal issues, and I could not help her until she was willing to help herself. Having contact with her only drew us into her problems, and our family had bailed out her far too many times—more than I care to mention here.)

For me this vacation initially was a mixed blessing. On the one hand it was really wonderful to have everyone in one place. It continued to amaze me how well those who came got along; we seemed to enjoy being with each other. Everyone took part in all of our activities, including playing lots of games. Each couple took turns cooking and we have so many great cooks in our family! We had time alone and also did things as a group, like touring the Saugatuck area, which has a lot to offer, and everyone loved that community. We were also lucky to have some delightful weather while we there. The beach was about a five-minute walk, and all of us made use of being so close to the water. One of the more important aspects of this trip was that everyone got to know each other much better, which was why Shirley and I wanted to host this occasion for everyone.

However, with all that being said, there was another issue that I was dealing with. On the other side of the fun part, there was a very painful and stressful part of the week for me. By this time Judah and Anna had been legally adopted by a family who on the surface was just perfect for them. We had prayed and hoped that they would now receive the love and stable environment that would allow them to become the people that God created them to be. As promised by the adoptive parents we were permitted to stay in their lives, and for a while Shirley and I had frequent contact with them. Then about a year before this vacation something changed in our relationship with the parents. They began putting up road blocks that prevented us from having much contact with Anna and Judah, and then suddenly things got even worse. Over time we were basically not able to see or talk to them. However, we continued to try, and we had hoped that doing this vacation together would allow us to once again be in their lives. Little did we know that was not going to happen.

When we picked out the rental house for this vacation, we chose a place with lots of room and enough bedrooms and bathrooms so that everyone could have their own personal space. At first, this couple said that they would come, as long as Anna was doing all right. From time to time, she had some behavioral issues as a result of her reactive attachment disorder. In my heart I desperately wanted them all to come, for I hoped they would bond with our blended family. I wrote them an extra note outlining all of the neat things about the rental house and the area. Shirley and I were paying for the rental house; all it would cost them was the gas to drive from Ohio, and to then help share the food costs. Both parents had very good paying jobs, so we knew money was not the issue.

After we got to the house and started our vacation, they were not there and never called us about their plans. I continued to pray and fervently hope that they would show up at some point. I wrote something every day in my journal about them not being there and I kept anticipating that they would arrive. I was really crushed and depressed when they did not come. On Friday morning July 11, 2008, this is what I wrote in my journal: "Lord the 'family' did not make it. But please continue to help me to let them and their actions or lack of actions go. Help me to just focus on the future (not the past things that this couple has done). Help me to let go of my negative thoughts and my hurt feelings of being unfairly treated. May I let them go and let me just hold on to your love and the future you hold in your hands, knowing that you love Judah and Anna more than anyone else. Lord, help me to hold on to that above all else. Lord, help me let go and trust you."

Later on, we found out the couple took Anna and Judah and actually went to the father's parents' house in upstate New York. That really ticked me off, and I was still upset that they did not come or call. However, in hindsight, even with all of my wishing and wanting, we figured out that things were better off because they did not come. Their negative attitudes would have put a damper on things. Later on, I wrote in my journal that it was really good that they were not there, for the whole dynamic of our week would have changed. I also noted that it was a wonderful vacation after getting over the hurt of them not being there.

## A MESSAGE

Later, on that day, July 11, *I was blessed to have an encounter with one of God's human-messenger angels*! Some of our family had begun to leave the rental house to get back to their homes. A friend of ours from the seminary who also was a pastor, Diane Bareis Greble, came by to stay with us for one night. Diane, Shirley, and I all went into Saugatuck for the day. Those two were going to walk around the town and take in the sights. I had brought my Bible, devotional books, and journal stuff, and had planned to sit by the pier and have some prayer and reflection time. At first, I sat underneath a shelter, but then I got cool and went to sit in the sun.

While under the shelter, there were three other people having lunch. It was about 1:00 p.m. when one of the women came up to me and started talking. Her first name was Doreen and she was visiting from England with her son and daughter-in-law. While they were driving to the pier area, she was told by God in a vision that she would see a man bending over and reading a book, and she was instructed to tell that man something. While I was under the shelter, I did bend over for a bit, but did not think much about it at the time.

She asked me if I was a Christian. I gave her a quick rundown of my life, then told her about Shirley and me going to the seminary and what was going on in our lives. I showed her the materials that were with me, the Bible, and other devotional materials, and how I was preparing to supply preach at a church on the following Sunday. She told me that she believed that there had been a shift in heaven, that God would be changing people here on earth as they prayed and studied the Bible. That people like us would be led to do things for God and God's kingdom. Just as she was led to come and talk to me, and like I had been guided to come to the park that day and read and reflect, the Lord would be directing our steps.

Doreen said that she was told by God to tell the man who was bending over and reading a book, *"That whatever problem was affecting him would be corrected or solved. That the challenge in that person's life/family would be okay. Additionally, that God loved this man and that God's favor was on him!"* Doreen was a real person, talking directly to me and to no one else. Those words totally blew me away, for they were so amazing to me! Yes, I have read countless times about God's love—about how God loves all of creation, and that we are all a beloved child of God. But hearing these comments in this manner gave those beliefs a totally new meaning and left me speechless.

Believe me, it took a really long time for me to reflect on that moment and realize what had actually happened. Needless to say, that was the one and only time something like that has ever happened to me or to anyone I know. I cannot tell you for sure why this occurred to me at that time, and in that manner. Shirley and I discussed it later and had a few ideas about it. However, at first, the entire encounter was a total mystery to me. After thinking upon this, we definitely believed that message referred to the situation with Judah and Anna. Because I had spent so much time worrying about whether or not they were coming, we believe that God was trying to reassure me about the future. Little did I know that, after that week, it would be several years before we were able to have contact with them again. Everything was out of our hands. We could hope and pray and try to keep communications open; but there was an intentional road block on their parents' part, and they controlled the flow of correspondence.

Reflecting back today on Doreen's message, it appears that God was letting me know, in addition to the fact that I was loved, that in time this issue would be corrected or resolved. That what happened or did not occur that particular week was not going to be the final outcome. That, in time, things would work out. Today I still read her message as part of my evening devotions. Anna and Judah's stories are still being written as they have become young adults who have had some really tough times, through no fault of their own. However, these words remind me that they will be all right in the long run. I will always be grateful for that message of love and support from God through Doreen. For, at that time, it helped me get past some of my negative feelings of that week, and gave me hope for the future.

## ANOTHER MOVE

Shirley and I continued to enjoy living in the greater Louisville area. There were a lot of fun things to do, it had a very diverse community, and for most of the year the weather was quite moderate. Shirley enjoyed doing ministry at Saint Paul; she was able to try new things and encouraged the congregation to become involved in outreach ministries. I was able to do a number of things related to my ministry. Also, I had written materials and had grained insights that would be used in future endeavors that I would become involved with. It was a fruitful time for both of us, which we will always be grateful for. However, no matter what was tried, Saint Paul was unable to grow very much, and over time the financial situation grew worse. As you may recall, when they called Shirley, she was informed that they had money for two years for a full-time pastor. A number of changes were made by Shirley and the church council, in order to save money. Because of that she ended up being there nearly eight years.

In May of 2011 at her suggestion, she was put on a half-time salary. She, however, still felt called to full-time ministry, and she put her name into the call process, which meant that she would be looking for a new congregation and, in time, leaving Saint Paul in Louisville. It was a very difficult and painful decision to make that came about through much prayer and discernment. She probably would have stayed longer, if they could have afforded her, but that was not to be.

I will not go into the long and difficult process that Shirley went through to get another call from a congregation. But over time she was offered a new call to Saint Paul Lutheran Church, in Alpena, Michigan. I had never heard of the town before, but it is in the northeast corner of northern Michigan (the lower peninsula, not the upper), and the town is located on the shore of Lake Huron. It was a larger congregation that had experienced a split about two years before they called Shirley. They had a real passion for ministry/mission and especially for outreach into the community. The congregation and Alpena community were very welcoming and warm to us.

Saint Paul was financially sound and could afford a full-time pastor and staff. Thus, on July 1, 2012, she began her call there. By living in Alpena, we were near family for the first time since we got married. Matthew, Angie, and Dana, Shirley's son, daughter-in-law, and granddaughter, were within two hours away. The shores of Lake Huron were minutes from our house, and we loved being able to be so near to such a large body of water.

## DISCIPLESHIP—A LIFELONG SPIRITUAL PILGRIMAGE

While still in Louisville, I was guided to start putting together the materials and insights that I had gained as a spiritual consultant and a director of small group ministry. The presentations that I had used became an outline for what I began to write. Over time, a small manuscript came out of it. I had written articles for insurance magazines while in the insurance industry, and one for *Angels on Earth*, but had never thought about writing a book before. Believe me, even though it was a small composition, it required a lot of trial and error on my part, for I had no clue what I was doing. However, here again, I felt that it was what I was supposed to be doing at that time; so, I continued on in faith trusting God about what was to come next. A number of my friends and Shirley were so wonderful in helping me by reading my draft and offering some very meaningful input.

After I had something that I thought was somewhat okay, I started contacting various publishing sources to find someone to print it for me. I started out by writing one place, and then would wait for an answer. Often, no response came back at all, and if one did, it was a no. Later on, I began writing a few at a time; I got pretty good at filling out the applications, or submission packets, for each company wanted something different. I started contacting publishing houses and literary agents while living in Louisville, but was unsuccessful. However, after we moved to Alpena and I kept contacting places, amazingly, Wipf and Stock Publishers, out of Eugene, Oregon, agreed to publish it for a small fee. After contacting over thirty different publishers and getting nowhere, I was happy to find one to help me out with it and was willing to pay their fee if that is what it took to get it published.

*Discipleship—A Lifelong Spiritual Pilgrimage: A Disciple's Reflection on Actively Living in God's Kingdom Today*, was published in August of 2013. Besides a number of friends helping me out, I was also blessed to have Professor Mark Allen Power, of Trinity Lutheran Seminary, and Bishop John David Schleicher, of the North/West Lower Michigan Synod of the ELCA, agree to write back page endorsements for the book. I was so grateful and honored to have it printed. I wrote the book to offer support, tools, and guidance to those who wanted to learn more about becoming a lifelong disciple of Jesus Christ. The focus of the book outlined a few basic points in establishing some spiritual practices. The chapters came right out of the presentations that had been put together for the work that I had done in Louisville; also included were reflections concerning my own life journey in striving for God's kingdom.

After my contract was signed and I began working on all of the requirements needed in order to meet the publisher's format, my son, Kevin, gave me a great suggestion. He noted that getting the book printed was just the first step; for he mentioned that I was an unknown and needed to do something to become better known. He recommended that I start a web site outlining my ministry and letting people know about me, and the work that I had been called to do. I had never thought about that before. He gave me a few suggestions and eventually, with a lot of trial and error, I set up a ministry web site. Additionally, I added a ministry Facebook page. The web site outlined who I was and what I had to offer to congregations relating to their spiritual pilgrimages. It was suggested that in order to keep the site fresh, something new should be added on a steady basis. Thus, I started writing a blog, based on the spiritual practices to becoming a lifelong disciple of Jesus Christ. I did not know it at the time, but those blogs were the foundation for my second book, a daily devotional.

## LIFE IN ALPENA

The town of Alpena had a population of about eleven thousand in 2012. Even though the church and the community had warmly welcomed both of us, it was not a very diverse area. It was not geographically close to any large city, thus finding people of any color was a challenge. However, as noted, we were within two hours of family for the first time; plus, Shirley has always loved being near bodies of water. After a short time in Alpena, I became a lover of big bodies of water as well. It was a real gift and pleasure to be so near a Great Lake with lots of inland lakes, rivers, and trees all around. Having those natural aspects to enjoy, in addition to how loving the church and overall community was, overcame some of the shortcomings of being so far removed from the amenities that a larger metropolitan city provides.

Fortunately, Alpena held potential for more ministries for both of us. Shirley loved being the pastor at Saint Paul in Alpena, for they were also open to trying new things. She additionally was able to impact the wider Alpena community in a number of different ways, especially ecumenically. Over time I got involved in different activities, one of which was as a member of the Alpena Martin Luther King Jr. Day Celebration Committee. That committee organized a full day of events for the community on Dr. King's birthday, to honor his work and to educate the community on how important it was to continue to strive toward making positive change happen racially and socially.

An aspect of the area's ecumenical ministry that we both were involved with included different denominations hosting services for the wider community. Shirley and I were fortunate enough to have been a part of something special when we lived there. In Alpena a group of churches lived out a little bit of how God's kingdom can look in this present age as they joined together to take part in various activities. This group was formed and operating before we got to Alpena and hosted several functions during the year. (Shirley has since retired from full-time ministry, and we have moved away, but these activities continue.) The most unique event was the midweek Lenten worship services. Each Wednesday during Lent the evening worship services were rotated from church to church, starting with a simple soup and bread supper, followed by a worship service with a different clergy person preaching each week. It was truly meaningful and wonderful to have so many faith traditions gathered together to break bread and worship together.

We got to visit the churches, hear different speakers, and take part in a variety of worship styles. Even though each week the format is unlike the previous week, the worship is centered around praising God and being in fellowship with other believers. Each year a specific Lenten theme was used for all of the services, and the sermons delivered were based on that theme. In my mind this is a real example of God's kingdom present in the here and now. The churches that are involved in Alpena were the United Methodist, Presbyterian, United Church of Christ, Episcopal, Lutheran (ELCA), and Roman Catholic faith traditions. While there Shirley and I really loved it and felt it was a blessing to be able to take part in these Lenten services and other ecumenical events that were put on during the year.

## MIDDAY DEVOTIONAL TIME

My midday devotional routine that had been started many years ago continues to be a part of my spiritual practices yet today. When I was working in the insurance business and was not on the road traveling for business, I maintained the midday devotional practice. I generally found a church that was open during the noon hour, and I spent my lunch hour praying and reflecting, I did that once or twice a week. After I left the insurance industry and entered Trinity Lutheran Seminary, I continued this habit. Trinity had Schenk Chapel, which was a small space away from the classrooms. Thus, between classes, I would take some reflection materials there, with my Bible and journal, to reflect on, and was able to have some meditation time during the day.

After Shirley received her call to Saint Paul Lutheran Church in Louisville, I again looked for churches that were open during the noon hour, so that I could pray and have my contemplation period. I found a Catholic church about a ten-minute walk from where we lived, and I visited that church once or twice a week. In time I discovered that in downtown Louisville, the Cathedral of the Assumption held noon Masses every week day. I started attending there once a week as part of my devotional routines. I did not want to park in downtown Louisville, so I would leave my car along the river front, about a half hour away. As I went to church, the path to get there partly followed the Ohio River; I would admire the view, and pray and meditate on the way to church. Thus, the walk was a reflective time for me as well. Most of the year, that was a pretty awesome hike.

When Shirley was called to Saint Paul Lutheran Church in Alpena, I found a Catholic church that was open where I could continue to light a candle for our family once a week. As noted before, the Alpena churches held joint worship services together during Lent. One such service was held at Trinity Episcopal Church in Alpena. I found out that they had a noonday service every Wednesday. Thus, I started going there most every week. I felt very comfortable there, for that congregation was again very open and welcoming to me, and I was could receive Holy Communion from them. Over the years, I attended there rather frequently and got to know the people there fairly well. I even read the Scriptures there every once in a while. They became like a second church home to me and also became part of my devotional practices.

Since Shirley retired and we left Michigan for Colorado, we have been blessed to find another church, Saint James Episcopal Church, which has a noon Wednesday service. Shirley and I both go to that weekly service. Again, even though we only attend on most Wednesdays, the community has warmly welcomed us and we enjoy being a part of that congregation, if only on a somewhat limited basis. Thus, a practice that was started by me many years ago continues today. Additionally, after we moved to the Denver metro area we have been able to join Lutheran Church of Hope (ELCA) in Broomfield, Colorado. Another community that has been very welcoming to us as well.

If you have read materials from any number of wonderful spiritual writers, their messages have a few common themes that are expressed in one form or the other. Having a set of spiritual practices, performed on a regular basis, done individually or with a community, is part of the spiritual pilgrimage. These rituals help us to daily strive for God's kingdom in our lives and also assist us in becoming the person that God wants us to be. For me, attending a church to have a reflection period, or to pray in, or to attend a midweek worship service has been an important part of my pilgrimage.

## NOURISHMENT FOR THE SPIRITUAL PILGRIMAGE

In 2017 while still in Alpena, I was privileged to have a second book published: *Nourishment for the Spiritual Pilgrimage: Daily Devotions for Christian Disciples*. To me, this book is somewhat different from many other devotional books because the principle focus is on the reader becoming a lifelong disciple of Jesus Christ. Jesus taught by his words and actions. He gave us guidance about what to pray, how to pray, and why to pray. He also was very familiar with the Hebrew scriptures. Thus, if we want to become a lifelong disciple of Jesus Christ, it seems apparent that we should follow the model of his life and teachings. In my mind this second book helps in this process.

I again do so appreciate getting some wonderful help in putting this together; Shirley was a huge support in reading the drafts and helping in the editing of it. In the book, I also thank people and events who over my lifetime have also indirectly helped in writing the book, because all of them are part of who I am now and have impacted how I see life and this spiritual journey. Basically, anyone with whom I have had a relationship is in my words and actions. Additionally, I am greatly indebted to the three who were kind enough to write a back-page endorsement for the book: Walter F. Taylor Jr., PhD, Trinity Lutheran Seminary; Jim Stuck, bishop emeritus, Indiana-Kentucky Synod, ELCA; and Craig Alan Satterlee, PhD, bishop, North/West Lower Michigan Synod, ELCA.

Sometimes it is very difficult for me to believe that the good Lord has guided me to write as much as I have over the years. Way back when I was nineteen, I failed my first college course, which was a basic communications class, because of my very poor writing skills. I have gotten a little better, but that will always be a learning curve for me. However, God has blessed me with people who are better than me in this regard and have greatly helped me along on this journey. My late wife, Judy, was really good in this, and was a big help with my college papers after we were married, and then with some of my business writings. Shirley also is much better at this than me, and has been a wonderful aid in some of the things that have been published. None of us is an island. We have all been supported, encouraged, given wisdom from many different sources; I know that I have, and am very grateful for all of them.

## REFORMATION 500: A PILGRIMAGE OF REMEMBERING

Another highlight for Shirley and me when we lived in Alpena was in May of 2017, when we took a tour to mark the five hundredth anniversary of the Protestant Reformation. We visited places in Germany related to Martin Luther's life and ministry. We of course learned more about Luther's life, the basis of the Reformation, and the fallout from it. We also spent time in Italy visiting historic vistas and cities. However, this excursion was also very much a pilgrimage, for we took time daily to pray and reflect, and had occasions to be part of worship services along the way. The trip was full of many of the sights and sounds of a normal tour, but had this very spiritual theme flowing through it, which we very much appreciated.

In my mind two events stood out for me. One was when we were at the Vatican, and were able to see Pope Francis up close in his popemobile and hear him give a short homily. Our tour guide got us there early, so we could get seats fairly close to his route as he passed by. He seemed to be a very loving and caring person as he took time to pick up and kiss little children and reached out and touched some of the people in the crowd.

Another truly moving moment for me was when we were in Munich's English Garden City Park, one of the largest urban city parks in the world. We met our German friend, Caroline, who took us around for a day and brought us to this garden. In this garden is an enormous beer garden. Now I do not drink any alcohol at all; however, Shirley and our friend Caroline had a beer. What struck me was that in this huge beer garden there were hundreds of people, simply sitting around eating and drinking beer, just talking, sharing stories, listening to music, laughing, and enjoying the beautiful day. I did not see anyone who had had too much to drink. There were young and old, families of all types, everyone just hanging out.

The reason this really amazed me was because this is how all of humanity should be: people willing to just be with each other, socializing no matter the age or background. Being there at that instant really made an impression on me of how God's creation and all humans are all connected and meant to live in harmony. (I know I am living in my own little world while thinking this way, but why can't we?) This was one of the best moments that I experienced on this trip, witnessing people just being people. Our friend Caroline noted that, in Germany, beer brings people together to socialize, to have fun, and to bond with one another.

There were of course many other aspects of the trip that were wonderful to have been a part of. It was my first time overseas, and I really enjoyed the bulk of it. What was reinforced to me again was that no matter where you go, most of the time people are just people, who want to get along and be loved and valued at some level. When we returned Shirley and I did two presentations for the community of Alpena that highlighted the main aspects of our journey, and we included a number of pictures that supported our lectures. The local newspaper wrote an article about our tour and presentations. It was rewarding to share our experience with others, and to also emphasize the importance of the Reformation and how far reaching it was and how much the world was changed because of it.

## DISCIPLESHIP MINISTRY

My Discipleship Ministry was enriched and continued after we moved to Alpena. After my first book was in print, I had to find ways to let the public know about it. My publisher did do some marketing for it, but I also needed to do my part. However, I was an unknown author. In a larger market, it would have been much harder to get the word out about my new book. However, living in the small community of Alpena made this task a little easier. Again the Saint Paul congregation where Shirley was pastor and the larger community were very welcoming and supportive to both of our ministries.

Fortunately, the city newspaper, the *Alpena News*, gave the book's release some free press. The local Christian bookstore, the Olivet Book and Gift Store, was very helpful to me as well. I was able to hold a book signing at the store, which did quite well, considering that I was fairly new in the community. I also held a signing at Saint Paul after worship. The people at Saint Paul were extremely supportive of my work. After my second book came out, Saint Paul, the newspaper, and the bookstore all offered help again. I will always be grateful for how much that community aided my ministry, with getting my books into the hands of readers.

Having that first book published opened other doors for my ministry. I was able to give workshops at various Lutheran (ELCA) synod assemblies. I presented for the North/West Lower Michigan Synod, and for the Indiana-Kentucky Synod. At a few of the Synod assemblies I was able to have more book signings. I also was a part of signings in other places in northern Michigan, and did a few more workshops and retreats around the state. I never imaged that when we moved to Alpena so many opportunities would become available for my ministry.

The one aspect that I enjoy the most about doing my Discipleship Ministry is giving workshops, retreats, and presentations. I welcomed and enjoyed any opportunity that came my way where this could be done. I love the interaction between myself and those who want to learn more about becoming a lifelong disciple of Jesus Christ. People on this journey are hungry for ideas, support, and guidance to aid them on their trek. When individuals are eager to learn, and open to change, it is a joy for me to walk with them as they strive to become the persons that God intended for them to be.

FOURTEEN

# One Final Move—Going West

> I asked, "What am I to do, Lord?" The Lord said to me, "Get up and go to Damascus; there you will be told everything that has been assigned to you to do."
>
> —ACTS 22:10

## ANOTHER MAJOR CHANGE COMING

THIS VERSE IS PART of an often-quoted story about Saul's conversion, when he was on the road to Damascus. He was blinded by a light and heard the voice of Jesus. He was told to go to Damascus and then he would be told the next step. Because he was blinded, he had to be led by his companions. He had to go and trust that what he needed to know would be given to him at some point. But he did not know what was to come after that. Likewise, discernment on this spiritual pilgrimage is about being open to where the Lord, through the Holy Spirit, may be leading us. Sometimes we can only see our next step and then have to trust God about the step after that. We may not have an experience like Saul had, with the blinding light and unseen voice; however, the guidance may come in a dramatic or a very quiet manner. Listening for guidance may be the easy part; listening and then *following* the message we have been given is the more difficult aspect to undertake.

In most of the major moments over my lifetime when the Holy Spirit offered me guidance, it was up to me to listen and then follow those directions. Leaving the insurance industry and entering the seminary, when I did not fully know why I was going, is a prime example of this. Additionally, Shirley's calls to Louisville and then to Alpena were very much directed by the Holy Spirit. I could note other times where that was the case as well. Making a major change or making a geographical move, especially when you cannot see how things will turn out, requires faith on our part to take the next step. That certainly was the case when Shirley began thinking about retiring from full-time ministry.

## THE DISCERNMENT PROCESS

In the months preceding her retirement, Shirley started thinking and talking about whether it was time for her to leave full-time ministry. She still very much loved the community of Saint Paul Lutheran in Alpena, as she had loved the community of Saint Paul Lutheran in Louisville. She had always been grateful for the opportunity to be their pastor, and had felt that she was meant to be with them during that time. She enjoyed most of the aspects in her role as pastor; however, certain facets of the call were starting to take a lot more energy to perform. She was concerned about giving the congregation what they needed. So early on in our discernment process, we went over the pros and cons of when to leave. She decided to stay a year longer, which she did, and things seemed to work out for everyone. However, during the summer and fall of 2017, we began those discussions again. We both prayed for guidance and agreed that the summer/fall of 2018 was when she would announce her retirement. Of course, that was the easy part. The more challenging thing was that we had to figure out where we would be moving to and when. Additionally, letting everyone know about it was going to be difficult as well.

In the Lutheran (ELCA) church, a retiring pastor cannot worship in the church from which they have just retired. Thus, we could not stay in town and continue to worship at Saint Paul. Additionally, because of the size of the town, when we were out and about, we could easily run into people from Saint Paul who might still look at her as their pastor. Therefore, the only thing that we could do was to move out of Alpena once she retired. At our age, most people do not have to make that choice of where to live; generally, individuals just stay where they have lived the majority of their lives. Being a pastor carries with it many situations that others do not have to face, especially at retirement.

## WHERE TO MOVE

The decision to move, and then thinking about where to go, took a lot of discernment, prayer, and discussion on our parts. Before going to the seminary my work in the business world involved a number of transfers, mostly to take a new job or to relocate with an existing one. Prior to Shirley's going to the seminary, she had moved a couple of times, but these were mainly in southwestern Michigan. Additionally, after getting married to Shirley, and her getting a call, we made two relocations together. However, what would be coming after her retirement would be a different kind of change for both of us.

Thus, our thinking process centered around where we wanted to move to retire and live for the rest of our lives. We knew that at our age, we would not have the energy or desire to do numerous relocations. Even though I had lived in various parts of the US, I had spent the majority of my time in the Midwest, and felt comfortable with the culture and values of those who lived there. Thus, my first choice was to stay in the area somewhere, but where became the issue. We did not think that we should go anywhere that we had lived before as a couple, nor where we had lived individually, before we got married. Therefore, we did not think it would be a good idea to go back to the Columbus, Ohio metro area, where I had lived twice before, nor to Kalamazoo, Michigan, where Shirley had lived before going to the seminary. We realized that if we went back to where either of us had established friends, the other person might have a harder time adjusting. Thus, during our discernment process, we began looking for places we had not lived before.

We both knew that we were still called to take part in some kind of ministry, individually or as couple, wherever we went. Even though she was retiring from full-time ministry, there would be something for her to do in time, no matter where we ended up. It was the same for me; I felt called to continue writing, doing my blogs, and eventually taking part in whatever activity was presented to me, as it relates to assisting individuals or congregations on their spiritual pilgrimage. Thus, we believed that no matter where we landed, it would be a place that the good Lord through the Holy Spirit would direct us to. We never thought of moving south to get out of the winters; we were okay with dealing with some cold and snow, for we were Midwesterners at heart. We were both very much open to the leading of the Spirit in this discernment process.

Initially, we both had thought about staying in Michigan, but moving to a larger city like Grand Rapids or Lansing that could provide opportunities for ministry for both of us. Since she was very young, Shirley has always loved being around water. She and her late husband, Bob, and family had lived on an inland lake for years, and thoroughly enjoyed it. Thus, when we moved to Alpena, which was on the shore of Lake Huron, she was in seventh heaven. While in Alpena, I too had come to appreciate being so close to a big body of water, and enjoyed spending time just being near it whenever I could. Michigan is full of inland lakes and bordered by three of the Great Lakes. Thus, if we stayed in Michigan, we would never be very far from a body of water of some type. At first, I was okay with this, for the state had a lot to offer us. However, that was not to be.

About once or twice a year during Shirley's vacation time we would travel to the Denver metro area to visit Shirley's daughter, Amy, and her family. After Amy had Isabella and Brody, those trips became more regular, as we wanted to be a part of our grandchildren's lives, as much as possible. After Shirley decided to retire, we were still discerning where to move and we made one of our visits to spent time with Amy's family. Each time we went, Shirley and I would take the time to see some new towns, around the greater Denver metro area. On one such trip in August of 2017 we visited the small community of Louisville, Colorado. We took Isabella with us as we strode through the town. We walked into the Louisville Historical Museum, and talked to the director about what it had to offer in the way of exhibits. The director was over the top friendly, took a lot of time with us in explaining everything. Isabella, who was about seven at the time, asked a lot of questions and the director was very patient and thoughtful in addressing them.

Now this act of kindness on the director's part was a very revealing moment for me concerning our upcoming move. You have to understand that I have had some troubled memories of my time living in California. My feeling was that people who lived in very large metro areas could be cold and inhospitable. I know that is not the case for everyone, and I should not paint each person with the same brushstroke; but that is what was in my memory about living there. For some reason how this director interacted with us caused a very huge light bulb to go off in my head. I had not thought about moving to Colorado before that day. I had told myself that we would be too far from our family members and friends in the Midwest, that it would be too costly to move and live in

Colorado, plus, people in large metro areas could be very distant and aloof at times. In the short time in that museum something like scales fell from my eyes, and I had an epiphany and made an adjustment concerning our next move. Those moments with the museum director caused me to start thinking that we were called to move to Colorado versus any other location.

## COLORADO BOUND

Having decided to move to Colorado after Shirley retired, the next major items were making all of the plans to make the move possible, along with letting everyone know about it. As noted, we enjoyed most of the aspects of living in Alpena. We had made good friends, had gotten involved in a number of different activities around the community, and had a routine set up in our daily lives. Additionally, we both had roles with our synod that allowed us to interact with the wider Lutheran community. Thus, telling the synod bishop, Bishop Satterlee, our friends, our family, and the wider Alpena community was bittersweet.

However, letting the members of Saint Paul know was one of the more challenging aspects of this move for us. Even though we were also close to the Saint Paul congregation in Louisville, they knew that after Shirley went part-time, she would be leaving at some point. Saint Paul in Alpena did not think that she would be retiring when she did and that took a number of people by surprise. However, when they found out that we would be moving to Colorado, partly to be closer to children and grandchildren, most people were very happy for us. They knew that we often went out there to visit, and because of being a pastor, often spent holidays in Alpena alone. We did get to visit with Shirley's son, Matt, and his family in northern Michigan; however, it was not the same as having family really close by.

After the people at Saint Paul got over the initial shock of Shirley retiring, they were very kind and supportive and provided us help in various ways. They gave us a really fun going away party, to which they invited people from the entire Alpena area, due to our involvement with activities beyond the congregation. We had a number of people who attended, and many were folks from the community and surrounding area. It was a good time to reflect and give thanks for the ministry that had been done during our six plus years there.

Even though we visited in the Denver metro area many times, there were still a lot of unknowns to be dealt with. We believed that the good Lord would be in the present and future, helping us along the way. Overall, the move went fairly well. However, it took a lot of prayers, sweat, energy, planning, support from others, and nervous moments to make it work. Thankfully, we enjoy living in Colorado, and know that this is where we are meant to be. We have had many opportunities to make some wonderful memories since moving here!

## ELIZABETH

Several months after starting our new life in Colorado, we heard indirectly about my daughter, Elizabeth. On June 11, 2019, we learned that she was having surgery. A mass and swelling in her brain dictated that the surgery be done immediately, and also a biopsy was needed. This was a huge shock to us, because we had not heard anything from her in several years. We knew that she had gotten married to Hewitt (Tuey) Harris, and they had started a ministry together, but we had no direct contact with her. Additionally, since Judy had died from issues with brain tumors, we were also concerned about the possibility of her having brain cancer.

The next thing that floored us was Tuey's message regarding Elizabeth's feelings. The message was that Elizabeth wanted most of all to see my face and hear my voice and tell me how sorry she was for what she had done, and to tell me how much she loved me. *Wow!* You could have knocked me over with a feather; that really got to me! Supposedly, after all of these years, and the countless time, effort, pain, and financial burden that she had caused our family and me, she wanted to say that she was sorry. That was a huge revelation for all of us. After more communications with Tuey, my son, Kevin, got involved and spoke directly with Elizabeth, which I was told was a really emotional conversation. After much prayer and many discussions between Shirley and me about what was going on, we decided to drive back to Columbus, Ohio (a nearly two-and-a-half-day drive) to personally visit them face to face. I was looking forward to seeing Elizabeth and hearing what she had to say about our past history together.

We met with Tuey and Elizabeth at two different restaurants, over two days, for about six hours total. We covered a lot of topics; however, Elizabeth *never* told me what Tuey had said she wanted to say. She never told me that she was sorry for the things that she had done to our family and me or that she loved me. That was of course a huge disappointment, to have driven that far, and to have not heard those words. It was as though those words were not important any more, and apparently the fact that we had come so far to see her was enough for her. On the one hand I was glad that we went when we did, for she was doing fairly well at that time, and later on she would have more issues related to her cancer. However, the letdown that I felt was hard for me to understand and deal with.

After we got back home, we continued to communicate with both of them, and of course pray for them. I understood what they going through because of my experience with Judy. Over the upcoming months they went through a lot of treatments and doctor visits, and their journey had many highs and lows. However, the lows became more frequent, and she eventually passed away from this cancer. The comparisons to Judy's death are very similar. Judy died at age fifty and a half on January 23, 1999; Elizabeth died on January 11, 2020, at age forty-nine. They both had two brain surgeries and lots of treatments to try to deal with the cancer and its side effects. Though the brain tumors were not exactly the same they were sort of cousins to one another. Regardless, it is so sad for both of them to have endured all of this at such a young age.

We flew back to Ohio for her funeral and, after the service, our family got together and talked about Elizabeth's life, which was good for all of us. At that time, we also contacted her other son, Charles. Charles is younger than Anna and Judah, lives in the Chicago area, and had been raised by his father, until his father passed away. Our family knew about Charles, a year or so before Elizabeth died, but we did not get to see him and talk to him until then. Elizabeth left a lot of questions unanswered about her life. Everyone impacted by her can only move forward and live without knowing many of these details. Her death closed one chapter in my life, which over time had caused many others and me much pain and sorrow. Elizabeth was a very gifted person who often did not always use those gifts very wisely; however, at her core, she was a very loving and caring person, but her shortcomings kept her from being able to live to her full potential until much later in her life.

## LIFE STORIES OF A DISCIPLE IN THE MAKING

Little did I know that I would be blessed to be led to my two marriages, when deciding to attend Youngstown State University and Trinity Lutheran Seminary. These two institutions were largely unknown to me before attending them. Both were a risk and involved drastic change for me, and caused me to walk into an unknown future. However, in time, I was in a position to receive the loving gifts from God, when I met and married Judy, and then Shirley. I am not saying that you will find someone to marry when you follow the Lord's direction through the Holy Spirit. However, only be willing to follow where you are being led to go; for you may encounter aspects in life that you were not aware of before. Yes indeed, God can be a God of surprises.

In my writings I have tried to share with you stories from my life that have helped to shape me in my journey to becoming a lifelong disciple of Jesus Christ. On this spiritual pilgrimage none of us have yet reached our final goal on this side of God's kingdom; we are all still being made new every day. We are all a *disciple in the making*. Additionally, any one of us can come up with life stories that have helped to mold us into the people that God wants us to be. I would encourage all of you to reflect on your own history; think of some of the important saints in your past that have shared their wisdom with you and supported you on this journey. Also, think about how the Holy Spirit has changed you on this trek. Furthermore, remember the times that you have been led to take a step in faith, into the unknown, which involved risk; recall the lessons learned from those moments and if there were some revelations that were revealed only by moving forward.

If any of my stories have aided you in your journey, that is great and a blessing and honor for me. As you reflect on your own travels be receptive to where the Holy Spirit may be guiding you to be a support to those around you. Often just being who you have been called to be is enough; but sometimes, the sharing of one's faith journey is required to assist someone else. Be bold in your life and witness to others when you are being led to do so. Friends, trying to stay on this spiritual pilgrimage to become a lifelong disciple of Jesus Christ is not for the faint of heart, and requires courage, patience, and perseverance. May God's Holy Spirit surround you with love, support, and guidance as you continue in the way of being a disciple in the making.

# Acknowledgments

THIS BOOK HAS COVERED some of my highlights and events as they mostly related to my spiritual pilgrimage. My life has been no better or worse than others who have had some of the same circumstances as myself. However, there is only one Vernon T. Jones from Youngstown, Ohio, with the experiences that I have had. I felt the need to list persons and occurrences that have gotten me to this point in my life. My low self-esteem, while younger, caused me to be open and receptive to what I read, as well as to those around me who offered help and guidance. The people noted below are just some of those who were so helpful in getting me to this point in my life. Some in small fashions, others in very major ways, are part of me right now and in all that I do. My sincere apologies to any I have inadvertently not mentioned here or elsewhere; you are still an important part of my life.

## MY MOM

As you know my parents were divorced and my mother pretty much raised my brothers and me on her own. Both sets of my grandparents were also divorced. This situation presented many challenges to all of us. My brothers and I knew we were loved and cared for by my mom, even when we did not have much in the way of material things, and especially compared to what some others had around us. Mom had to deal with some really demanding situations, not all of her own doing; however, she endured through them all. Overall, I feel very fortunate and blessed to have been raised by Emma B. (Coleman) Jones. She raised us to respect ourselves and others and not be bitter or negative about what life had dealt us. I am grateful for the solid foundation that was given to me.

In addition to making sure that we were in church every Sunday and that we behaved whenever we went out, I want to highlight just one other specific example about my mother's impact on my life. After high school I got a job in a steel mill in Youngstown. After working there for a while, I talked with her about wanting to do more with my life. She encouraged me to take college courses while still working as a way to improve things for myself. I started taking classes and, about eight years later, I earned my college degree and was able to move on. If not for her encouragement, support, and guidance I might have still been at the mill when it ceased operations about four years after I left there with my college degree.

## JERUSALEM BAPTIST CHURCH

Jerusalem was attended by my maternal grandmother and her family, and I was basically born into it and attended there until I left town after finishing college. I attended Sunday worship and Sunday school nearly every week. Over time I became the youngest Sunday school superintendent, taught the high school Sunday school class, and did a number of things with the youth. With the youth group, we visited other churches of different faith traditions and races. I was in charge of the youth ushers and played piano for the Sunday School and for one of the worship choirs. Through my various roles there I developed skills in a number of areas including working with people collaboratively to get things done as well as learning to give presentations.

Those activities, plus a number of people, helped me on my life journey and spiritual pilgrimage. One man who was an example of someone who daily lived out his faith was Deacon J. R. Moore. I saw him as someone who was honest and always tried to do the right thing, even when he was facing a lot of opposition. It is amazing how much conflict can occur in a worshiping Christian community, and Deacon Moore firmly stood his ground when others around him were going off in other directions.

Theodore Venable was someone who taught me the importance of always greeting people with a positive attitude and a welcoming smile. Theodore was one of the adult leaders who came with the youth group when we visited other various faith traditions. He was always open to those who were different than himself; he was great role model for our youth and me. There were many others at Jerusalem who are still a part of me now and who helped mold me.

Sometime after becoming the Sunday school superintendent, I became involved with a group made up of various Sunday schools from other congregations. I eventually became president of this Sunday school association, and we worked collectively on various programs for the churches. One individual I came to know from that period who became a wonderful mentor for me was James Smith. He was in charge of the YMCA on the north side of Youngstown. Mr. Smith was connected to many activities and organizations in the area. He was a wealth of wisdom and understanding about life, people, and how to have a spiritual journey in the midst of all of the negative things that go on around us. He also shared with me that he saw me in a vocation, ministering to people; but not necessarily tied to any specific denomination. He said that in the late 1960s, long before I ever thought of going to the seminary. His comments were right on, but way ahead of their time. I will always be grateful for the insights and knowledge that he shared with me.

## SCHOOL TEACHERS

During my school-age years I had a number of quality teachers. Tony Davanzo was my sixth-grade teacher at Covington Street School and had a huge impact on my young life. He, like some others, inspired me and saw a potential in me that at times I could not see and often did not know how to develop. My East High School senior class Problems of Democracy teacher, Arthur Schwartz, is someone else who stands out for me. I remember him as an older man who had an impact on my young life. I do not have a good memory for easily remembering a lot of facts and data. He suggested that I write information over and over until it stuck in my brain. That helpful bit of insight has helped me all of my life. The other thing that I recall from his classes was this statement about life, that "as soon as you solve one problem, you create another one." I have used that thought many times in my life, and it has served me well. There are others that I could mention, such as my assistant high school football coach, Joseph Bernard, or my high school choir director, Richard Campbell; these plus many others have influenced my life in various ways.

## YOUNGSTOWN SHEET AND TUBE COMPANY

At the Youngstown Sheet and Tube Company, Campbell Works, Open Hearth Department, a number of people had a hand in my tutelage during that time. However, two men stand out who greatly influenced my journey while there. One was Kenny Venable, who attended my church; however, he influenced me more at work than at church, because I was around him more. When I started in the mill it was still segregated in certain sections and especially in the Open Hearth Department where we worked. The pay was better in that area than in most other departments in the mill. Thus, for many years, no persons of color were allowed to get any of those high paying jobs on or around the furnaces. Kenny was the first African-American person to run a crane there. Over time he became an operator of the charging machines that loaded raw materials into the furnaces. Kenny was a wonderful source of support and wisdom for me, especially during my early days in the mill. From watching how Kenny carried himself, when he worked with this rainbow collection of people, and in a highly visible and sometimes stressful job, he helped me learn how to deal with different people. I came to appreciate how much of a straight shooter he was, and he always gave his honest opinion about things. He and his wife, Voncile, became very supportive friends to Judy and me when we were first married.

Another individual whom I remember as welcoming and supportive of me at that time was Gus Karas. People referred to him as Gus the Greek. He was a second helper when I started; however, as time went on, he got into the management side of this department. Gus was concerned about me and was interested in what I was doing overall. He was one of the few people in the mill who took a real interest in my college work. He wanted me to finish so I could move on to something outside of the mill. He gave me insight about working there and about life in general.

## JUDITH ANN

I feel extremely fortunate to have been married to two very faith-filled and loving women. Both were pure gifts from God for me. Each taught me much and have shown me wonderful love. They have enriched my life in more ways than I have room to comment on. They have some similar traits in common, such as their faith, their own spiritual pilgrimage, how they loved life, and the way they treated others in a loving manner. Both of them have a passion for ministry as well. Of course, they are also different in many aspects of life and indeed are very much their own persons.

When Judy and I decided to get married, we had a number of challenges to deal with besides the normal ones that young people have. I was still working and taking classes at YSU, she had not finished her degree work yet, we were from very different backgrounds, and she was expecting. When we were married none of her family came, only her friends. However, later on we got closer to her side, and her parents, Stella and Vito, became a really significant part of our family.

There are many things that I could write about Judy; because we worked through so many challenges over the nearly twenty-eight years that we were married. One major point she helped me immensely with was regarding my communications skills. When we got married, I had a very hard time expressing my feelings. While growing up I knew that my mom loved me; however, it generally was not expressed in words. Thus, I never learned how to verbally share my emotions. Judy, on the other hand, was one of those people who very freely shared what was going on; it just came naturally to her. This issue was a real struggle for me early on in our marriage. This caused her a lot of pain and frustration. However, she helped me through this, and over time I got slightly better in this regard. Sometimes I still have to work with this, but considering where I was when we were first married, I have come a long ways. I will always be indebted to Judy for walking with me through this.

Another gift given was her love and support for me, which surrounded everything we did. When Shirley and I were married we acknowledged to those in attendance that we were who we were in part because of our marriages to Bob and Judy. Also, that Judy and Bob would always be a part of us and that their love given to us would continue in our lives. This was physically shown to me by way of an unusual miracle (at least in my mind it was a miracle). At some point in our marriage Judy got me using a face moisture cream under my eyes, in order to keep me from getting dark circles. For years I continued to buy the cream and use it faithfully every morning. After Judy passed away, this practice was maintained. However, over a long period of time I noticed that the four ounce container of cream that was being using when she died was not running out and lasted for several years. Hard as that is to believe, that container of cream lasted for years after she died! It did eventually run out and I got another container and that one also lasted for years.

I started to keep track of the beginning and end of each container and it was always used for years, and that routine has lasted all of this time. The last bottle that was totally used up lasted from November 10, 2016 until February 7, 2022. Over the years I have been amazed at how long the containers have lasted and I am not totally sure why this all happened. However, one of the reasons for these miracles may have been another way of God showing me that God's presence would be with me even after Judy passed away. Another possible reason is that it could be a way of showing that Judy's love and care for me would always be a part of me no matter what. This is the first time that I have told this story publicly, but in my book, it shows that love given continues on in those who are loved. I will always be grateful for the love given me by Judy, Shirley, and so many others.

## FATHER BOB BONNOT

When we decided to get married, Judy very much wanted to get married in a Catholic church and we approached a priest about helping us out. Father Bob was a priest at Sacred Heart Catholic Church on Youngstown's east side. Now remember that this was a time when marriages across religious, cultural, and racial lines were not done very frequently. Thus, we were stepping out on a limb with the faith that with God guiding and helping us, we could handle anything that came up. Of course, at that time we had no clue what was in front of us.

I feel extremely fortunate that Father Bob was there when he was. I now know that if we had had many other priests, we would have had a lot more road blocks thrown up in front of us, as compared to the bridges that he tried to build for us. The way he expressed his loving-caring manner and how he shared his thoughts made me feel very comfortable with how he dealt with us. After talking with him, I was okay in going ahead with the wedding.

## BETH BREWER AND EDNA MCDONALD

Needless to say, there were a lot of things going on for both of us when we got married. Often, I felt that I was completely overwhelmed. However, at times like that, God places people in our lives to give us what we need to help us make it through what we are facing at the moment. Mrs. Beth Brewer was that person for me back then. She worked in the social studies office at YSU and I came to know her when I became involved in some of the groups on campus.

During that period, she listened to me go on and on about what Judy and I were facing as we approached our marriage. Even though I was not really good about sharing my feelings, I felt very comfortable trying to let her know what was going on with us. She had a caring ear and a very strong faith herself. Her glass was always more full than empty, and the people around her could feel her positive love and outlook. Her love and listening ability are something that I will always remember.

Mrs. Brewer worked in the same office as Mrs. Edna McDonald, a professor of mine whom I took a few courses with. Both ladies attended the same church and were good friends and together they helped a lot of people besides myself. While in school, a couple of times I thought I was a better student than I actually was. Thus, twice I was thrown out and could not take classes, and had to wait out on probation before beginning again.

Because Mrs. McDonald was a professor in my major field of study, she helped me make it through probation until I could get back into good standing. It really humbled me and made me reevaluate what the most important things in my life were. She was very gracious in the way she helped me; she kept the standards of the course work high but was able to assist me in working through my issues. I was aware that I created my own problems, but she was still willing to help me out.

## VITO

Vito, Judy's father, was a kind person who had a lot of love for life, his family, and his church, even though he could seem to be a little tough on the outside. Our marriage initially caused him a lot of pain. However, because he was a very loving person in his inner being, eventually that love allowed him to see us differently.

After we had been married for a while and he and his wife, Stella, had not come around to see us, I was led to go to a Catholic church, where I lit a candle for them. That was something this Baptist-bred man had never done; but I did it. I lit a seven-day candle and said a prayer for them. On the seventh day, they came to see us. After that point they were in our lives in a major way until they passed away. He was such a wonderful example of how genuine love can overcome barriers that society may attempt to set up. He taught me a lot of life lessons just by how he lived, and I came to respect and love him immensely.

## BOOKS

As mentioned before, I had a low self-esteem and sometimes did not have a lot of direction as a young teenager. After I started working in the mill, and thought about taking college courses on a part time basis, I began reading books about life and about making something of yourself by being more focused. Some I loved to read, and I came to learn a lot from certain authors. I want to note a few, for their thoughts and writings are certainly part of whom I am today.

Norman Vincent Peale is an author that I have read and come to use and previously reread more than any other. *The Power of Positive Thinking*, and many of his other books, helped me with my low self-esteem and gave me more focus and direction about the journey that I was on. Many of my routines that I still do today came directly or indirectly from his writings. However, I do not read his books anymore, for my readings take more of a spiritual pilgrimage view then what his books have to offer for me. However, I will always appreciate the influence his wisdom, suggested faith practices, and spiritual insight had on my life.

A few of the other authors who have contributed greatly to my spiritual pilgrimage are Henri Nouwen, Richard Foster, James Martin, and Joan Chittister. These writers plus many others have given me wisdom, suggested ways of being on this journey, and supported me during the low points of my life. They also gave insights and directions about how to continue becoming the person that God wants me to be: a lifelong disciple of Jesus Christ.

During the interim winter session of my first year at Trinity Lutheran Seminary, I went on a spiritual retreat for a few days. At that retreat I started journaling, and that practice has become part of my daily prayer routine. For this retreat, we also had to buy the *Book of Common Worship: Daily Prayer*. I started using it then and continue using it today. It has been a wonderful way to add some structure to my daily prayer/Bible study/reflection habits.

## THE INSURANCE INDUSTRY

During my property and casualty insurance career of nearly twenty-eight years, my jobs mostly revolved around the marketing area. I was able to experience some distinctive work environments and locations and meet and work with a wide cross-section of characters. One unique person was Saul Sokol, who owned an agency in Columbus, Ohio. Saul was one of the smartest insurance minds I ever worked with, and he earned a number of insurance degrees and designations.

I got to know him pretty well and, after finishing my course work and earning my CPCU designation, I told him I wanted to do more than I was doing. (This was similar to me talking with my mom after working in the mill for a year. From that she inspired me to begin taking college courses.) Saul had written a book on insurance, and he suggested that I think about writing. From his encouragement, I started writing insurance articles. These pieces were printed in a number of different insurance trade magazines. That was good advice for me at that point. It is amazing that I started writing and have been writing ever since: things for the insurance industry, lots of papers at Trinity Seminary, various articles, and now books. Never thought I would be where I am now with this skill. But I am grateful to Saul for his friendship, wisdom, and guidance.

There are many other people that I was blessed to have worked with or for during this career. I was also fortunate enough to have been able to live in, or travel to, a number of different places in the US. This gave me the chance to see so many wonderful sights this country has to offer, plus meet a wide variety of people with all of their distinctive personalities and backgrounds.

## EPIPHANY LUTHERAN CHURCH AND PASTOR DAVE SHUGERT

Epiphany and Pastor Dave were both noted in my book; however, I would like to mention them again, because of how much they supported my family and me.

- After my home congregation, Jerusalem Baptist, Epiphany Lutheran is the faith community that had the second greatest influence on my spiritual pilgrimage and life journey.
- Epiphany warmly welcomed Kevin and me with open arms while visiting them the first time, and I stayed there for nearly fourteen years.
- They were extremely generous in helping Elizabeth get a second chance of a "normal" life after being released from jail.

- Pastor Dave embodied many traits that a good pastor should have: patience, compassion, love, and a prayer essence, also, a vision of what God's kingdom could look like in this time and space.
- He helped me understand the basics of Lutheran theology, which assisted me with being comfortable worshiping at Epiphany.
- During my years at Epiphany his presence and wisdom aided my spiritual journey.
- Epiphany helped out with meals, prayers, support, and human angels during Judy's battle with cancer and afterwards while under hospice.
- Our family will always appreciate Pastor Dave's act of kindness and love with his welcome presence on the night that Judy died.
- His preaching at Judy's funeral Mass was a good example of different faith traditions coming together to take part in a challenging service. His sermon was meaningful and captured Judy's love-filled life.
- His prayer, actions, and support gave me the direction to attend Trinity when I did, and the funds to pay for it.
- Pastor Dave did premarital counseling for Shirley and me and co-officiated at our wedding.
- Pastor Dave is no longer with us on this earthly journey, but he remains a part of many lives who are still around today.

## SHIRLEY

Shirley was raised in South Bend, Indiana; however, she spent most of her married life in southwest lower Michigan. We did not know each other before we went to Trinity Lutheran Seminary. We got married at Trinity, because that is where we met. The wedding was such a wonderful event for those who could come. Most of the people who attended had been through the high and low points in our lives. Some had walked with us when we lost Judy and Bob. Now they could celebrate with us at this wedding, *really cool*!

There are numerous things that could be said about Shirley and how much she has meant to my life. She is a very caring, compassionate, and loving person. She has a number of wonderful traits that she was able to use in her role as a Lutheran pastor. However, one aspect that stands out is how willing she is to be so accepting and inclusive of all people in her personal life and in her ministry. One of my many shortcomings is when I judge individuals based on how they look, their personal lifestyles, or how they carry themselves. I have gotten better over the years and know that my spiritual pilgrimage has helped me in this matter. However, Shirley's very open attitude and her welcoming spirit have had an influence on the person that I am today. How she treats and looks at all folks has certainly impacted me.

## STOPS IN LOUISVILLE, KENTUCKY; ALPENA, MICHIGAN; AND THEN WESTMINSTER, COLORADO

After Shirley finished her course work and pastoral requirements, she received a call to St. Paul Lutheran Church in Louisville, Kentucky. That St. Paul was a small church, but it was a great place for Shirley to develop her expertise as a pastor. It was also a good location for me to continue on my journey with my personal spiritual pilgrimage and to acquire skills for my own ministry. In Louisville, I was able to function as a spiritual consultant and the main worship leader for Bethany Lutheran Church. Around the same time, I became the director of small groups for Christ Lutheran Church and preached once a month for them. Those roles and the people we came into contact with, lived around, and worshiped with all had an impact on my life.

After she received her second call from St. Paul Lutheran Church in Alpena, Michigan, and we moved there, we both had another new range of experiences. That St. Paul was much larger, and Shirley was again able to expand on the things that she had done before as a pastor and was blessed to add new aspects to her ministry. During my time in Alpena, I was fortunate enough to set up a ministry web page and a ministry Facebook page, have my first two books published, and become involved in various activities in Alpena. Shirley and I both feel that even though Alpena was a much smaller city than Louisville, the people there and in the surrounding area were very warm and welcoming to both of us. Because we were surrounded by water (Lake Huron and many inland lakes), we used that opportunity to reflect on all of the wonderful gifts the good Lord gave us.

When Shirley was pondering her retirement, we spent a lot of time thinking about where we wanted to relocate. We did a lot of praying, researching, and reflecting on where God was calling us next. We both felt that we were still called to continue doing ministry of some type; we just did not know exactly what that would be. We ended up moving to the Denver metro area in Colorado, in a community called Westminster. Besides being near family and two of our grandchildren, we have also found a very loving faith community, Lutheran Church of Hope, in Broomfield, Colorado, to be a part of. As part of my midday devotional practices when we lived in Alpena, I attended Trinity Episcopal Church's Wednesday service. When we moved to Colorado this practice has been continued, for Shirley and I attend St. James Episcopal Church's (in Wheat Ridge, Colorado) Wednesday noon service; it is a blessing to have been connected to those faith communities

In these three areas, Louisville, Alpena, and Westminster, like all of the other places lived, a number of people have become lifelong friends. I certainly feel very blessed to have encountered so many caring people, and to have had so many wonderful experiences wherever I have lived. I realize that I have come across my share of negative folks, and have also had moments of pain and challenges, but overall, if I could, I would not change much about these relocations.

## BEING THANKFUL

I know that I have been extremely fortunate and blessed to have been married to Judy and now to Shirley. A lot of people would love to have what I have been given, to have a special someone to walk together with on this pilgrimage. However, many have gone through life without having just one wonderful relationship where they can love and be loved. My heart goes out to those who wished to have what we have been given but were not able to.

Additionally, it has been noted often that we all are made of the people and events that have come across our paths and influenced us. Just as Bob is still a part of Shirley, Judy is still a part of me. Additionally, Shirley and I are a part of each other's lives, and of course how we are impacted by each other changes daily. We did not get to where we are today alone, without countless folks, many different communities, our families, along with books, events, and the good and bad coming into our lives. On our spiritual pilgrimage, God is able to use all of these individuals and occurrences to help us become the person that we were meant to be. Our role is to be willing to allow the Holy Spirit to direct our lives and to be open to what the good Lord has in store for us. Each day we make choices; do we strive for God's kingdom, or do we seek after our own agenda?

The people and events highlighted here are a few of those who have helped me and are a part of my journey to become a lifelong disciple of Jesus Christ. I have not gotten here alone. I will be always be thankful for all of these aspects of my life that have helped me get to where I am today. I have made my share of wrong turns and dumb mistakes, and have had my portion of joy and sorrows—often at the same time. However, my plan is to continue to lean on what has happened to me in the past so I can have hope about the future.

We each have our own stories, and mine is no better or worse than any other. However, my prayer and hope are that what has been written here may assist you in leaning on what has happened to you in your past. That you may have faith about your future based on all of the people and events that have helped get you to where you are today. *God's blessings on your spiritual pilgrimage!*